D0893371

Biodiversity
and
Conservation

Gabriel Melchias

Science Publishers, Inc.

Enfield (NH), USA   Plymouth, UK

CIP data will be provided on request.

SCIENCE PUBLISHERS, INC.
P.O. Box 699
Enfield, New Hampshire 03748
United States of America

Internet site: *http://www.scipub.net*

sales@scipub.net (marketing department)
editor@scipub.net (editorial department)
info@scipub.net (for all other enquiries)

ISBN 1-57808-146-7

Published by Science Publishers, Inc., Enfield, NH, USA.
Printed in India

Preface

With each passing day the debate over issues of environment and biodiversity is getting deeply entrenched into every facet of human activity and governance. Unfortunately far from being a road map enabling the creation of a framework, the debate often boomerangs into a virtual roadblock. The biological diversity of our planet, the foundations of agriculture and food production, once seemed inexhaustible. Now a different picture is emerging of a finite, yet renewable resource. Wisely managed, it can support the world's peoples into the foreseeable future. It is no exaggeration to say that the future of human civilization could depend on our ability to defend and make sustainable use of biological diversity.

Humanity's place in nature is still not widely understood. Human influences on the environment are all pervasive; even those ecosystems that appear most "natural" have been altered during the course of time. Starting some 12000 years ago, our ancestors, have created a rich diversity of productive ecosystems. This heritage which spans the generations is threatened by the recent rapid pace of change, undesirable side effects of industrialization and the continuing expansion of the world's population.

The international community led by the FAO is pressing for the highest priority to be given to saving biodiversity, not as a museum piece but as a source of continuing development. But who will finance the multifarious tasks of conservation? How can this funding be sustained? Most of the burden will inevitably fall on the principal economic beneficiaries of biodiversity. The international community has still to agree, however, on how to draw equitably on the wealth generated by biodiversity or how to distribute the funds fairly for the conservation and sustainable development of natural resources.

A serious weakness of the international economic system has been its inability to assign a value of exchange to biodiversity and other environmental components. Finding out how to incorporate the cost of conservation into that of production is a challenge we must meet in order to fulfil our obligations to future generations and halt the continuing impoverishment and misuse of biodiversity. Genetic resources have become a tool for profit - and fuel for political concern. The extension of monopoly rights over plant varieties, their genes and characteristics is a further threat to world food security. As crop diversity diminishes, farming systems and farmers themselves are growing more vulnerable to an array of pressures. Together, genetic erosion and the privatization of genetic resources are undermining the very base of sustainable development. For over two decades now, governments, NGOs and inter-governmental agencies have been immersed in an intense debate over the conservation and development of plant genetic resources. Once the least-known and least political aspect of the world's food supply, why is it that the myriad little genes that comprise plant varieties have become the cause of so much controversy?

Stripped of their technical and political jargon, plant genetic resources are quite simply the first link in the food chain. Without them - or without a lot of them - sustainable agricultural development would be an unattainable dream. We hope to draw attention to such issues and mobilize action to halt the continuing loss of biodiversity. The message is clear: the cost of conserving biodiversity is far less than the penalty of allowing its degradation. Once lost, this heritage cannot be recovered or restored. It is a challenge for each and everyone of us.

This book is an attempt to appreciate and inform those who can influence a balanced opinion for the cause of valuing and protecting nature's treasures for future generations. I gratefully acknowledge among others the University of Amsterdam, The Netherlands; GRAIN, Barcelona and the FAO, Roma for their generously sharing information that helped me to shape the message. I received immense help from a number of good people who encouraged me through constructive criticism, evaluation and timely consultation. They include Rev. Felix George of *Pontificio Collegio Beda*, Rome; Dr. M. Patrick Gomez, the Head of Botany & Biochemistry Department of *St. Joseph's College;* Dr. Adrian Elangovan of *National University of Singapore* and my colleagues at *St Joseph's College,* Tiruchirappalli, Tamilnadu, India. I take immense pleasure in thanking The Lord Almighty who strengthened me in the completion of the book. J. Charles of *Golden Net Computers* deserves special word of thanks for the type-setting of the manuscript.

DR. GABRIEL MELCHIAS
January, 2000

Acronyms

AGR	Animal Genetic Resources.
BDM	Biotechnology and Development Monitor, Univ. Amsterdam, The Netherlands.
Bt	*Bacillus thuringiensis.*
CBD	Convention on Biological Diversity .
CGIAR	Consultative Group on the Intl. Agric. Res.
CIAT	Intl. Centre for Tropical Agric. (of the CGIAR).
CIMMYT	Intl. Maize and Wheat Improvement Centre (Mexico) of the CGIAR.
CITES	Convention on International Trade in Endangered Species of wild fauna and flora.
DEEP	Development Education Exchange Papers, UN FAO, Roma, Italy.
EAAP	European Association for Animal Production, Hannover.
EC	European Commission.
EPA	Environmental Protection Agency of the US.
EPO	European Patent Of.
EU	European Union.
FAO	Food and Agric. Org. of the UN.
FDA	Food and Drug Administration of the US.
GATT	General Agreement on Trade and Tariff.
GEF	Global Environment Facility (WB).
GEOs	See GMOs.
GIFT	Genetic Improvement of Farmed Tilapia.
GMOs	Genetically Modified Organisms.
GRAIN	Genetic Resources Action International, Barcelona, Spain.
HGDP	Human Genome Diversity Project.
HGP	Human Genome Program.
HGSP	Human Genome Sequencing Project.
HUGO	Human Genome Organization.
IARC	Intl. Agric. Res. Centres (of the CGIAR).
IATP	Institute for Agric and Trade Policy, MN USA.
IBC	Intl. Bioethics Committee.
IBPGR	Intl. Board on Plant Genetic Resources.

ICGEB	Intl. Centre for Genetic Engg. and Biotechnology.
ICLARM	Intl. Centre for Living Aquatic Resources Management, The Philippines.
ICRAF	Intl. Centre for Res. in Agroforestry, Nairobi, Kenya.
ICRISAT	Intl. Crops Research Institute for the Semi Arid Tropics.
IDRC	Intl. Development Research Centre, Canada.
IFPRI	Intl. Food Policy Res. Institute.
IIED	Intl. Inst. for Envir. and Develop., London.
ILCA	Intl. Livestock Centre for Africa.
ILO	Intl. Labour Organization.
ILRAD	Intl. Laboratory for Research on Animal Diseases.
ILRI	Intl. Livestock Research Institute.
IPGRI	Intl. PGR Institute, Rome.
IPM	Integrated Pest Management.
IPR	Intellectual Property Rights.
IRRI	Intl. Agric. Res. Institute, HQ Manila, The Philippines.
ISNAR	Intl. Service for NAR.
IUCN	World Conservation Union, Switzerland.
IWGIA	Intl. Working Group of Indigenous Affairs, Copenhagen.
LMOs	Living Modified Organisms.
MNCs	Multinational Corporations (TNCs).
NAFTA	North American Free Trade Agreement.
NARS	National Agric. Res. System.
NGOs	Non-governmental Organizations.
NIH	National Institutes of Health, USA.
NP	Natural Product.
ODA	Overseas Development Administration, Great Britain.
OECD	Organization for Economic Cooperation and Development.
PBRs	Plant Breeders' Rights.
PGR	Plant Genetic Resources.
PTO	Patent and Trademark Office of the US.
RAFI	Rural Advancement Fund Intl. Canada.
RBG-KEW	Royal Botanical Gardens, Kew, UK.
RFSTE	Rural Foundation for Science, Technology and Education, Dehra Dun, India.
SSE	Seed Savers Exchange, USA.
TNCs	Transnational Corporations (MNCs).
TRIPS	Trade-Related IPRs/Disputes.
TWN	Third World Network, Malaysia.
UNCED	UN Conf. on Envir. and Development.
UNCTAD	UN Conference on Trade and Development.
UNDP	UN Devel. Program, New York.
UNEP	UN Envir. Program.
UNESCO	UN Edu. Sci. Cultural Org., Paris.

UNIDO	UN Industrial Devel. Organization, Vienna, Austria.
UNRISD	UN Res. Inst. for Social Development, Geneva, Switzerland.
UPOV	Intl. Union for the Protection of New Varieties Geneva.
USDA	US Department of Agric.
VIR	N. Vavilov Inst., Russia.
WHO	World Health Organization.
WIPO	World Intellectual Property Organization.
WRI	World Resources Institute, Washington.
WRM	World Rainforest Movement.
WTO	World Trade Organization.
WWF	World Wide Fund (for Nature) International, Switzerland.

Contents

PART III

BIOTECHNOLOGY AND BIODIVERSITY

PART IV

BIODIVERSITY PROSPECTING

PART V

CONSERVATION

PART I

BIODIVERSITY : AN OUTLINE

1

Introduction

Biodiversity is a popular way of describing the diversity of life on earth, it includes all life forms and the ecosystems of which they are a part. World Food Day—the anniversary of FAO's founding on 16 October 1946—celebrates, in particular, that part of biodiversity that nurtures people and contributes to long-term food security for all. Biodiversity forms the foundations for sustainable development. It is the basis for the environmental health of our planet and the source of economic and ecological security for future generations.

In the developing world, biodiversity provides the assurance of food, countless raw materials such as fibre for clothing, materials for shelter, fertilizer, fuel and medicines, as well as a source of work energy in the form of animal traction. The rural poor depend upon biological resources for an estimated 90% of their needs. In the industrialized world access to diverse biological resources is necessary to support a vast array of industrial products. In the continuing drive to develop efficient and sustainable agriculture for many different conditions, these resources provide raw material for plant and animal breeding as well as the new biotechnologies. In addition, biodiversity maintains the ecological balance necessary for planetary and human survival.

Biological diversity is made up of all species of plants and animals, their genetic material and the ecosystems of which they are a part. The word 'biodiversity' is a contraction of 'biological diversity'. It refers to variety within the living world. This term biodiversity is commonly used to describe the number, variety and variability of living organisms. In general, biodiversity is defined in terms of genes, species and ecosystems, corresponding to three fundamental and hierarchially related levels of biological organization.

Genetic diversity refers to the variation of genes and genotypes between and within species. It is the sum total of varied genetic information contained in the genes of individual plants, animals and microorganisms that inhabit the earth. Diversity within a species gives the ability to adapt or resist changes in environment, climate and agricultural methods or the presence of new pests and diseases. In other words, the heritable variation within and between populations of organisms is genetic diversity. This represents variations in genes (DNA or RNA). Ultimately this is due to the variations of sequences of bases in nucleic acids, which constitute the genetic code.

The genetic variations are due to gene and chromosome mutations, and in organisms with sexual reproduction these can be spread by recombination. Other kinds of genetic diversity can be identified at all levels of organizations, including the amount of DNA per cell, chromosome structure and number. The pool of genetic variation present within an interbreeding population is acted upon by selection. Differential survival results in changes in the frequency of genes within this pool and this is equivalent to population evolution. The genetic variation thus enables both natural evolutionary change and artificial selective breeding to occur.

Only a small fraction (often less than 1%) of the genetic material of the higher organisms is outwardly expressed in the form and function of the organisms, the purpose of the remaining DNA is still not clear. Each of the estimated 10^9 different genes distributed across the world's biota does not make an identical contribution to the overall genetic diversity. In particular, these genes which control fundamental biochemical processes are strongly conserved across different taxa and show little variation, although such variation that does exist may exert a strong effect on the viability of the organisms, the converse is true of other genes.

Species diversity refers to the variety of species within a given area. Biodiversity is very commonly used as a synonym of 'Species Diversity', in particular of "species richness", which is the number of species in a site or habitat. Global biodiversity is typically presented in terms of global numbers of species in different taxonomic groups. An estimated 1.7 million species have been described to date; estimates for the total number of species existing on earth at present may be around 12.5 million (the majority of these are insects and microorganisms). Evidently the crops are numerically smaller as can be seen in Fig. 1.

Species level is generally regarded as the most natural one at which to consider the whole organism's diversity. Species are also the primary focus of evolutionary mechanisms and therefore the **origin** and **extinction** of species are the principal agents in governing biodiversity. Further, implicit within the term is the concept of **degree** or extent of variation, i.e., organisms which differ widely from each other in some respect by definition contribute more to overall diversity than those which are very similar. A site with many different higher taxa present can be said to possess more taxonomic diversity than another with fewer higher taxa but many more species. Marine habitats have more phyla but fewer species than terrestrial habitats, i.e., higher taxonomic diversity but lower species diversity.The ecological importance of a species can have different effects on community structure, and thus overall biological diversity. For example, a species of a tropical rainforest tree which supports an endemic invertebrate fauna of a hundred species makes a greater contribution to the maintenance of global biodiversity than an alpine plant which may have no other species wholly dependent on it.

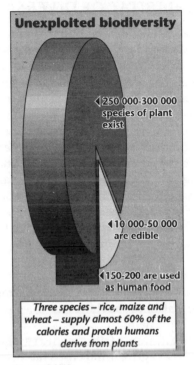

Unexploited biodiversity

◁ 250 000-300 000 species of plant exist

◀ 10 000-50 000 are edible

◀ 150-200 are used as human food

Three species – rice, maize and wheat – supply almost 60% of the calories and protein humans derive from plants

Source: CGIAR.

Fig. 1 The unexploited and exploited biodiversity : Global view.

ECOSYSTEM DIVERSITY

Ecosystem consists of interdependent communities of species (complex mixes of diversity between and within species) and their physical environment. The extent of an ecosystem or habitat is imprecise, a single ecosystem may cover thousands of hectares or just a few. They include major natural systems such as grasslands, mangroves, coral reefs, wetlands and tropical forests as well as agricultural ecosystems that, while depending upon human activity for their existence and maintenance, have characteristic assemblage of plants and animals.

Ecosystem differs from gene and species in that they explicitly exclude abiotic components (soil, water and climate). The quantitative assessment of diversity of the ecosystem, habitat or community level is problematic. Ecosystem diversity is often evaluated through measures of the diversity of component species. This may involve assessment of the relative abundance of different species as well as consideration of types of species.

HABITAT OF DIVERSITY

Species diversity in natural habitats is high in warm areas and decreases with increasing latitude and altitude. On land diversity is higher in areas of higher rainfall and lower in drier areas. The richer areas are undoubtedly tropical moist forests (high level of insects, microfauna). The forest area which comprises 7% of world surface area contains over 90% of all species. The reasons for large-scale geographic variation in species diversity, and in particular for very high species diversity of tropical moist forests, involve 2 interconnected questions; the **origin** of diversity through origin of species and the **maintenance** of diversity. Both involve climatic, edaphic and topographic conditions. Climatically warmth and moisture for long periods appear to be important. The loss of biological diversity may take many forms, but at its most fundamental and reversible it involves extinction of species. Species extinction is a natural process which occurs without intervention of man. But the extinction rate goes beyond the normal rate due to the direct or indirect interference of man.

FACTS

- Nobody knows how many species are disappearing (or being generated) on the earth: probably fewer than 10% of species have been given a scientific name.
- Since the beginning of this century about 75% of the genetic diversityamong agricultural crops has been lost.
- The rural poor depend upon biological resources for an estimated 90% of their needs.
- A 13.7 km² area of La Selva forest in Costa Rica contains almost 1500 plant species- more than all those found in the United Kingdom's 243500 km².
- Panama contains more species than all of North America.
- In the USA, 25% of all prescriptions dispensed by pharmacies are substances extracted from plants. Another 13% come from microorganisms and 3% from animals.

2

Why is Biodiversity Important?

Genetic diversity in agriculture enables crops and animals to **adapt** to different environments and growing conditions. The ability of a particular variety to withstand drought or inundation, grow in poor or rich soil, resist one of the many insect pests or diseases, give higher protein yields or produce a better-tasting food are traits passed on naturally by its genes. This genetic material constitutes the raw material that plant and animal breeders and biotechnologists use to produce new varieties and breeds. Without this diversity we would lose the ability to adapt to ever changing needs and conditions. Sustainable agriculture could not then be achieved in many of the world's different food production environments.

Diversity among individual plants and animals, species and ecosystems provides the raw material that enables human communities to adapt to change -now and in the future. Deprived of biodiversity, the ability of humankind to meet the challenges resulting, for example, from global warming and ozone depletion would be severely limited. The diversity found within the small number of plant and animal species which form the basis of world agriculture and food production remains a small but vital part of the earth's biodiversity. Through modern biotechnologies wild diversity can also be incorporated into crops and contribute to world agriculture development. It is evident that a certain level of biological diversity is necessary to provide material basis of human life; at one level to maintain the biosphere as a functioning system and at another to provide materials for agriculture and other utilitarian needs.

The most important direct use of one species is as **food**. Although, relatively a large number of plant species, perhaps a few thousand has been used as food stuffs, and a greater number are believed edible, only a small percentage are globally of nutritional significance. A few dozen species, mostly mammals, are managed in some kind of husbandry system, and a handful of these are globally significant. Similarly, very many species are eaten (mostly fishes) but only a very small percentage are globally of nutritional significance.

Medical drugs derived from natural sources make an important global contribution to health care. An estimated 80% of people in less developed countries, rely on traditional medicines for primary health care, and this shows no signs of decline, despite the availability of western medicine. Some 120 chemicals extracted in a pure form from around 90 species are used in medicine throughout the world.

Forests play an important role in watershed regulation and stabilization of soils. They protect a variety of organisms under their cover and have an important role in climate. There are a variety of uses of forests and forest products (flora and fauna). The role of mangroves in coastal zone stabilization and nursery areas for fishery species is very significant. Coral reefs rich in flora and fauna support fisheries. Natural ecosystem then is protected as national parks —an advantage towards tourism.

BIODIVERSITY FOR SUSTAINABLE DEVELOPMENT

The biological resources of each and every country are important, but not all are equally endowed. In general, a small number of countries lying within the tropics and subtropics account for a very high percentage of world's biodiversity. The most important food crops, however, appear to have originated in areas that have pronounced seasons. This tends to coincide with arid and semi-arid zones, which include famine-prone countries such as Ethiopia. It makes sense, therefore, to look for sources of certain food crop diversity in such areas. A single Ethiopian barley plant, for example, has yielded a gene that now protects California's annual barley crop from yellow dwarf virus.

The fact that the richest nations are home to the smallest pockets of biodiversity while the poorest are stewards of the richest reservoirs underscores the interdependency of all nations, and the urgency of crafting common strategies for sustaining biodiversity that share both responsibility and benefits. On the eve of the twenty-first century, the challenge for the global community is not to save biodiversity for its own sake, but to ensure that biodiversity is managed and used sustainably and equitably for human development. While it is evident that at present a relatively small proportion of the world's biological diversity is actively exploited by man, other elements of biological diversity may be important for different reasons. They have values which are unused or unknown at present but which could enhance the material well being of mankind if these values were discovered and exploited. They may become useful or vital at some time in the future owing to changing circumstances.

Thus, biodiversity provides the raw materials, combinations of genes, that produce the plant varieties and animal breeds upon which agriculture depends. Thousands of different and genetically unique varieties of crops and animal breeds owe their existence to 3000 million years of natural biological evolution and to careful selection and nurturing by our farming and herding ancestors during 12000 or so years of agriculture. Whether they are used in traditional farming systems, conventional or modern breeding or genetic engineering, the genetic resources of plants and animals are a global asset of inestimable value to humankind. As genetic diversity erodes, our capacity to maintain and enhance crop forest and livestock productivity decreases along with the ability to respond to changing conditions. Genetic resources hold the key to increasing food security and improving the human condition.

3

Plant Diversity

Crop Plants and their Relatives

The plant genetic diversity used in agriculture—the crops that feed us and their wild relatives—is being lost at an alarming rate. Just nine crops (wheat, rice, maize, barley, sorghum/millet, potato, sweet potato/yam, sugarcane and soybean) account for over 75% of the plant kingdom's contribution to human dietary energy. None of the world's staple crops is likely to disappear. Yet they too are threatened—not by the loss of a single crop species such as wheat or rice, but by the loss of diversity within species.

SEEDS OF SURVIVAL

All major food crops, the staple crops grown and consumed by the vast majority of the world's population, have their origins in the tropics and subtropics of Asia, Africa and Latin America. Over the years, farmers selected and domesticated all major food crops on which humankind depends today. Wheat and barley originated in the Near East, soybeans and rice came from China. Sorghum, yams and coffee came from Africa. Potatoes and tomatoes originated in the Andes of South America and maize in South and Central America. Crop genetic diversity is still concentrated mainly in regions known as "centres of diversity" and located in the developing world. Farmers in these areas, who still practice traditional agriculture, cultivate local varieties known as "land races" that have been selected over many generations. Closely related species that survive in the wild are known as "wild relatives" of crops. Together, land races and their wild relatives are the richest repositories of crop genetic diversity.

Thousands of different and genetically distinct varieties of major food crops owe their existence to millions of years of evolution and to careful selection and nurturing by our farmer ancestors during some 12000 years of agriculture. This diversity protects the crop and helps it meet the demands of different environments and human needs. Potatoes for instance, originated in the Andes, but nowadays they can be found growing below sea level behind Dutch dykes or high in the Himalayan mountains. One variety of rice survives on just 60 centimeters of annual rainfall, another floats in 7.5 metres of water.

AGRICULTURE'S VANISHING HERITAGE

The FAO estimates that since the beginning of this century about 75% of the genetic diversity of agricultural crops has been lost. We are becoming increasingly dependent on fewer and fewer crop varieties and, as a result, a rapidly diminishing gene pool. The primary reason is that commercial uniform varieties are replacing traditional ones—even, and most threateningly, in the centres of diversity. When farmers abandon native land races to plant new varieties, the traditional ones die out. The introduction, beginning in the 1950s, of high yielding grains developed by international crop breeding institutions led to the Green Revolution. The spread of the new varieties in the developing world was dramatic. By 1990 they covered half of all wheat lands, and more than half of all rice lands - total of some 115 million ha. This resulted in large increase in yields but large decreases in crop diversity.

Trees and Forests

About 30% of the world's ice-free land surface is forest or woodland. Forested areas of the world today comprise between 3000 million and 3500 million ha—an area equal to the size of North and South America. According to recent estimates, temperate forests cover approximately 1430 million ha in the industrialized countries and another 210 million ha in non tropical developing countries. Tropical forests, both moist and dry, cover an estimated 1760 million ha.

BENEFITS AND USE OF FORESTS

Forests supply food, fodder, medicine and timber, poles and fuelwood as well as raw materials for industry The income earned from trees and forests is of vital importance to both rural populations and national incomes. Forests are home for an estimated 300 million people—shifting cultivators and hunter gatherers—around the world. In the past, the slash-and-burn agriculture practiced by forest-dwelling people was sustainable, but population pressures are reducing the land available for shifting cultivation: shorter fallow periods and overuse are turning traditionally sustainable methods into destructive ones. Rural people living in and around forest areas depend on a large variety of forest products for subsistence. Forest foods form a major part of the diet of some population groups in rural areas in developing countries. They include leaves, seeds and nuts, fruits, roots and tubers, sap and gums, fungi and animals. Forest foods often increase in importance during the periods of hunger and drought which reach their peak just before crops are harvested, and when crops fail.

Woody species provide three quarters or more of the population in developing countries with their primary energy source. In developing countries, eight times more wood is used for fuel than is logged for industrial purposes. In many areas, fuelwood is being harvested faster than it is being replenished. By this year, nearly 3000 million people could face fuelwood shortages. Forests provide vital ecological functions, their absorption of carbon dioxide and release of oxygen through photosynthesis help control the level of greenhouse gases and provide an atmosphere essential to support life (Fig. 2). Forest vegetation helps recycle nutrients. Forest cover also reduces soil erosion by slowing the runoff of water, reducing the hazard of floods and the silting of reservoirs and waterways. Forest woodlands and other wilderness areas are increasingly valued as sites of natural and cultural heritage, as well as education and recreation. Ecotourism is a vital source of income for many countries of the South as well as the North.

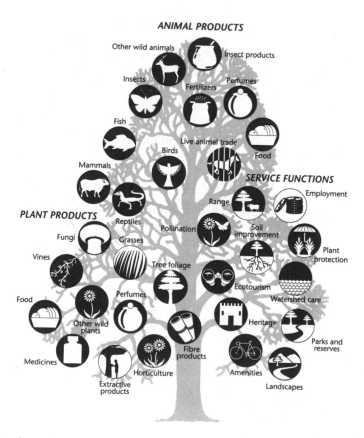

Fig. 2 Benefits and use of forests: plant products, animal products, service functions and others.

WORLD FOREST DECLINE

The world's forests are declining at unprecedented rates. Major threats are deforestation and atmospheric pollution. Another threat is the narrowing of the genetic base of tree species as a result of commercial forestry operations. Whereas reforestation of temperate forest lands now exceeds removal of trees, tropical forests were destroyed at an annual rate of 15.4 million ha between 1980 and 1990 according to a recent FAO survey. In terms of area, the greatest losses were in Latin America and the Caribbean (an average of 7.4 million ha per year) followed by Africa (4.1 million ha per year) and Asia and the Pacific (3.9 ha per year).

The causes of deforestation vary from region to region. The most important include; conversion of forest land to agriculture use; excessive use of fuelwood and charcoal; shifting cultivation where fallow periods are too short; unsustainable logging; expansion of urban and industrial areas; and overgrazing and fodder collection. Poverty is the underlying cause of many of these environmentally degrading activities. Despite a net increase in the forested area in Europe, pollution and forest fires have caused a severe decline in biodiversity and forest vigour. Forests in Germany and the former Czechoslovakia have been particularly affected. Less obvious, but equally alarming, is the decline in genetic diversity within forest species in both Europe and North America. This genetic erosion results mainly from deforestation, compounded for a few economically important species by intensive breeding for commercial forestry. The FAO estimates that about 400 tree species are endangered in whole or in significant parts of their gene pools.

When forests decline or are removed, much more than trees is lost. Forests harbour many animals and plants that depend on their environment for survival. Many of these species, their potential value to society and their ecological importance have yet to be discovered. Untapped treasures include possible crops, pharmaceutical, timbers, fibres, pulp, soil-restoring vegetation, petroleum substitutes and countless other products and amenities. The bark of the rare western yew tree *Taxus brevifolia*, which is now found only in the old-growth coniferous forest of the northwestern United States, was recently found to be the source of taxol, one of the most potent anticancer substances ever found. If forest felling continues at the present rates, new sources of scientific information are likely to be lost and inestimable biological wealth destroyed.

Even where conservation measures have been taken, they may not halt the decline in biodiversity and therefore the overall genetic resources of the forest ecosystem. At present less than 5% of the earth's land surface is allocated for conservation as national parks, scientific stations or other types of legally protected land. Conservation areas have been set aside for many reasons, but rarely with reference to the location of valuable gene pools. Frequently they are too small to maintain viable populations of the threatened species and varieties they do contain. At the same time, experience shows that policies to control and protect such reserves will not succeed without active support of the local people and complementary programmes aimed at meeting their everyday needs.

SUSTAINABLE DEVELOPMENT OF FORESTS

Properly managed, forest ecosystems can provide goods and services while, at the same time, perpetuating the genetic resources contained in them. Progress is being made towards new styles of management. The sustainable harvesting of non-wood forest products can improve food security and nutrition, while increasing income and job opportunities. **Agroforestry**—a farming system that combines trees, crops and livestock—enables farmers, even the poorest, to diversify agricultural production and reclaim degraded land. The degradation of forests can also be reduced by harvesting practices that enable logging to take place while promoting and conserving forest regeneration. The sustained utilization of forests, coupled with the maintenance of a network of areas dedicated to the protection of ecosystems and their functions, provides the only solution for lasting genetic conservation. A graphical comparison of forest area can be gauged from Fig. 3.

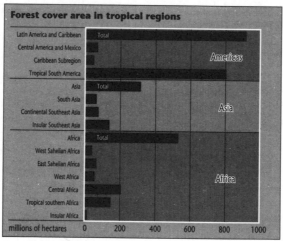

Source: FRA, 1993, FAO.

Fig. 3 Forest cover area in tropical regions.

FACTS

- Deforestation of closed tropical rain forests could account for the loss of as many as 100 species every day.
- Kalimantan, Indonesia, is an important centre of genetic variation for tropical fruit trees, including mango, breadfruit and durain. Of 16 species of mango in East Kalimantan Province, 13 are edible.

- Exports of chicle, allspice and xate (edible palm fronds) earn Guatemala US $7 million annually and support some 6000 families in the Peten region of the country.
- Collecting, extracting and processing the kernels of the fruit of babassu palm provides an estimated 25% of household income for 300000 families in Brazil's Maranhao State.
- In Cote d'Ivoire, harvesting giant snails (*Achatina achatina*) in the buffer zone around Taj National Park provides a source of food and income; each snail provides some 100 to 300 g of meat and the shells provide calcium for animal feed or crop fertiliser.
- More than 30 ta of mushrooms, mainly chanterelles (*Cantharellus* spp.) are gathered and consumed every year by the 700000 or so residents of the Upper Shaba area of Zaire.

4

Animal Diversity

Domesticated and Related Animals

Animal genetic resources include all species, breeds and strains that are of economic, scientific and cultural interest to humankind for agriculture, both now and in the future. Common agricultural species include sheep, goats, cattle, horses, pigs, buffaloes and chickens, but there are many other domesticated animals such as camels, donkeys, elephants, reindeer, rabbits and rodents that are important to different cultures and regions of the world. Animal domestication began some 10000 years ago when people began selecting animals for food, fibre, drought and other agricultural uses. Livestock provide valuable products, such as hides, wool and manure, that are important both for subsistence and as sources of income for rural communities. Livestock process forage and crop waste, inedible to humans, into nutritionally important food products. Approximately 40% of the total land available in developing countries can only be used for some form of forage production. An estimated 12% of the world's population lives in areas where people depend almost entirely on products obtained from ruminant livestock cattle, sheep and goats.

Centuries of human and natural selection have resulted in thousands of genetically diverse breeds of domestic animals adapted to a wide range of environmental conditions and human needs. Some are resistant to parasites or disease, for example, while others are adapted to humidity or drought or extremes of heat and cold. Animal genetic diversity, represented by this wide range of breeds, is essential to sustain the productivity of agriculture. Animals account for 19% of the world's food basket directly, but they also provide drought power and fertilizer for crop production, bringing their overall contribution upto 25%. In addition, livestock serve as a very important form of cash reserves in many of the mixed farming systems. Taking this into account, animals contribute an estimated 30% of total human requirements for food and agriculture.

A SINKING ARK

In Europe, half of the breeds that existed at the beginning of the last century have become extinct, a third of the remaining 770 breeds are in danger of disappearing over the next 20 years. In Germany, for example, only five out of at least 35 indigenous breeds of cattle remain. In North America, over one third of all breeds of livestock and poultry are considered rare or in decline. Much less is known about breeds in the developing world. As with plants, domestic animal diversity is greatest in the developing world. Asia, for instance, is home to more than 140 breeds of pig, while North America can claim only 19. Based on preliminary data, the FAO predicts that one in four of all non-European livestock breeds may be at risk of extinction, and more than half of them are likely to be found in developing countries. Worldwide, the greatest threat to domestic animal diversity is the highly specialised nature of modern livestock production. In the developed world, commercial livestock farming is based on very few breeds that have been selected for the intensive production of meat, milk or eggs in highly controlled and regulated conditions. The spread of intensive productive system to the developing world places thousands of native breeds at risk. Commercial breeds imported from North America and northern Europe are usually unable to sustain high production in less hospitable environments. They require intensive management and high levels of inputs such as high protein feed, medication and protective housing. Introduction of intensive animal production creates dependency on imported technologies; it is neither affordable nor sustainable for most farmers in the developing world.

After thousands of generations of controlled interbreeding most domesticated animals no longer have wild relatives from whom germplasm can be obtained. When a variety becomes extinct, an already narrow genetic base shrinks irreversibly. Commercial breeds suited to intensive production do not offer an adequate genetic reservoir for the future. Their genetic base reflects the emphasis on maximizing production. The BSE crisis of the main land Europe of the late 90s and the Foot-and-Mouth disease of the early part of 2001 have amply demonstrated the fact that methods aimed at maximizing production themselves are the cause of extinction of the very species. *Turkey* that is mass produced on factory farms in North America and Europe, for example, has been selected for such a meaty breast that it can no longer breed unassisted. This broad-breasted breed which accounts for 99% of all turkeys in the United States today would become extinct in one generation without human assistance in the form of artificial insemination. The level of risk faced by animals is presented in Fig. 4.

WHAT VALUE IS ANIMAL GENETIC DIVERSITY?

The genetic diversity now found in domestic animal breeds allows farmers to select stocks or develop new breeds in response to changes in the environment, threat of disease, market conditions and societal needs, all of which are largely unpredictable. Indigenous livestock breeds often possess valuable traits such as disease resistance, high fertility, good maternal qualities, longevity and adaptation to harsh conditions and poor-quality feed, all desirable qualities for low-input, sustainable agriculture. The rare *Taihu* pigs of China, for instance, offer valuable traits for swine breeders worldwide. This group of pigs has thick, wrinkled skin and long, droopy ears. They can use a high proportion of forage

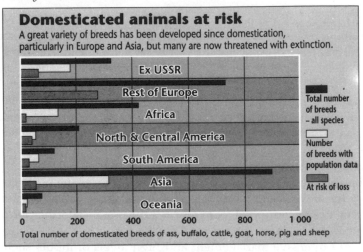

Fig. 4 Genetic diversity of domesticated animals at risk.

foods in their diet. The adult pig has little lean meat—hence the Chinese passion for suckling pig. But *Taihu* pigs reach sexual maturity in just 64 days and are extraordinarily fertile, producing an average of 16 piglets compared with only ten for western breeds. Researchers in Europe and the United States are exploring ways to incorporate these beneficial qualities into commercial breeds. A company in the United Kingdom, National Pig Development, has already produced a commercial hybrid of the *Meishan*, one of seven strains of *Taihu* pig. Announced in 1992, it combines the fecundity of the traditional Chinese breed with a higher lean meat content.

Thirty per cent of Africa's cattle population, approximately 160 million cattle, are at a risk from *trypanosomiasis*—a debilitating and frequently fatal disease transmitted by a fly in 36 African countries covering over 10 million sq. km. This devastating disease jeopardizes not only African milk and meat supplies, but important by-products and services such as hides, manure, fuel and drought power. Annual losses in meat production alone are estimated at US $ 5000 million. Several traditional African cattle breeds, among them the small humpless *N'Dama*, have developed resistance (trypanotolerance) over thousands of years of exposure to the parasite - a trait that relatively modern African breeds do not possess. This genetically based resistance offers hope of reducing or controlling the impact of *trypanosomiasis*. Small numbers of trypanotolerant *N'Dama* cattle have long been maintained by West African farmers in marginal farming areas. They thrive on low quality forage and, though less productive than modern breeds of cattle, their high survival and reproductive rates and longevity make them extremely valuable in harsh environments.

Using a technique known as "embryo transfer", the population of trypanotolerant *N'Dama* cattle has already been increased in order to conserve this rare breed, improve its performance and study its disease resistance. The

N'Dama's hardiness, heat tolerance and disease resistance have also been crossed with the *Red Poll*, an endangered British breed to produce the *Senepol* breed. The *Senepol* has been introduced successfully in the Caribbean and the Southern United States.

FACTS

- *Europe:* Half of the livestock breeds that existed at the beginning of the last century have become extinct and a third of the remaining 770 breeds are in danger. Almost 20% of breeds in the developing world are at risk.
- The sheep of North Ronaldsay island in Scotland have adapted to feeding on seaweed while *Ming* pigs have adapted to the cold winters and hot summers of northeastern China.
- The cattle of Secotra (an island off Yeman) are among the highest milk producing cattle per kilogram of body weight in the world.
- The broad breasted turkey which accounts for 99% of all turkeys in the United States today would become extinct in one generation without the assistance of artificial insemination.

Fish and Aquatic Life

Oceans, lakes and rivers cover four fifths of the earth's surface, but little is known about their living resources. Fewer aquatic than terrestrial species have been described, but there is no reason why aquatic biodiversity should be less. Tropical waters are the richest in terms of species diversity. The Indo-West Pacific Ocean, for example, contains an estimated 1500 species of fish and over 6000 species of mollusc, compared with only 280 fish and 500 mollusc species in the Eastern Atlantic. Inland waters are also rich in diversity, the greatest concentration once again being in the tropics. Thailand, for example, could have as many as 1000 species of fresh water fish, but so far only 475 have been documented. Brazil is believed to have more than 3000 fresh water fish species - three times more than any other country. For the most part, the aquatic harvest consists of wild rather than farmed species. According to the FAO, the world production, 90% of it finfish, stands at almost 100 million ta. Of this, only about 13 million ta come from aquaculture. Over 4 million ta of algae are also harvested annually.

IMPORTANCE OF FISHERIES

Fishing, fish processing and fish trading have provided food, employment and income to coastal and inland communities for centuries. Fish contribute substantially to the world supply of animal protein, either directly or through their use as foodstuff for livestock—almost a third of the fish catch is converted into meal and oil. The developing countries account for more than half the world catch. Their fisheries are dominated by small scale or artisanal producers.

Artisanal fisheries, typically using small boats and canoes, account for more than 25% of the world catch. They supply more than 40% of the fish used for human consumption. These fisheries are also a significant source of employment —an estimated 100 million people in the developing world depend upon them for all or part of their livelihood.

During this century, demand for fish is expected to exceed by some 20 million ta the productive capacity estimated at about 100 million ta of stocks now exploited by the capture fisheries. Increased income and appreciation of the dietary value of fish are spurring the demand for fish and fish products, especially for luxury products such as oysters, shrimp, salmon and tuna. In the developing regions, population increases and the need to tap every potential source of food and foreign exchange provides the main impetus for increased fishing activities. One response to the growing demand for fish especially the crustaceans (Fig. 5) and its falling availability has been development of aquaculture. This rapidly expanding source of food poses some threats to biodiversity by concentrating on a very small range of species and an equally narrow genetic base in these species. Large-scale escapes of cultured fish, or deliberate releases of stocks for ranching, are thought to influence the genetic composition of the wild resource.

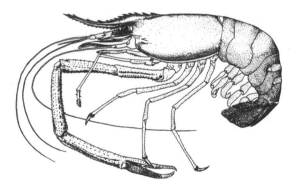

Fig. 5 Production of crustaceans, mostly from aquaculture, has increased dramatically over the past ten years.

TROUBLED WATERS

Aquatic biodiversity is threatened primarily by human abuse and mismanagement of both the living resources and the ecosystems that support them. Loss of habitats, overexploitation and introduction of exotic species are the prime hazards.

OVEREXPLOITATION

Fish stocks are a renewable resource, but already many of them are strained to the limit. Over the years, they have suffered from a widespread notion that the seas are inexhaustible. All fishing activities depend on a fragile resource base which, if mismanaged and overexploited, can easily collapse. Efforts to regulate marine fisheries can be traced back to the late 1800s with the creation in Europe of the Intergovernmental Commission for the Exploration of the Seas (ICES). Many fishery bodies for developing and regulating fisheries, in both marine and inland waters, have been established since then, nine of them under the auspices of the UN, FAO. Despite this appreciation of the threat posed by overfishing, stocks have continued to be exploited at a non-renewable rate.

All demersal (deep water) species such as cod, haddock and pollack are now either fully exploited, overfished or depleted. Larger pelagic (surface water) species such as herring, sardines and anchovy, stocks of which can fluctuate greatly from year to year, are in serious need of management. Crustaceans such as shrimp, lobster and crab are also overexploited. Only the bivalve molluscs, such as mussels and clams, and cephalopods such as squid and octopus, offer a lot of scope for expanded production.

The world fish catch has increased more than four-fold in the past 40 years, but the misuse of modern technology, coupled with government support for otherwise non-economic production, has had a devastating impact on fish stocks. Fleets using sophisticated fish detection, non-selective nets (upto 50 km long) and bottom trawls are driving some species to extinction. The FAO (1998) estimates that the cost of overexploitation amounts to some US $ 30000 million per year. The impact of overexploitation of fisheries may be the greatest in the developing world. Commercial fishing in tropical waters can often mean valuable foreign exchange for developing nations, but it can also lead to intense competition with declining catch rates for small-scale fisheries, many of which provide fish for local consumers and markets. Higher fish prices, the result of increased demand exacerbated by overfishing, are making fish unaffordable to an increasing number of poor people. Fish is no longer a cheap meat dish—a marketing slogan used in the United Kingdom in the 1950s.

SELECTIVITY OF FISHING METHODS
Traditional fishing gears, ranging from a simple harpoon to a basket work fishtrap, are typically selective for both size and species and are adapted to the diversity of fish captured, whereas commercial gears, such as the purse seine, large driftnet and trawl, often have a bycatch of unwanted species. The displacement of traditional fishing methods, combined with the introduction of new materials and highly mechanized fisheries, has contributed to overexploitation of resources in both marine and freshwater environments.

ENVIRONMENTAL DEGRADATION
To the pressure of exploitation must be added the degradation of aquatic ecosystems caused by pollution or competing uses. The oceans function as a sink for carbon dioxide, eroded soils, contaminants, fertilizers and human and industrial wastes. Most urban and industrial activities and indeed, much of human life, are concentrated close to coastal waters, rivers and lakes. Six out of ten people live in coastal areas, and migration towards them is increasing. The

development of intensive aquaculture has, in some cases, damaged coastal ecosystems and water resources, causing conflicts over land use and resources, and even undermining local sources of employment and food. In parts of Asia, thousands of hectares of rice paddy have been replaced by high value shrimp farming or have had their productivity reduced by salinization caused by neighbouring aquaculture enterprises. In the Indo-Pacific region, more than one million hectares of mangrove forests have been converted to aquaculture ponds. Mangroves provide spawning and nursery areas for many marine species and are vital to maintaining ecological balance and biodiversity.

INTRODUCTION OF EXOTIC SPECIES

The introduction of exotic fish species can have many unforeseen consequences. The release of the Nile perch in Africa's Lake Victoria is a classic example. Introduced in the late 1950s as a sports fish, its voracity and large size has driven many of the smaller indigenous species to extinction. Some scientists speculate that 200-300 species of fish may have been lost. The expanding population of Nile perch is making Lake Victoria one of the most productive lake fisheries in the world, yielding 200000 to 300000 ta per year. But increased productivity may have been achieved at serious ecological and social cost. The lake is increasingly providing fish for export rather than local consumption. Lakeside fishing communities have lost species that traditionally provided food and supported the local economy. The long-term example provides a valuable lesson for future introductions and transfers of fish species.

TILAPIA: AN "AQUATIC CHICKEN"

Tilapias, consisting of species of the genera *Tilapia* (Fig. 6), *Oreochromis* and *Sarotherodon*, have been widely distributed around the world from their original African home. They are now the mainstay of small-scale aquaculture for many poor farmers in the developing world, as well as for enterprises in the developed world. They are most widely cultured in Asia, particularly China, The Philippines and Thailand. Dubbed as the "aquatic chicken" tilapias possess many positive attributes that suit them for a range of aquaculture systems: excellent growth rates on a low-protein diet; tolerance of a wide range of environmental conditions; high resistance to disease and parasitic infections; ready breeding in captivity and ease of handling and wide acceptance as food fish.

As tilapias are so widely farmed in the developing word, the Philippines based ICLARM, the CGIAR centre devoted to fisheries, has established the Genetic Improvement of Farmed Tilapia (GIFT) programmes. Its aim is to increase production and income by and for small scale producers. The GIFT programme has collected strains of tilapia and evaluated their culture and growth in different environments. Scientists have discovered, for example, that tilapia breeds in Asia are deteriorating as a result of generations of inbreeding. Future breeding efforts must draw on a wide genetic base, incorporating genetic material from Africa. This underscores the importance of future conservation and utilization of Africa's native tilapia breeds.

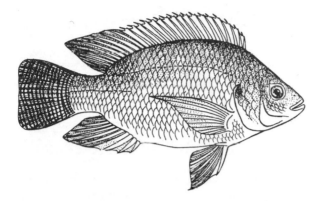

Fig. 6 *Tilapia*: an "aquatic chicken"

FACTS

- Capture fisheries have reached their sustainable yield at 100 million ta, leaving a gap between supply and demand which is estimated 20 million ta by this year.
- About 300 kinds of finfish are cultured for food, but 85% of production comes from carp while tilapias account for most of the remainder.
- In the northwestern United States, 159 genetically distinct populations of ocean migrating fish species are at high or moderate risk of extinction.
- Approximately 7000 species of marine fish have been described from Indonesia, which has over 13000 islands and the largest total coastline of any tropical country.

5

Marine Biodiversity

Though biodiversity encompasses all living organisms on earth, perhaps due to semantics, people generally tend to think of biodiversity in terms of terrestrial living organisms. Given the fact that nearly 70% of the earth's surface is covered by oceans, it is naturally of the highest importance that marine biodiversity be at least as well preserved as the terrestrial. At the same time one has to admit perforce that even scientists today have a better idea of the surface of the dark side of the moon than the depths of the oceans!. However, our understanding of marine biodiversity continues to increase and some of the most recent discoveries have shown that marine biodiversity, though not as well documented as the terrestrial, is probably far greater. For example, at least 43 of the more than 70 phyla (highest taxonomic grouping in biological kingdoms) of all life forms are found in the oceans, whereas only 28 are found on land. At the species level, taking into account the large amount of information extracted every day from samples gathered from diverse marine environments, it would not be far-fetched to assume that more than half of the earth's living species are to be found in the diverse marine and coastal habitats, ranging from coral reefs, mangroves, sea grasses, rocky or sandy beaches down to the soft sediments of the deepest ocean floors and all the water column in between.

WHY PRESERVE MARINE BIODIVERSITY?

Some people believe that marine conservation deserves less priority than terrestrial conservation. One important explanation is the general idea that the oceans host less biodiversity than land and even freshwater environments. It is true that the seas host perhaps only 20% of the total species that inhabit the earth. However, if insects, which represent 75% of all land animals, are left out, 65% of the earth's remaining organisms are marine. If we consider biodiversity at higher taxonomic levels, more phyla and even classes of living organisms are represented in the world's oceans than in terrestrial environments. Almost all (the exception being *Onychophora*) animal phyla exist in the seas, but some are exclusively marine. Furthermore, if we examine biodiversity in terms of functional relationships, types of reproduction, and biochemical strategies, among others, we find an immense diversity in the marine environment.

The preservation of marine biodiversity has been overlooked, for many reasons such as the remote nature and difficulty of monitoring and studying marine habitats and the complexity of the marine environment due to the tridimensional interchange of mass and energy. Finally, it could also be our terrestrial orientation and a prejudice against cold blooded organisms. Loss of marine biodiversity at specific levels is difficult to quantify. A partial list of extinct marine species includes: the Steller sea cow (*Hydyodamalis stellari*); the Atlantic gray whale (*Eschrichtius gibbosus*), the Caribbean monk seal (*Monachus tropicalus*); the sea mink (*Mustela macrodon*), the great auk (*Pinguimus impennis*); and the Labrador duck (*Camptorhynchus labrocorium*).

Why is it so important to preserve marine biodiversity? There are many reasons, ecological, genetic, food and biomedical resources to name only a few. In the first place it is estimated that 20% protein intake by humans is provided by fisheries, this percentage being much higher in many island states and coastal communities. Secondly, from an ecological and genetic point of view species diversity and intraspecies genetic diversity are key factors in ecosystem functioning, stability and resilience. Finally, biochemical compounds derived from marine plants, fish and invertebrates for medical applications are an active field of research today. In short, loss of biodiversity will be detrimental to the quality of human life. It is noteworthy to mention the recent addition by the International Union for the Conservation of Nature (IUCN) of 118 marine fish to its Red List of endangered animals.

THREATS TO MARINE BIODIVERSITY

The increase in world population by approximately 86 million people a year has provoked topographical alterations in shorelines due to the construction of new ports, airports, recreational developments, new cities, etc. Increased populations have also caused an escalation in pollution and infestation in marine habitats. A higher population means more mouths to feed. The harvest of fishery products from the oceans and other natural waters has peaked at about 100 million ta and may have started to decline. At present it is estimated that approximately 50% of fish stocks are fully exploited and 22% are overexploited. The long-term sustainable harvest may be around 100 million ta, which is the level recently attained. If present trends continue, fishery-induced changes in ecosystem trophic structure will inevitably lead to a collapse of many valuable fisheries.

Overfishing, increased number of fishing vessels, sonar and other sophisticated equipment, spotter planes, advanced technology (blast fishing) as well as more efficient fishing gears have greatly increased the harvest of fish from the oceans. On the other hand, destruction of nursery areas, the elimination of mangrove swamps, the construction of new ports, tourist developments and pollution have also caused a decline in our marine fisheries.

6

Human Diversity:
The Indigenous Peoples

Rural populations, especially indigenous communities have created, developed and transmitted technologies and arts for many centuries. They have mastered crop varieties and methods of irrigation, maintained delicate ecosystems, and used the medicinal, nutritional and other valuable properties of endemic flora and fauna. Through trial and error, they have learned to use their ecosystems, plants and animals to maintain or improve human health and well being. Even today, according to the World Health Organization (WHO), 80% of the world's population depends on traditional health care based on medicinal plants. In addition to sustaining health and the local economy, traditional knowledge, particularly that of tribal healers, is often of great local importance as a link to a community's cultural and religious values.

Habitat loss, population growth, and overharvesting of plant products for trade are causing the transformation of rural communities. Many indigenous populations face pressures that threaten their cultures and their very existence, often leading to their disappearance as a distinct group. By one estimate, 85 Brazilian Indian groups became extinct in the first half of this century. More than two-thirds of the remaining tribes have fewer than 1000 members. These losses raise serious human rights concerns and, in addition, mean that the undocumented and increasingly valuable knowledge of nearly 15000 existing cultures is disappearing before it can be transmitted to a new generation.

Biological diversity is also rapidly decreasing due to environmental damage caused by pollution, habitat loss through deforestation and overcultivation. It is estimated that, of approximately 1.4 million organisms already given a scientific name, one plant or animal species becomes extinct every day. By the end of the decade the rate is likely to reach one species every hour. The loss is incalculable: only about 1100 of the earth's species of plants have been studied by western scientists; as many as 40000 may have medicinal or undiscovered nutritional value for humans. In addition to the health consequences, there are enormous economic implications: the annual world market value of medicines derived from plants is currently estimated to be over US $ 43 billion.

The importance of known and anticipated benefits from biological resources and local knowledge has led to calls for wider access and greater dissemination.

The UN Convention on Biological Diversity calls on states to encourage and develop methods of cooperation for the development and use of indigenous and traditional technologies, and for the wider application of local knowledge, innovations and practices. As part of such programmes, access to, and use of traditional knowledge and resources should be regulated in order to minimize negative impacts on local communities and their ecosystems. In addition, local communities should be compensated for the real value of their contributions in ethnomedicine, plant breeding, and other forms of traditional knowledge. Increasing the economic value of local resources and traditional knowledge can promote resource conservation by making sustainable development a viable alternative to environmentally destructive activities, such as mining or monocultural agriculture. Regulated access and use, including a compensation scheme, can thus help to ensure cultural and biological diversity.

At present, ethnobotanists and collectors, mostly from the industrialized countries, are using local informants and guides to create profits from traditional knowledge about exotic flora and fauna. They collect plant species with horticultural potential, plants useful to develop pharmaceuticals, cosmetics and other household or industrial products, and seeds from crop plants. New enterprises have been formed especially for this purpose; in 1989 a group of scientists began Shaman Pharmaceutical, a California company that aims to commercialise the traditional pharmaceutical uses of plants. Substantial research contracts are being awarded to botanical gardens and other groups who collect and study plants. Seeds collected from farmers in developing countries are held in seed banks in the industrialized North. They are increasingly protected by intellectual property laws although they represent the experience of generations of rural breeders. In most cases, no compensation is provided to the donor states, communities or individuals.

Collectors turn to countries in the South because biological resources are not equally distributed around the globe, most of the northern hemisphere is "gene-poor" in living resources; Brazil has more than two-and-a-half times as many species as the Unites States, which in turn has ten times more than Germany. Our genetic interdependence becomes clear when we consider export commodities. Although the world's primary source of natural rubber originated in Brazil, the centre of production and many related innovations lies in Southeast Asia. Southeast Asia is also the centre of production of oil palm, although the crop's gene centre is located in Africa. Conversely, the centre for banana production is in South and Central America, although "home" for bananas and plantains is Southeast Asia. The centre of origin of the Latin American coffee industry is Ethiopia, while East Africa's sisal production is based on germplasm from Central America. Even the most genetically abundant regions of the world look beyond their own borders for at least half of the germplasm required for their staple foods. The main sources of biological diversity are the natural ecosystems of forests, savannahs, pastures and rangelands, deserts, tundras, rivers, lakes and seas. Tropical rainforests, located predominantly in developing countries, are of particular importance.

Biological resources and modern technology are also unevenly spread within countries. Areas rich in biodiversity are mostly distant from urban centres and are often inhabited by indigenous or tribal communities whose survival depends upon using natural resources in a sustainable manner. Technology, on the other hand, is concentrated in the urban scantness of industrialized countries. The Rio Earth Summit (1992) of the UNCED recognised that this uneven distribution of biological and technological resources makes cooperation essential between developing and developed countries and between urban and rural areas.

The twin goals are to protect biological resources and local communities. There are numerous interests to balance in achieving an equitable result for all the parties concerned; the communities and the state, the researchers and collectors, the companies that acquire, process and market the knowledge, and the consumers of the end products. Biodiversity is a "common concern of mankind", and in balancing the interests involved it is crucial to recognise that the marketing of local resources may actually accelerate the destruction of those resources unless protective programmes are implemented in full recognition of the human rights of local communities.

7

Indigenous Knowledge and Biodiversity

The wealth of living things on the earth is the product of hundreds of millions of years of evolutionary history. Since the emergence of *Homo sapiens* from the ranks of humanoid primates, biodiversity and humanity have become inextricably linked. Human cultures have adapted to many diverse habitats. They have used, altered and nurtured biological resources to meet countless needs. As a result of plant and animal domestication and resource harvesting, a tremendous interdependence has evolved between "natural" and "human-induced" biodiversity.

For centuries rural people have encouraged and relied upon biodiversity for their livelihood. Farmers have managed genetic resources for as long as they have cultivated crops. For some 12000 years, they have selected varieties of crops and livestock breeds to meet environmental conditions and diverse nutritional and social needs. The immense genetic diversity of traditional farming systems is the product of human innovation and experimentation both historic and ongoing. This has been recognised in the FAO by the resolution on farmers' rights that acknowledges the past, present and future contributions of farmers in conserving, improving and making available plant genetic resources, and that they should be rewarded for their contributions.

For a large number of developing countries, self reliance in food production will depend on improving low-input agriculture in difficult environmental conditions. The raw materials for these improvements are the biological resources sustained in forests, rangelands, fields and farms. The accumulated knowledge of farmers, coupled with access to modern technologies, provides the key to developing sustainable agricultural systems. In many parts of the world, wild species and natural habitats still help support household food security—access by all people at all times to the food they need for a healthy life. In Nepal, for example, 135 tree species are used as fodder. In Ghana, three-quarters of the population look to wildlife for most of their animal protein.

Access to advanced science and technology contributes to reducing human suffering and promoting economic development. But there is a growing recognition of the value of indigenous knowledge to address global agricultural, health and environmental problems. There is increasing awareness that conservation and use of biodiversity must be concerned not only with genes, genotypes, species and ecosystems, but also with the traditional knowledge that has helped to produce and maintain this diversity (Panels 1 and 2).

TRADITIONAL MEDICINES

An estimated three quarters of prescription drugs derived from plants were discovered because of their prior use in indigenous medicine. Forest dwelling indigenous people employ at least 1300 plant species for medicines and related purposes. Over 60 species of plants are used to treat skin infections in the Amazon region alone.

TRADITIONAL FOOD PLANTS

For generations, subsistence farmers have been producing or gathering plants in the wild or semi-wild that have long been accepted as desirable sources of food. At least 1000 million people are estimated to use such traditional plants to satisfy their food needs. They are essential to the diets of rural subsistence

Panel 1
Traditional system of resource use. Negative feedback cycle prevents excessive long-term use of local environment (Colchester, 1994 a).

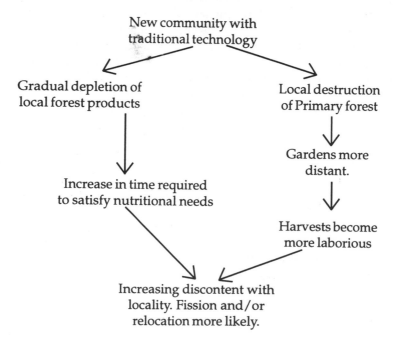

Panel 2

Modern system of resource use. Positive feedback cycle exaggerates speed of environment destruction leading to increasing dependence on outside society (Colchester, 1994 a).

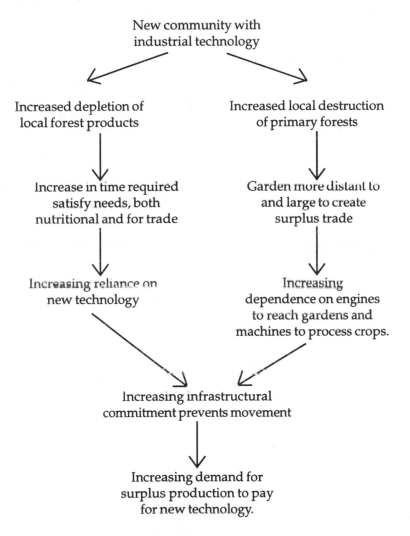

households throughout the developing world, providing sources of energy, vitamins and minerals.

Many countries, However, are experiencing a shift away from traditional foods, resulting in a narrowing of the food base. Failure to appreciate their benefits, together with a growing demand for imported foods, is reducing availability and consumption of these foods. Since 1985, the FAO, in cooperation with governments, has been endeavouring to reverse this trend. In association with research institutions the FAO is also promoting genetic improvements in traditional plants and development of technologies for preparing foods based on these plants that are acceptable in urban markets.

TRADITIONAL EXPERTISE FOR FISHERIES DEVELOPMENT

The International Centre for Living Aquatic Resources Management (ICLARM) in the Philippines, is tapping traditional knowledge to conserve and utilize fish genetic resources. Together with the FAO, it is assembling a comprehensive database on all of the 24000 species of cartilaginous and bony fishes in the world. In addition to scientific and technical information, the database incorporates indigenous knowledge—common names, traditional management practices and practical or symbolic uses of each species.

TRADITIONAL PLANT FOR DISEASE VECTOR CONTROL

Endod (*Phytolacca dodecandra*) commonly known as the African soap berry, is a perennial plant that has been cultivated for centuries in many parts of Africa where its berries are traditionally used as a laundry soap and shampoo. Dead snails were found floating in the water, where people were washing clothes with endod berries. This observation led to further research, which revealed that sun-dried and crushed endod berries are lethal to all major species of snails but do not harm animals or people, and are completely biodegradable.

For Africa, where one of the most serious diseases, *schistosomiasis*, is transmitted by freshwater snails, discovery of a low cost and biodegradable lumicide represents a major breakthrough. According to WHO, more than 200 million people are infected with *schistosomiasis*, which kills an estimated 200000 people every year. With support from international donors, endod is undergoing further toxicological studies to ensure its safety. Dr. Lemma views it as a product of traditional knowledge that can be developed by and for African communities.

NATURAL INSECTICIDE FROM A TRADITIONAL TREE

For centuries, Indian farmers have used seeds from the neem tree *Azadirachta indica* as a natural insecticide to protect crops and stored grain. Drawing on traditional knowledge and practices, scientists have isolated compounds that are extremely effective against insects, even in minute quantities. They reportedly control more than 200 species of insects, mites and nematodes, including major pests such as locusts, rice and maize borers, pulse beetles and rice weevils. Yet neem extracts do not harm birds, mammals and beneficial insects such as bees. Unlike most synthetic pesticides, insects apparently do not develop resistance to neem extracts because they contain several biologically active ingredients.

The commercial potential of neem-based pesticides had attracted the attention of companies in India and in the industrialized countries. In 1993, the world's first commercial - scale facility designed and built for neem-based natural biopesticide production opened in India, capable of processing 20 ta of neem seed per day. Scientists continue to study the potential of neem for treatment of diseases and, in particular, as a contraceptive agent. Neem is also reported to have fungicidal, antibacterial and even antiviral properties.

AGROSILVICULTURE AND THE ALDER TREE

In Nagaland, India an agricultural system has evolved that centres on the alder tree *Alnus nepalensis*. The tree is a source of fuelwood, timber and mulch while bacteria that grow in nodules on its roots capture atmospheric nitrogen adding to soil fertility. In the fields, alongside the alder trees farmers grow crops of maize, millet, potato, barley and wheat and secondary crops of chilli, pumpkin and taro. The alder tree cycle starts when the tree is pollarded. The main trunk of a 6-10 year-old tree is cut off at a height of about 2 meters from the ground. It then sprouts 50 to 150 shoots or coppices, all of which except for 5 or 6 are cut when they are 1 year old. Many of these trimmings are burnt together with crop waste to add fertilizing wood ash to the soil. A second crop is grown in the fertilized field. The field is then left fallow for 2-4 years to allow the trees to grow. After this time, when the remaining coppices are about 6 meters long and 15 centimeters in diameter, the tree is pollarded again. The main uses for these larger coppices are for fuelwood and poles. About 120 ha of alder plantation can provide all the fuel wood needed by 100 Naga families.

TRADITIONAL ROLE OF WOMEN IN RESOURCE MANAGEMENT

Women have played a silent yet central role in the sustainable use of biological resources. In most of the developing world they have the primary responsibility for house-hold food security. Women produce an estimated 80% in Asia and the Pacific and 40% in Latin America. Their roles as producers and gatherers of foodstuffs, medicines and fuel, and as drawers of water, involves them daily in the management of natural resources. In some parts of the developing world, home gardens cultivated by women represent some of the most complex agrosilvipastoral systems known. As a result of their knowledge of forests, crops, soils, water management, medicinal plants, growing techniques and seed varieties, women hold considerable responsibility for and knowledge of sustainable agriculture systems. Until recently, their role as conservers and users of genetic diversity, and as natural resource managers, was largely ignored. Now, there is a growing recognition that conservation and sustainable use of biological diversity will not be possible unless women are involved in decision-making and in the control of resource management and production.

More voices, it seems, are joining the chorus of praise for indigenous knowledge every day. While the litany has gotten louder, the meaning of the words is not necessarily clearer. Certainly, indigenous knowledge is about what local people know and do, and what they have known and done for generations—practices that evolved through trial and error and proved flexible enough to cope with change. But to outsiders this knowledge often remains elusive. Imported western methods and technologies fail too often in a new setting because the "experts" simply do not understand the people they were trying to help, and failed to take local knowledge and attitude into account.

THE SILENT GENIUS

Indigenous knowledge is not always visible, and even when it is, not always easy to understand because it is incorporated in the way of life—part experience, part custom, religion, tribal law and the attitude of people towards their own lives and those of other living things. What little is recorded in black and white is often found only in anthropologists' anecdotes or merely mentioned in scientific dissertations on tropical agriculture, forestry or veterinary medicine.

But even better observation and recording will not be sufficient: understanding is needed. It is important to know how people define and classify soil types and varieties of crops and how they use these classifications in the decision-making process. It is important to know a host of factors—from how people perceive different trees to how land tenure systems and inheritance rights influence decisions. And priorities must be appreciated. The small farmer with a hungry family to feed every day of the year will reject high-yielding varieties even if they do not require high inputs. Several different low-yielding varieties that mature at different times and under different climatic conditions may take more time and effort to cultivate but they spread the risk i.e. from conditions of no food at all to one of less food.

Some investigation has been possible thanks to the relatively new concept of cognitive anthropology, or "ethnoscience," in which a culture's perception of its universe is studied through its language. But this requires an in-depth knowledge be studied "scientifically". Will this risk destroy the data? Is it possible to integrate "scientific" and indigenous knowledge at all? Can indigenous methods be used to disseminate knowledge? Can indigenous knowledge be extracted from its socio-cultural context and transferred to other parts of the world?

FACTS
- In Africa, 80% of vitamin A and more than a third of Vitamin C are supplied by traditional food plants.
- Apart from the macadamia nut of Australia, all the fruits and nuts used in western countries were grown first by indigenous people living there.
- The world market value of pharmaceuticals derived from plants used in traditional medicine exceeds US $ 43000 million, but less than 0.001% of the profits has gone to the indigenous people who led researchers to them.

- Indigenous populations and their knowledge are threatened with imminent destruction. In the Amazon alone, over 90 different groups of Indians are thought to have died out during this century.
- More than 200 varieties of sweet potato can be identified by the *Ifugao* of Luzon in the Philippines; *Jivaro* farmers in the Amazon grow over 100 varieties of cassava; and in the central Andes 50 to 70 potato varieties can be found in a single locality.
- Mixed farming using crops and livestock is frequently the most sustainable form of agriculture in a region.

INDIGENOUS—DEFINED

There is no commonly accepted definition of who indigenous peoples are. In its most literal sense the term "indigenous" only implies *long-term residence in a given area*. Yet in international law the term has begun to be used in a more precise way to apply to *culturally distinct ethnic groups that have a different identity from the national society, draw existence from local resources and are politically non dominant* (ICIHI, 1987). In a similar vein, the World Bank identifies indigenous peoples as "*Social groups with a social and cultural identity distinct from the dominant society that makes them vulnerable to being disadvantaged by the development process*" (Word Bank, 1990). The International Labour Organization (ILO), whose Conventions treat both indigenous and tribal people, places more emphasis on the notion of *prior residence in an area, before conquest, colonization or the establishment of present state boundaries*. However, the ILO (1989: Article 1) notes clearly that: *Self-identification as indigenous or tribal* shall be regarded as a fundamental criterion for determining the groups to which the provisions of this Convention shall apply.

For their part, many ethnically distinct and marginal people are increasingly adopting the term "indigenous" to describe themselves because of the rights that they believe are associated with such a term—rights to their lands and territories; to maintain their cultural traditions, religions, languages and practices; to exercise their customary law; to govern themselves through their own institutions; to represent themselves through their own organizations; to control their own natural resources; to self-determination, and the recognition of their right to be different.

Estimates of the number of people classified as "indigenous" vary widely, not only because definitions vary but because census data are often poor or absent in the remote areas such people inhabit. Figures from organizations such as the ILO, Survival International and the International Working Group on Indigenous Affairs range between 300 and 500 million worldwide (Fig. 7). More importantly, "indigenous" people speak the vast majority of the world's languages and represent the majority of cultural diversity.

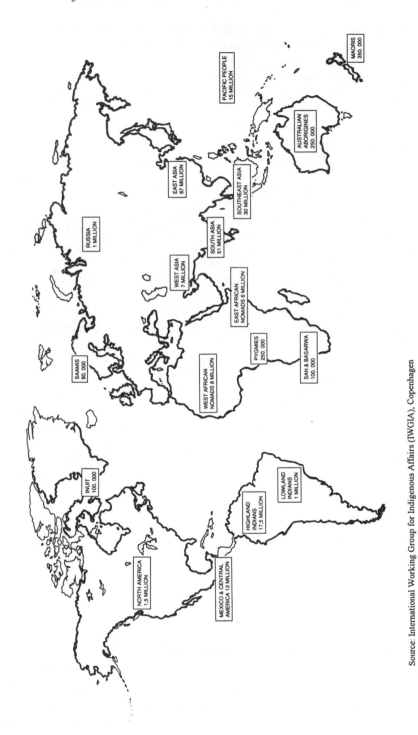

Fig. 7 Where indigenous peoples are.

Source: International Working Group for Indigenous Affairs (IWGIA), Copenhagen

PART II

GENETIC RESOURCES

1

Crop Genetic Diversity

Soil, water and sunlight are essential for food production but a lot of people do not realize that there is a fourth, equally important resource; the genetic diversity. Plant genetic resources give us crop varieties of different shapes, colours and sizes, with strategic characteristics such as resistance to disease or pests, or tolerance of drought or frost. Today, these resources are threatened by genetic erosion, particularly with the introduction of new varieties that have been promoted as part of the green revolution. While potentially high-yielding under certain conditions, the uniformity of these new varieties can lead to crop failure with profound consequences.

Non-agriculturalists find it hard to understand the importance of plant genetic diversity. It is helpful to describe "rice", for example, in the same way as "people". In the same measure that human genes determine a person's colour, shape, size and quality, plant genes determine the growth, harvesting, processing and cooking characteristics of rice. The more genes there are available to breeders, the more choices there are for adapting crops to new environmental or market conditions. When there are fewer genes available for breeding, there is little or no room to manouvre should climatic variation, global warming, ozone depletion, new pests and diseases or new processing technologies demand new genetic characteristics in our food supply. The world's food supply is losing its capacity for change and its ability to manoeuvre through new pressures and opportunities.

This century has witnessed a truly massive explosion in crop yields. Current breeding strategies have made it possible for us to keep pace with the world's growing population. The side effect, however, has been for breeders to concentrate on a relatively limited number of plant varieties with special genetic characteristics. As farmers plant the new seeds, the old seeds are eaten. With seed, the means of production is also the end product of consumption. Ten thousand years of agricultural development can meet extinction in a morning bowl of porridge. Since the middle of this century, a large proportion of the genetic diversity of the world's top food crops has disappeared from the farmer's fields. This genetic erosion of the world's food security is continuing at a current annual rate of 1 to 2%.

FACTS

- Several thousand plant species have been used for human food in history, but now only about 150 are cultivated and no more than three supply almost 60% of the calories and proteins derived from plants.
- Since the beginning of this century about 75% of the genetic diversity of agricultural crops has been lost.
- Kenaf (*Hibiscus cannabinus*), an East African plant related to cotton, provides an alternative source of pulp for making paper.
- From wild pineapples found in the dry open Chaco of South America, breeders have imparted high-sugar content and a distinctive "wild fruit" flavour to cultivated varieties.
- Genes transferred from a wild relative of the tomato found on the shores of the Galapagos islands has conferred salt tolerance to cultivated varieties so that they can be irrigated by one-third sea water.

The Centres of Origin(Figure 8)

1. Chinese-Japanese Region

Soybean	Orange
Rice	Tea
Millet	Mustard
Bamboo	Peach

3. Australian Region

Macadamia nut

4. Indian Region

Rice	Mango
Banana	Bean
Sugarcane	Eggplant
Chickpea	Citrus

6. Near Eastern Region

Wheat	Barley
Lentil	Rye
Grape	Almond
Melon	Fig
Pistachhio	Pea

8. African Region

Wheat	Sorghum
Millet	Telf
Yam	Oil Palm

2. Indochinese-Indonesian Region

Banana	Coconut
Sugarcane	Rice
Grapefruit	Yam
Bamboo	Mango

5. Central Asian Region

Wheat	Rye
Grape	Apple
Apricot	Plum
Pear	Melon
Onion	Carrot
Pea	Spinach
Bean	Walnut

7. Mediterranean Region

Wheat	Oats
Olive	Beetroot
Radish	Lettuce
Fava bean	Grape
Cabbage	Celery

9. European-Siberian Region

Hops	Apple
Pear	Cherry
Chicory	Lettuce

10. *South American Region*

Potato	Sweet Potato
Cassava	Tomato
Pineapple	Lime bean
Groundnut	Cacoa
Squash	Papaya

12. *North American Region*

Sunflower	Blueberry
Jerusalem Artichoke	

11. *Central American and Mexican Region*

Maize, French Bean
Potato, Squash
Pepper / Chilli

The Areas of Diversity for Major Food Crops

Banana	Southeast Asia
Bean	Latin America, Meditterranean South America, South Asia, India
Cassava	Northern South America
Groundnut	South America
Maize	Central America
Millet	Horn of Africa, China, Japan
Oats	Eastern Mediterranean
Oil-Palm	Africa
Pea	Near- East
Potato	Andes
Rapeseed	Mediterranean
Rice	India
Rye	Near- East
Sorghum	Horn of Africa
Soyabean	China, Japan
Sugar bean	Southeast Asia
Sweet potato	Central America
Wheat	Horn of Africa
Yam	Horn of Africa

The value of genetic diversity to modern plant breeding is enormous. The US Government estimates that a 1% gain in crop productivity means a US $ 1000 million benefit to the American economy. Italian scientists calculate that the benefits of exotic germplasm for a single crop, drum wheat, amount to US $ 300 million per year. Not only cultivated species but also the genes from wild relatives are enormously valuable. Between 1976 and 1980, wild species contributed an estimated US $ 340 million per year in yield and disease resistance to the farm economy of the US. In the developing world, crop genetic diversity enables farmers to select crops suited to ecological needs and cultural traditions.

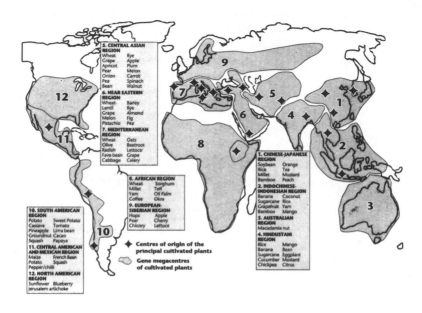

Fig. 8 The twelve megacentres of origin of cultivated crop genetic diversity.

Without this diversity, options for long-term sustainability are lost. This is particularly true in marginal areas with highly varied environments. The variety to a large extent determines the need for fertilizers, pesticides and irrigation.

Communities that lose traditional varieties that are adapted to local needs and conditions over centuries, risk becoming dependent on external sources for seeds and the inputs needed to grow and protect them. Without an agricultural system in harmony with a community and its environment, self reliance in agriculture is impossible. To feed an increasing world population, all available genetic resources, including wild relatives, will need to be tapped. Modern plant breeding as well as new biotechnologies offer the potential to exploit little-known plant species as sources of food, and to enhance the qualities of those plants that are underutilized, especially traditional plants of special significance to poor people, such as local grains, legumes, oilseeds, fruits and vegetables.

Traditional food crops, often grown by rural families to see them through the "hungry season" just prior to harvest, offer many advantages. Many of them are drought resistant, can be grown without expensive inputs and have good storage qualities. For many developing nations, self-reliance in food production will depend on low input agriculture in poor production environments. The capacity to grow varieties, particularly those resistant to pests and diseases and adapted to marginal lands, is vital for sustainable agriculture and food security.

2

Uniformity vs *Diversity*

HISTORIC ROOTS : DIVERSITY AS NECESSITY

Agricultural history is a story of continuous movement of domesticated biodiversity into new areas. In the case of farm-to-farmer movement it is called 'diffusion'. In the case of movements facilitated by explorers or scientists, it is called "introductions". While diffusion of germplasm is strongly linked to associated knowledge and culture, the transfer in the form of introduction is normally limited to genetic stock only. Diffusion means the spread of a farm technology element with enough associated diversity and skill to ensure the continued evolution of both the crop and the cropping system. Introductions very often come with a narrow genetic base—a limited scope for evolutionary adoption and a dangerous vulnerability to diseases and pests. History since the time of Colombus has a number of examples of such introductions. For example a few clones of potatoes coming to Europe and a single coffee tree which was propagated and distributed in enormous areas in Latin America.

These stories are, however, a couple of centuries old. The more recent examples, the introduction of *Brachiaria decumbens*, a tropical forage grass, into South America, and *Nile tilapia*, a farmed fish species, into Southeast Asia. When researchers started to work on the forage grasses of Latin America, it was soon shown that *Brachiaria* had been introduced with a too narrow genetic base. More introductions became the first priority. They had to go to the home of the species, the East African savannas, for more collections. *Nile tilapia* is also a species of African origin. Introductions into Southeast Asia occurred approximately 30 years ago. But when researchers started to work on the locally available stock, they found it to be highly inbred and genetically uniform. Also in this case, new introductions from Africa became the first priority.

In such cases, hardly anybody would dispute the wisdom of widening the genetic diversity by new introductions. But why, then, go in the opposite way in places where crops have arrived by diffusion and a wide diversity is already present? Why consider farm-level diversity of wheat and rice to be a "problem" and try to have it replaced with uniform modern varieties? We are told that the traditional varieties, the landraces, are low-yielding and the modern varieties are high-yielding. Protests against the eradication of traditional genetic variation are put down by a demagogic question: "Do you want them to starve?". We have to raise a new question. Is it really true that technology based on genetic uniformity is the only possible way of meeting growing food demands? Considering the ecological and political implications of removal of genetic diversity from farm level management and custody, there be ample reasons to explore other alternatives?

MODERN SYSTEMS: UNIFORMITY AS A NECESSITY

What has made development technology go for uniformity? Plant breeding is often blamed. However, the breeding is but one of several components of the commercial seed system. Before we pass the verdict, let us have a quick glance at those components.

The Commercial seed system

Basic plant breeding
↓
(Genetic resources : information and access, germplasm enhancement)
Applied plant breeding
↓
Variety testing
↓
Release and IPR-formalities
↓
Multiplication
↓
Certification
and Dissemination

Firstly, the variety testing and the release and IPR formalities require the varieties to be stable and distinct. These requirements are met through a high degree of uniformity. Secondly, the system is, for economic and practical reasons, unable to make local varieties. Broad adaptability to make the varieties useful in huge areas is necessary. Many plant breeders know that diversity would be an advantage from an agricultural point of view. However they know no other way of reaching the farmers except through a commercial seed system and therefore have to present their achievements in the form of uniformity as a necessity.

TECHNOLOGY ISSUES

It is commonly assumed that modern institutional plant breeding is "advanced", while traditional farmer breeding is "primitive". While this may be true if we consider breeding methods, it is not true if we consider breeding strategies. Breeding strategies within the formal system are dictated by formal requirements, such as those of the IPR bureaucracy of the Plant Breeders' Rights System (UPOV). Farmer breeders are independent and only consider the local agricultural needs. Their strategies may be closer to a biologically optimal breeding strategy. The main differences of breeding strategies between institutional and informal plant breeding are:

- Breeding targets in scientific breeding programmes may be different from those of small-scale farmer breeders.
- Traditional farmer breeding allows natural crop evolution to continue, while scientific breeding produces stable varieties which are supposed not to evolve or undergo any change once they are released.
- Traditional farmer breeding is tolerant of intra-varietal diversity, while formal breeding requires uniformity.
- Farmer breeding will be for local specific adaptation while scientific breeding will be for wide adaptation.

This last point, that of local or wide adaptation, is essential. The drive towards wide adaptation is taken to the extreme by the International Centre for the Improvement of Wheat and Maize (CIMMYT), an International Agricultural Research Centre (IARC) sponsored by the Consultative Group on International Agricultural Research (CGIAR). CIMMYT's breeding strategy is designed to develop broadly adapted germplasm that performs well in various zones or regions around the world under both high-input and low-input conditions: that is, germplasm with spatial-, temporal-, and system-independent yield stability.

Many would question the desirability of having one super variety which could be the top yielder on every farm across CIMMYT's ecogeographic "mega-environment". An increasing number of experts also question this approach. Discussing breeding strategy, a representative of the International Rice Research Institute (IRRI, another CGIAR centre) has said that, "Breeding for wide adaptability has associated costs. Varieties selected may not be best for a specific locality." This admission of advantages with local selection would be endorsed by most plant breeders, and within the CGIAR system this view is reflected in an increasing number of research reports.

This is also becoming a policy issue. Jim Ryan, Director General of the International Crops Research Institute for the Semi-Arid Tropics (ICRISAT, also of the CG family) has made the following remarks: "I wonder if our recent policy in India of not releasing finished cultivars and working more closely with National Agricultural Research Systems[NARS] Breeders in the provision of segregating materials and in cooperating breeding programmes, might not lead to greater genetic diversity in farmer's fields, and hence be conducive to biodiversity and conservation?". If local breeders and farmers access these heterogeneous segregating and early generation materials and graft them onto local land races, presumably this will lead to a plethora of region-specific and perhaps even village-specific cultivars, rather than just a few cultivars which might emerge from the previous ICRISAT approach of releasing finished products. May be this is plant breeding heresy, but it seems to be an issue worth exploring as we map out our future directions, and more importantly begin to measure our impact on sustainability and environmental concerns. CIAT, the CG's International Centre for Tropical Agriculture, has taken this reasoning to its logical consequence and started experimentation with farmer participatory breeding in their bean programme in East Africa.

DANGERS OF GENETIC UNIFORMITY

The erosion of crop genetic diversity poses a serious threat to food supplies. To maintain pest and disease resistance in major food crops, for instance, or to develop desirable traits such as drought tolerance or improved flavour, plant breeders require fresh infusions of genes from the farms, forests and fields of the developing world. Developing the high yielding, elite cultivars of modern agriculture depends on a steady stream of new, exotic germplasm. Plant breeders continuously try to develop new varieties to keep one step ahead of thousands of pests and diseases. Without access to traditional land races and their wild relatives, modern agriculture would be seriously endangered.

Industrialized agriculture favours genetic uniformity, typically, vast areas are planted to a single, high yielding variety—a practice known as mono-culture—using expensive inputs such as irrigation, fertilizer and pesticides to maximize production. In the process, not only traditional crop varieties, but long-established farming ecosystems also are obliterated. Genetic uniformity invites disaster because it makes a crop vulnerable to attack—a pest or disease that strikes one plant quickly spreads through out the crop.

GENETIC "WIPE-OUTS" IN HISTORY

Every year somewhere in the world, crop genetic uniformity leads to production losses. Ever-mutating pests and diseases overwhelm plant variety defences and sweep through fields. This sometimes results in lost markets and sometimes in lost people, as happened to the Indian cotton farmers in 1998.

- The genetic uniformity of the Irish potato crop of the 1840s exposed the country's staple food supply to devastating disease and massive production losses. Before it was over, two million people had died and millions more had fled to North America.
- In the 1870s, Sri Lanka's coffee crop was swept away by rust. The result was that the British became a nation of tea drinkers; the culprit was the genetic uniformity of Sri Lanka's coffee crop.

- The great Bengal famine of the 1940s—and the millions of deaths that resulted-may be partly traced to the genetic vulnerability of the region's rice crop to brown spot disease.
- A new maize blight, which first appeared in the Philippines in the 1960s, crossed the Pacific to devastate the United States' maize crop in 1970. With as much as half the crop lost in some southern states the country's farm revenues dropped by US $ 1000 million that year.
- Three years later, the genetically uniform cold-sensitive winter wheat in the former USSR was decimated in an unusually harsh winter and the world grain markets were thrown into chaos as a result.
- Throughout the 1970s, in Asia repeated attacks of brown planthoppers in rice crops slashed harvests by as much as 30 to 50% in some years.Once again, crop genetic uniformity was a major contributing factor to the consequent food losses.

Most of these problems were overcome by first identifying genes for resistance and adaptability in the areas of diversity of each species and then introducing them into the cultivated varieties of the production areas.

3

Agricultural Biodiversity

Agricultural biodiversity is of unquestionable importance. Its overwhelming value draws from it being the backbone of agriculture worldwide. Industrialization of farming and food systems and intellectual property schemes are threatening the survival and availability of the biodiversity. The main sectors in the conservation and use of agricultural biodiversity have been, and continue to be the millions of farmers and local communities who use and maintain this resource pool as the basis for their livelihoods. It is not only logical, but also urgent that the issues affecting the future of agricultural biodiversity are dealt with in a clear and comprehensive manner. The most appropriate way forward is to club all these issues into a special protocol on agricultural biodiversity, as an integral part of the Convention.

For the first time in history, one legally binding instrument (the Convention on Biological Diversity) signed by virtually all nations attempts to bring together national and international efforts to safeguard what is left of the biological resources on which peoples' basic livelihoods depend. It outlines a basis for committed national action in a framework of international cooperation. It firmly asserts that biological resources are subject to national sovereignty of the country that harbours them. It makes a worthy attempt to specifically consider local communities as valid actors in these efforts, and tries to be bold in looking beyond just how to conserve and use the planet's treasure chest and address the forces that are depleting this resource base in the first place.

SPECIAL ACTORS : THE FARMERS

Based on thousands of years of hands-on experience and a deep knowledge of their needs and their agricultural production systems, rural communities have developed multiple strategies for their farming systems, almost all of which hinge upon sophisticated management of genetic diversity. Farmers developed, and continue to develop, thousands of different crop varieties—each of them adapted to specific needs within their farming systems. While the public imagination in industrialized countries is dominated by concern for the biological diversity of the tropical rainforest ecosystems and rare or threatened animals, the biologically under-recognised wealth found in farmers' fields underpins global food security. The true actors in this mega conservation scheme are not nature park officials or environmental organizations, but the millions of small farmers and local communities.

Farmers developed crop varieties and maintain their diversity to meet the needs of their families and farming systems. But their contribution in the creation and conservation of this tremendous biological treasure goes much further. The importance of agricultural biological diversity is almost beyond imagination. Especially the citizens of the industrialized world benefit from this contribution by Third World farmers. For example, wheat growers in the USA gain as much as US $ 500 million per year from the use of Third World wheat genes incorporated into their seeds. What is true for wheat is true for virtually any major crop grown in the industrialized world. Farmer-developed biological diversity forms the basis of much of our contemporary agriculture, moving tremendous amounts of resources Northward without any recognition or acknowledgement flowing back to those who developed and conserved this resource base in the first place. Beyond its monetary value, the richness of agricultural diversity allows for present and future stability and resilience of farming systems and the food supply.

THE THREATS

Wild biodiversity gets lost when bulldozers move into the rainforests. Agricultural biodiversity goes extinct when farmer-bred varieties are replaced with a handful of laboratory-developed uniform seeds. The loss of biological diversity in the farmers' fields undermines the very sense of "sustainable development" as it destroys options for the future and robs people of a key resource base for survival. Genetic erosion means more than just the loss of genetic diversity. In essence it is an erosion of options for development, especially at a time when humanity has to deal with radical climate changes and other environmental hazards. While destruction of agricultural biodiversity is one threat, its monopolization is another. In the past decade, some countries have passed a legislation on intellectual property rights that give private interests ownership over genetic materials. Under such legislations, and free trade treaties such as GATT and NAFTA, most of the benefits from biological diversity flow to industries in the North.

The dangers involved in the genetic erosion of our food base have prompted numerous reactions to do something about it. The formal scientific sector reacted by going out to the farmers' fields, before the seeds and breeds "disappeared", to collect samples for storage in genebanks. Currently some four and a half million samples of crop varieties are in *ex situ* storage—most of them in, and under the control of the industrialized countries. The "informal" sector—farmers, communities, their organizations and NGOs working with them—have taken a different approach: on-farm genetic resources conservation and management, in a system where farmers continue to use and breed the genetic diversity they have been custodians for centuries. Both approaches have their problems, but both are also necessary. At the international level, discussions have been going on for over a decade on how best to conserve and use this agricultural treasure chest. The UN Food and Agriculture Organization (FAO), in particular, has tried to bring together the different concerns; those worried about scientific quality, those pushing for political equity, those working on *ex situ* gene banking, and those concerned with grassroot approaches and farmer empowerment. The emerging *Global System on Plant Genetic Resources* embodies some consensus on the issues at stake.

In most parts of the world, agricultural genetic heritage is under siege. The push to "modernize" and "industrialize" the world's rural landscape has already taken a heavy toll on plant and animal diversity. In fact, the worse might be yet to come. Yet community organizations, independent farmers and NGOs are struggling at the local level to document, conserve and revive biodiversity in innovative farming systems throughout the world. Many large tropical countries, such as India are characterized by complex mosaics of distinct agro-ecosystems, differentiated by their climatic, soil, geological, vegetational and other natural features. These agro-ecosystems are separated by natural features and crop growing periods. Each of these agro-ecological zones is in turn comprised of myriad micro-habitats. It is within this diversity of habitats that an amazing variety of crops and livestock have been developed over the millennia of farming. But it is the genetic diversity within each species which is even more mind-boggling.

THE PROCESS?

Over generations, the rural farmers have continuously adapted and modified the rich genetic material available to them from nature. The diversity of crops and livestock is not only accidental, nor is it purely natural; it is more the outcome of thousands of years of deliberate selection, planned exposure to a range of natural conditions, field-level cross-breeding, and other manipulations which farmers have tried out. In other words, a single species of rice collected from the wild some time in the distant past, has diversified into 50000 varieties as a result of the ingenuity and innovative skills of the farming communities. But why did the farmers do this in the first place? One obvious answer is the prevailing diverse environmental regimes. The crop varieties and livestock breeds got adapted further to the diverse local conditions of growth and survival that were available. What is even more striking is the use of a large diversity of the same crop within a single village, and sometimes within the same field. The diversity was spread over both time (seasonal) and space (geographical), both vertical and horizontal layers within the same field, and both within and between species. Even the much maligned and misunderstood systems of shifting cultivation in some Third World countries encouraged the use of a large diversity of crops. More than mere physical adaptation, a host of economic, cultural, religious and survival factors have played a role in this diversification. Several varieties of rice and other crops were grown just for their use during festivals, marriages or other auspicious occasions; several others were grown for their taste, colour, or smell; yet others for their pesticidal or soil-fertilization characteristics. The stability of a biodiverse agriculture is perhaps its most important characteristic.

4

Green Revolution: The Cost and Remedy

The last three decades have seen dramatic changes in world agriculture. With the advent of the Green Revolution in the mid 1960s, a handful of laboratory-generated varieties have been promoted over vast areas. Given a high input of irrigation and chemical fertilizers and pesticides, these varieties produce high yields (High-Yielding Varieties or HYVs). It is understandable for farmers who can afford such inputs, or who are offered bank loans, to take enthusiastically to these varieties. Agricultural schemes have also attempted to homogenise growing conditions, for example by surface irrigation, so that where there was a complex mosaic of diverse micro-habitats earlier, there are now vast stretches of uniform agricultural landscape. Intercropping is replaced by monocropping, reinforced by uniformity, a wide diversity of species is replaced by a handful of profitable ones, and the great genetic diversity within the same crop species is replaced by a narrow genetic range of financially lucrative varieties. The net effect of these practices had been a massive displacement of indigenous seed varieties, and with them the people.

There is no available figure for the overall loss of crop diversity worldwide, some idea can be gauged by the fact that a handful of HYVs are now grown over 70% of the paddyland and 90% of the wheatland of India with the resultant loss of traditional varieties. Thousands of varieties of rice, cotton, minor millets, pulses, and other crops are no longer in use. Livestock diversity has also faced a serious threat. It is estimated that over 50% of goat breeds, 20% of cattle breeds, and 30% of sheep breeds are today threatened. The greatest factor in the loss of domestic animal diversity has been the deliberate cross-breeding with exotics, carried out extensively in order to increase the yields of milk, meat or other animal products. Semen banks have generally stored the semen of exotics. While all kinds of livestock are affected, perhaps the worst off is poultry population, with disastrous effects on indigenous breeds. The current thrust towards export-oriented poultry production is likely to intensify the loss. This erosion of agricultural biodiversity, a fallout of the green revolution, threatens the long-term sustainability of agriculture itself, in many ways.

- It erodes the genetic base on which scientists are depending on for continuous improvement of crops and livestock. The majority of the

HYVs themselves have been developed from genetic material taken from traditional varieties and wild relatives of crops.

- The failure of a single HYV crop due to any natural calamity will be a crippling blow for a farmer who has no other crop to fall back on. And since the same variety may now be grown over thousands of hectares, its failure entails suffering and destitution for a vast number of farmers.
- Both the above features result in an increasing dependence of the farmer on the industry-dominated market and the market-dominated government for seeds, irrigation, fertilizers, pesticides, credit, subsidies and support prices. Farmers are facing the economic treadmill, spending more and more to achieve the same output.
- Several other effects of the green revolution have brought insecurity in the lives of farmers.

Modern agricultural policy is based on *introductions,* a type of deliberate movement of germplasm effected previously by explorers and scientists, and now by MNCs. The germplasm comes with a narrow genetic base and hence is vulnerable to attack by diseases and pests. The result is the undermining of food security locally and the loss of biodiversity globally. Increased outputs are tied up with intensive external inputs. New farming techniques require farmers to invest more. The HYVs, and the hybrids in particular, often require a never-ending breeding replenishment to sustain the output. Policies that govern the GR technology are the brainchild of the CGIAR, the conglomerate for agricultural research for developing countries, with the stated objectives of poverty alleviation and food security. The programme of the CGIAR are funded by the WB, FAO, UNDP, UNEP and the First World. The CGIAR is the world's most influential agricultural research network armed with the 16 IARCs that pride themselves for producing the technologies underpinning 75% of the world's rice, wheat, maize, potato and other food crops. In the 70's and 80's the GR technology did come out successful in quantitatively pushing the yield output in most countries.

WHAT WENT WRONG ?

But in the Third World, especially in the late 90's, this did not lead to the betterment of the small farmer or slowed the increasingly vicious cycle of rural poverty and environmental degradation. For the GR concentrated on farmers at the top of the gradient, hoping that " progressive or advanced" farmers would serve as examples to others in a sort of "trickle-down" technology diffusion process. The high inputs of fertilizers and pesticides in the long-run led to soil degradation and salinization, chemical pollution, environmental imbalance and loss of biodiversity.

It is well-known that plants grown in genetically homogeneous monocultures often do not have the ecological defence mechanisms to tolerate disease outbreaks and climatic fluctuations. Uniformity only boosted yields under optimal conditions. Monoculture being the structural base of the agricultural

system, the increasingly vulnerable crops call for equally destructive and prohibitively expensive protective measures. The GR targeted the best of the irrigated
lands in the Third World to begin with, but even in these favourable areas, the
farmers are beginning to abandon the high input technology. Still worse, the
poor farmer faces a bigger threat of complying with the IPR regime that endows
the MNCs with ownership of the seeds and with that the cropping systems.
Having accepted the CGIAR's high input GR model he stands to lose the ownership of the very seeds he grew, evolved and harvested. The noose around his
neck is getting tighter by the day as technology after technology stress is laid on
the gains of the MNCs rather than of the farmer. It is no surprise then if a group
of US citizens and farmers have taken the five leading MNCs to court for damages.
The petitioners argue that their own as well as the world agriculture has been
hijacked by these giants for ransom, ever since the MNCs started insulating
their stranglehold on the farmers with IPRs and technology protection systems.
The *terminator* and *traitor* technologies are just a few examples.

THE REVIVAL

In February 1995, the masterminds behind the GR paradigm gathered in
Switzerland to review the existing IARC strategy. Following this in October the
IFPRI of the UN launched *2020 Vision*, a call for a new agricultural strategy to
fight poverty and malnutrition in developing countries. The policy document
calls for the *second green revolution*. It agrees with the fact that there is no
alternative to the continued use of crop and livestock diversity in the farmers'
fields and the pastoralists' rangelands. In its recognition of sustainable agriculture as an ideological bridge that brings development and environment
together, there seems to be a belated realisation of the following :

- GR agriculture attempted to homogenise growing conditions.
- Stress-free environment is hard to achieve and even harder to sustain.
- Global climate change is destined to put new pressures on the GR
  crops, requiring their never-ceasing adaptation.
- External inputs were intended to reduce environmental heterogeneity
  that people had earlier coped with by means of varietal diversity.

SUSTAINABILITY THE ANSWER

The CGIAR, bowing to internal and external pressures, has been trying to renew
itself by combining biotechnology with sustainability goals. Its *External System
Review Panel* made an internal soul-searching and presented its draft report
during the CGIAR's 1997 *International Centres' Week*. Among other things it
recommended the inclusion of NARSs, private industries and NGOs in programme planning and implementation. The NGOs, suspicious of the CGIAR's
involvement, are yet to commit themselves. However, they pointed out the
fundamental flaw in the GR model. That is, in the GR package yields are not
considered intrinsic to the seeds, rather, are intimately tied to purchased inputs

of seeds, chemical fertilizers, pesticides, fuel and a host of intensive irrigation practices. Hence Dr. Palmer of the UNRISD renamed, the HYVs as high-responsive varieties (HRVs). Native cropping systems involve an interaction between the environmental resources, plant genetic resources and human resources. GR agriculture replaced this interaction with the integration of costly inputs.

Since the early 90s the CGIAR experienced a serious crisis of confidence and orientation. It felt the pressures of declining research funds and increasingly intriguing donor queries. Declining yields and the rising cost of inputs were among the factors that prompted the head of the FAO's Regional Office (Asia-Pacific) in 1996 to realise and recognise the need to move away from the GR model. The CGIAR's mission statement now is "to contribute to promoting sustainable eco-friendly agriculture". This objective, to increase food security while conserving the resource base, requires profound changes in strategic research agendas. The concept of sustainable agriculture aims to develop agro-ecosystems with minimal dependence on agrochemical and energy inputs, and in which ecological interactions and synergy between biological components provide mechanisms for the systems to sponsor their own soil fertility, productivity and crop protection. Such a biological agriculture encourages tapping farmers' knowledge and skills in assembling diversity, productivity and food security together. In other words, it means development that meets present needs without compromising the options of future generations.

5

Who Controls Genetic Diversity?

International cooperation with respect to biodiversity has been complicated by the efforts of some industrialized countries to extend intellectual property rights to genes, plants, animals and other living organisms, which inevitably leads to restrictions on access to genetic resources. With the advent of genetic engineering, for example, the biotechnology industry has promoted the extension of industrial patenting regimes to living organisms—an approach popularly known as "life patenting".

Proponents of patenting argue that it stimulates innovation by rewarding patent holders and enables companies to recoup their research investment. In the 1980s, precedents were established for extending the concept through "life patenting". As a result, genes, plants, animals and microorganisms—whether discovered in nature or manipulated by genetic engineers—could be rendered the intellectual property of private interests. Patenting of useful genes found in nature is particularly controversial. For farmers and consumers in the developing world it could mean paying royalties on products that are based on their own biological resources and knowledge. Under the patent law, a farmer breeding a patented animal and selling its offspring without payment of royalties would be contravening the law. Similarly, it would be illegal for farmers to save seeds from a patented variety for replanting.

Proposals are now being considered at various international fora to :
- Promote the extension of patenting and/or plant breeders' rights in the developing world.
- Expand the scope of industrial patent law to cover all biotechnology products and processes.

In promoting mechanisms for rewarding innovators of new biotechnologies, little or no consideration has been given to the impact on the future conservation and exchange of biological resources. The *FAO Commission on Plant Genetic Resources* has warned: ".. if the patent system is applied universally to living matter, including plants and animals, and their genetic resources, then the principle of unrestricted access will be severely eroded".

The danger is that claiming intellectual property rights, without reciprocal benefits and compensation for developing nations, could set up formidable barriers preventing access to genetic resources. In the wake of new intellectual property proposals, developing nations are questioning the concepts of free access and heritage of humankind. They may react by restricting access to germplasm on their territories. Clearly, present proposals could have grave implications for future economic development and world food security.

GEOPOLITICS OF PLANT GENETIC RESOURCES

Historically, scientists from the industrialized countries have ventured Southwards in search of exotic plants for plant breeding. Seeds found in tropical centres of diversity have been freely collected and later deployed in plant breeding. As a result, a lot of the origin has come to be stored in the Northern hemisphere or in gene banks established by the developed countries (Figure 9). The issue of control, ownership and access to plant genetic diversity has come to the fore over the past two decades. Plant breeding in the industrialized world has become increasingly commercialized and is now dominated by transnational seed and agrochemical corporations. To promote innovation and to enable breeders to recoup their research investment, many governments in the industrialized world have adopted a system of "plant breeders' rights". This gives patent-like protection to breeders with limited monopoly rights over the production, marketing and sale of their varieties for a period of upto 20 years.

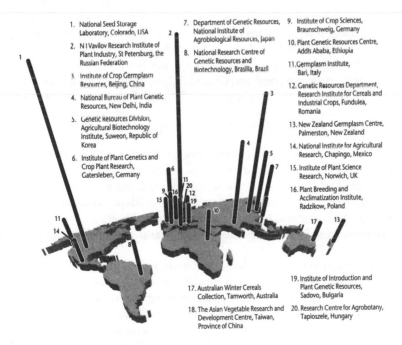

1. National Seed Storage Laboratory, Colorado, USA
2. N I Vavilov Research Institute of Plant Industry, St Petersburg, the Russian Federation
3. Institute of Crop Germplasm Resources, Beijing, China
4. National Bureau of Plant Genetic Resources, New Delhi, India
5. Genetic Resources Division, Agricultural Biotechnology Institute, Suweon, Republic of Korea
6. Institute of Plant Genetics and Crop Plant Research, Gatersleben, Germany
7. Department of Genetic Resources, National Institute of Agrobiological Resources, Japan
8. National Research Centre of Genetic Resources and Biotechnology, Brasilia, Brazil
9. Institute of Crop Sciences, Braunschweig, Germany
10. Plant Genetic Resources Centre, Addis Ababa, Ethiopia
11. Germplasm Institute, Bari, Italy
12. Genetic Resources Department, Research Institute for Cereals and Industrial Crops, Fundulea, Romania
13. New Zealand Germplasm Centre, Palmerston, New Zealand
14. National Institute for Agricultural Research, Chapingo, Mexico
15. Institute of Plant Science Research, Norwich, UK
16. Plant Breeding and Acclimatization Institute, Radzikow, Poland
17. Australian Winter Cereals Collection, Tamworth, Australia
18. The Asian Vegetable Research and Development Centre, Taiwan, Province of China
19. Institute of Introduction and Plant Genetic Resources, Sadovo, Bulgaria
20. Research Centre for Agrobotany, Tapioszele, Hungary

Fig. 9 The words's major national plant gene banks.

The disparity between unrestricted access to genetic resources, including farmers' land races, and the existence of proprietary rights (breeders' rights) on improved varieties has fuelled an intense debate over the inequity in the flow of germplasm from the developing world to the industrialized world. At the United Nations, representatives from the developing countries ask : why are patented seeds, originally from developing countries, bringing profits to seed companies in the industrialized countries without corresponding compensation for the developing world? What compensation will be made to those who have tended and nurtured the world's crop genetic diversity and continue to conserve and make it available today?

TANGLED GENES

The overwhelming majority of plant genetic resources are found in developing countries. There are many more plant species in the area covered by Botswana, Lesotho, Namibia, South Africa and Swaziland than in any other region of the world of a comparable size. Each one of the world's 20 key food crops originated in Africa, Asia and Latin America. This has led to the popular notion that geopolitical boundaries govern the control of genetic diversity and that the North - although "grain-rich" - is "gene-poor".

However, tracing the creation and flow of plant genetic resources is a tangled proposition: wheat, for example, originated in the Near East but the specific genes that inspired semi-dwarf wheats and propelled the green revolution came from Japan; disease-resistant genes found recently in Brazil may support crop yields as far away as India; tomatoes originated in Latin America but some of their most useful processing qualities have come from the Philippines, and when corn blight struck the Southern United States, resistant genes were found not only in Mesoamerica, the crop's genetic "home", but also in West Africa.

UNTANGLING TOUGH QUESTIONS

In the late 1970s, the international community became aware that the seemingly abundant genetic diversity of food and agriculture was eroding, even though our technical capacity to use and transform germplasm was increasing. This little-known and even less understood resource suddenly became scarce and the subject of global concern. Among the issues raised were :
- What system is best for the collection and safe storage of priceless crop genes?
- Who controls the access to genetic material?
- How does the world community share the benefits of genetic diversity?

In November 1983, the FAO Conference adopted resolutions on the International Undertaking on Plant Genetic Resources and on the establishment of the Commission on Plant Genetic Resources. Member Nations pledged themselves to work together, through FAO, to resolve these vital problems. When the Commission first met, in 1985, the gap between the "donors of germplasm" (the South) and the "donors of funds and technology" (the North) seemed unbridgeable. Having lost much of their own crop diversity, industrialized countries were the first to recognize the need to collect and conserve seeds, and the bulk of the seeds collected in developing countries are now housed in or controlled by the industrialized countries. An unknown proportion - some say half - of these are duplicates of each other. It has been estimated that the international collections of the CG centres represent 35% of all original materials, making these specific collections very important for food security.

The benefits of the *ex situ* conservation are quite straight forward. The diversity currently held in gene banks is for all practical purposes, the most immediately accessible form of breeding materials used by the breeding and biotech industries. On the negative side, *ex situ* conservation has been criticized from many angles. As a philosophy, *ex situ* conservation has the drawback of cutting plants and animals off from evolution. Specimens that are frozen in time will only adapt to their new institutional settings, not to a changing environment. Thus, valuable characteristics will be lost or forgone in time. As a centralised and technology-dependent form of storage, gene banks suffer power shortages, lack of trained personnel and inadequate funding. Finally, from the geopolitical angle, today's *ex situ* collections of crop, microbial and animal genetic resources are by and large controlled by the North, whilst the bulk of the material is taken from the South. The Convention's approach to *ex situ* conservation is to treat it as a com-plement, a second class approach, to *in situ* conservation. Essentially, it calls for governments to establish and maintain facilities and regulate collection of samples so as to make them true representatives of their respective populations.

ACCESS AND CONTROL

Beyond calling for more seed banks and nature parks, the CBD lays out general rules on access to genetic resources. These rules stipulate that countries have sovereign rights over the resources that occur in their territory. Access shall be granted on mutually agreed terms and subject to prior informed consent. However, this only applies to states which are "countries of origin" of the genetic resource in question or to states which acquired the resource under the provisions of the Convention. This last point raises an important problem. All the currently held *ex situ* collections of biodiversity are subject not to the rules of the Convention but to the convenience of the powers that be. This neatly accommodates the commercial interests of the industrialized countries. Today, the North effectively controls 61% of all crop germplasm collections (national holdings plus those of the CGIAR): 85% of all fetal populations of domesticated livestock and 86% of global microbial culture collections.

6

Animal Genetic Resources

ALARM FROM ANIMALS

The UN's Food and Agriculture Organization (FAO, 1994) has released a new and important alarm. Not only is the vital diversity of our crops and forests succumbing to erosion under the guise of "development" programmes, but one - third of the 4000 or so breeds of animals used worldwide for food and farming are dangerously facing extinction. The issues surrounding animal genetic resources parallel in many ways the problems that have been plaguing plant genetic resources. However, we know a lot less about it. Animals—domesticated and wild—are extremely important components of people's livelihood systems. This chapter is a background overview of the status of animal genetic diversity and resource use, and what is being done to safeguard and improve the benefits people can derive through the riches of the animal world.

Without a doubt, global concern over biological diversity is skewed by the North's fascination with grizzly bears, tropical rainforests and other majestic "wonders of the world". The diversity crucial for agriculture and the daily struggle of farming communities gets little attention at all. Still, where agriculture does get attention, most of it is directed to food crops, and mainly to the "starchy staples", cereals, roots and tubers. Animals, especially those which help sustain local people and their integrated farming systems, are grossly missing from the scene. Compared to crops, little is known about the livelihoods, but we do know that it is disappearing fast. Despite the dearth of data, an important challenge lies before us to upgrade the conservation and use of animal genetic diversity in order to secure benefits to local people and develop more sustainable production systems.

A GLOBAL PORTRAIT

It may be hard for those living in the big cities of the industrialized world to imagine, but pigs, cattle and poultry formed a world population of some 13 billion heads (and bodies) in 1990, most of them being chickens. This is more than twice the human population of the planet. The FAO (1994) calculates that animals account for 19% of the world's food basket directly, but they also provide drought power and fertilizer for crop production, especially in developing countries, bringing their overall contribution to global agriculture upto 25%. While evolution has produced more than 40000 species of vertebrates, less than 20 make a significant contribution to the world food supply. Of those 20, just a small number of them dominate global production. The bulk of global meat production comes from pigs, cattle and poultry, while the world's milk supply is almost entirely provided by cows. Of course, all these data omit "minor" species such as camel, rabbit and deer, as well as fish and game, which are vital at the local level. They also mask regional differences. In India, buffaloes contribute more milk than cows do. And in China, 80% of the meat production is from pork.

While some 70% of all cattle and 60% of all pigs and poultry live in developing countries, only 30% of all the milk and 40% of all the meat is produced there. This bias has a lot to do with the way the Europeans and North Americans organize their livestock production : in many cases it is highly intensive, concentrated, disconnected from crop production, and based on a very limited number of super-breeds. It also reflects a tremendous North/South bias in the place and role of these animals in agriculture. In India and sub-Saharan Africa only 2% of all the grain is consumed by animals, while in a country like the USA this figure is as high as 70%. Every hectare of agricultural land in the Netherlands is backed up by 8 hectares of land somewhere in the Third World—whether it is cassava in Thailand or soyabean in Brazil—the feed is grown for its intensive livestock industries.

VALUE OF ANIMALS TO LOCAL LIVELIHOODS

Still, for the majority of the farm animals and the majority of the farmers in the world, the picture is quite different. Rather than seeing farm animals as single milk and meat machines, they also provide other important services such as traction, fertilizer, soil management, pest control, fuel, clothing, etc. On many farms, animals make a major contribution to crop production and energy supplies in the form of manure. Dung and urine enhance the fertility of soil and contribute to plant nutrition; dung is also burned as fuel. For many poor farmers in the South, manure is the only form of applied fertilizer that is available and affordable. In many farming systems, there is a strong interdependency of cropping and livestock keeping. A drop in animal numbers (for example, after drought), means less manure and lower crop yields.

In many countries, animals make cropping easier. Not only can animals plough the fields, they can also transport water and fuel to the home, goods to and from markets, fertilizer to the fields, and crops to the granary. While some animals such as rats and goats can be veritable pests themselves, destroying crops with voracious appetites, chickens and ducks can be of excellent assistance in pest control strategies. Deployed in the field, they feed on weeds, insects, snails, larvae and other threats to crop production.

Beside farming, domestic livestock are a vital form of capital, especially for the poor. Many people raise animals as an eventual source of cash when times are bad or a heavy investment has to be made. They are used for loans, collateral and dowries, and can always be quickly converted into currency - without interest payments! Women often take charge of fattening pigs or raising small animals to barter or trade for household needs. For many communities as well, animals also play an important role in sacred or religious traditions. People depend on wild animals for many of the same purposes. Rural folk manage the undomesticated environment to secure a wide range of needs, especially in times of stress such as drought or harvest loss. Wild animals which can be hunted or trapped provide food, skins, bone and a source of income when the products of the wild can be sold on the market or as a source of recreation for tourists. Most of the aquatic foods people rely on in the South—fish, shrimp, crabs, frogs and snails are wild or semi-wild, whether they are farmed or caught.

ORIGIN AND DIVERSITY

The domestication of animals started some 11000 years ago, shortly after the domestication of plants, when settled farming became a new option for food supply. According to archaeologists, goats and sheep were the first animals to be tamed, followed by pigs and cattle, in today's Near-East. As in the case of plants, the vast majority of domesticated animals have their origin in developing countries. Apart from the animals in the Near-East, chickens came from Southeast Asia, turkeys from Latin America, and buffaloes from India. Not to forget a whole series of "minor" species which are very important to local communities such as guinea pigs, yaks, musk oxen, as well as miscellaneous owl and small ruminants.

Despite our overall dependency on a limited number of animal species for global production, farmers managed to develop a vast amount of diversity among them. Just as we speak of different varieties of crops, we can also distinguish different breeds of animals. If chickens have a discrete centre of origin in Southeast Asia, there are countless, locally-adapted breeds spread all over the world today. Over time, domesticated animals spread mainly with people and settled into new environmental niches. The natural pressures that livestock had to beat include extreme temperatures, feed supply, humidity, parasites disease and other factors. Together with mating strategies employed by rural folk to combine desirable characteristics in offspring, selection and breeding have resulted in a range of indigenous types.

For example, the *Criollo* cattle in South America were developed from initial introductions coming from Spain and Portugal in the 1500s. Over the past five hundred years, they have developed traits that allow them to live on poor nutritional supplies and withstand environmental extremes. Several traditional African cattle breeds have developed resistance against *trypanosomiasis*—a debilitating and often fatal disease affecting 30% of Africa's cattle. Chinese farmers breed the rare *Taihu* pig, which can use a very high portion of forage food in its diet, reaches sexual maturity in 64 days and produces an average litter of

16 piglets. In general, Asians can boast of developing more than 140 different breeds of pigs, while North Americans can only claim 19.

However, the concept of a "breed" is really limited to the setting of the industrialized countries. Only in the past 150-200 years, have farmers and herders in the North begun intense, controlled breeding practices to develop uniform animal types, duly registered in herdbooks. As their pedigree is so strictly controlled, they can be identified as distinct breeds. In most developing countries, however, this kind of pedigree breeding for uniformity was never employed. Thus, a genetically diverse population of many millions of cattle in northern India goes by the encompassing name *Haryana*, while the difference between a Holstein cow and the Red Holstein cow in northern Europe draws down to one single recessive gene. When experts talk about the important diversity of European livestock, they refer to the amount of visually different breeds developed, and not necessarily to the amount of genetic diversity they embody.

7

Erosion of Animal Genetic Diversity

While intensive livestock breeding in the North over the past centuries helped to develop numerous different breeds, it also sowed the seeds of diversity's destruction worldwide. The sharp differentiation between breeds prompted a tendency to favour certain "superior" types over others. As with crops, economic pressures brought farmers to concentrate on new production systems. Since a few decades, the industrialization of farming practices and new technologies for breeding are resulting in an incredible impoverishment of animal genetic diversity. The FAO calculates, for example, that half of the breeds that existed at the beginning of the century in Europe have become extinct. One-third of the remaining 770 breeds are in danger of disappearing over the next 20 years. Other sources indicate that one single breed—the Friesian—now constitutes 60% of the dairy cattle community in the European Union, having gradually replaced other breeds over the past decades.

Agricultural policies in the North promote intensified livestock production systems, where animals are often reared inside special buildings and are forced to produce higher yields through a combination of genetics and management practices. Leaving aside the question of how these animals feel in such production systems, the genetic push has been nothing short of impressive. Compared with 30 years ago, the average dairy cow in the United States produces over twice as much milk. Fat thickness in Danish pigs has been cut to half. Today's broiler chickens mature in six weeks instead of three months. And industrial turkeys have been bred for such a wide breast that they cannot mate naturally any more. Not mating at all has a lot to do with this dangerous trend. The development of artificial insemination techniques and the use of frozen embryos means that one bull can "donate" sperm to hundreds of cows without ever seeing them. Other techniques (such as "super ovulation") are making it possible to produce upto a hundred offspring from a single female, and a few years of *in vitro* fertilization is likely to increase the number of possible - and virtually identical - offspring to thousands of cows (as with the cloning by Dr. Ian Wilmut).

Together, intensification of animal and the new reproductive technologies are posing a major threat to indigenous livestock breeds worldwide. The lure of high productivity from superstocks has resulted in developing countries importing exotic temperate breeds at an increasing rate. Imported strains are either shelled up in local versions of the "factory farm" (often under contract to processors and traders from the North) or they are crossed with indigenous breeds. With a backing from the World Bank, all the zones of Central and South America, as well as parts of Africa, are producing hamburger meat and broiler chickens for the Northern fast-food consumers under the most intensive conditions. Frozen sperm and embryos are also being flown from Europe and the US to all corners of the South in the name of improving stocks. For industry in the North, this is simple business. Dr. Walton of the company University Genetics sees it this way : "You can ship cows to China, which is an expensive process, or you can get 10000 of them under your seat on the plane." His company already signed a $9 million contract with the Indonesian government to buy Holstein cow embryos and a similar contract was signed with China.

Unless controlled, regulated and assessed on their real value, the new bio-technologies that allow for massive shippings of embryos under airplane seats spell disaster for indigenous breeds everywhere, but also for farmers depending on them. The replacement of indigenous breeds by airplane embryos means the loss of important genetic adaptations to unique local conditions. The International Livestock Centre for Africa (ILCA) already warned against importing the Northern superbreeds or crossing them with the local ones in Africa : "Evaluations have shown that the productivity of indigenous breeds is equal to or greater than that of many exotic genotypes under local conditions".

OBVIOUS IMPORTANCE

Given their obvious importance, not only to developing countries, but developed ones as well, it is critical that the genetic resilience of the relatively few species on which world agriculture depends be maintained. First cattle which account for 90% of world's milk and 32% of the world's meat production, followed by buffalo, sheep, goat, pigs, horses, camels and fowl.

Amongst civilized people, other considerations ought to enter the equation as well. Since *Homo sapiens* are the dominant species on Earth, we should think that people have an absolute moral responsibility to protect what are our only known living companions in the universe. Human responsibility in this respect is deep, beyond measure, but urgent nonetheless. The genetic diversity among animals deserves to be preserved for future generations as much as other manifestations of our cultural heritage, such as art or architecture. Developed over hundreds, perhaps thousands of years by breeders responding to the changing fortunes of history, domestic breeds are, as much as any work in paint or stone, the fruit of human genius.

ANIMAL GENE BANKS

In 1992, the FAO announced the launch of a five-year *Global Animal Genetic Resources Programme* that aims to rescue local animal breeds such as the *Shiwal* cow of Pakistan, the *Taihu* pig of China, the *N' Dama* cattle of West Africa and the

South American *Criollo* cattle. The FAO hopes to include the US$ 15 million programme in the World Bank's Global Environment Facility. In the 1980s, already the FAO Animal Genetic Resources Group decided that the most appropriate mechanisms for the preservation of endangered breeds are regional animal gene banks for cryogenic storage of semen, embryos, DNA and later, if feasible, oocytes. During 1988, regional gene banks were established in Africa (Ethiopia and Senegal), Asia (China and India) and Latin America (Argentina, Brazil and Mexico). These centres are located in national facilities in each country with necessary equipment and supplies coming from the FAO. There is more than one centre in each region so that split samples can be stored to reduce the risks of loss. Countries wishing to store germplasm of their endangered breeds are responsible for the collection of samples and their shipment to the bank. Legally, ownership of the germplasm remains with the country of origin. Provisions are made for access by third parties presenting valid claims for use. Users are expected to replenish the gene bank when possible with semen or embryos from regenerated animals. The FAO's animal gene bank system is supported by a global animal genetic database of the European Association for Animal Production (EAAP) based in Hannover. Originally set up for Europe, EAAP's database has been extended to cover all countries of the world.

8

Aquatic Diversity

The industrialization of fishing and the global markets are putting increasing pressure on marine ecosystems and the diversity they contain. Overfishing, the introduction of new species, restocking and aquacultural development very seriously affect diversity in continental waters. Both at sea and inland, small-scale fishing communities and the poor are paying the price for the scarcity of resources. The world-wide coverage in 1995 of the capture of the Spanish freezer trawler "Estai" by Canadian coastal guards as it fished for Greenland halibut in international waters, has drawn public attention to increasing international conflicts over marine living resources. Most of these conflicts are rooted in the fact that fish is a dwindling resource due to the explosive growth of the amount of fish which is being taken from the water.

OVERFISHING, AN INDISPUTABLE REALITY

Since the late 40s marine fish landings (the amount of fish brought ashore) have increased almost five-fold from around 18 million ta to over 86 million ta in 1989. The spectacular growth in catches resulted from technological innovation, greater accessibility to fish resources and low fuel prices. It derived from a basic assumption that has proved to be dangerous : the notion of the unlimited marine living resources as mankind's property. This assumption survived until the 1970s and, unfortunately, still seems to be alive today in the minds of many managers, scientists, shipowners and fishermen alike.

There are clear signs that the current situation is far from sustainable. In a report issued in June 1994, the FAO points out that 69% of the global fish stocks for which assessments are available, are considered either fully exploited, overfished, depleted or slowly recovering from depletion. This figure masks regional differences : in the Northern Pacific, nearly 100% of the studied fish stocks are in those categories, and more than 60% in the Eastern Atlantic. By 1992, the FAO had recorded 16 major fishery species whose global catch had declined by more than 50% over the previous three decades. Overall nine of the world's 17 major fishing grounds are now in precipitous decline, and four are "fished out" totally from a commercial point of view.

This situation is reflected in the increasing difficulty to keep up with the current fish landings. Since 1989 the growth of total landings started declining and by the early 1990s they started showing a decreasing trend. The message is clear : under current exploitation patterns we simply do not leave enough fish in the water to regenerate their stocks. Unless some drastic measures are taken, we will see a further decline in the amount of fish that can be brought ashore.

All this happens despite—or perhaps better—because of a tremendous increase in the size of the global fishing fleet. Between 1970 and 1989, fishing fleets grew at twice the rate of fish landings. In 1993 the FAO estimated that there were 1 million large-scale (more than 24 m long) and 2 million small-scale fishing boats operating around the world. To some the solution to overfishing is simply the reduction of the amount of boats out there and, as will be seen below, preferably the smaller ones. But the international fisheries scene is not that simple. A crucial factor in overfishing is technology. Large modern fishing vessels—most of them controlled by large transnational corporations started incorporating improved shelf positioning, fish detection, fish aggregation, fish catching and on-board fish preservation technology. This allowed them to become more efficient hunting machines competing for scarcer fish. Another factor is the increasing internationalization of fisheries, turning fish into a post —GATT international commodity that increasingly features in import and export statistics. Yet another one is the policy of many nations to subsidise, at whatever cost, their national fleets, in a race to continue the depletion of marine biological resources.

Growing fleets, dwindling resources and huge losses of capital have characterised the fishing industry. The FAO calculates the overall losses in 1989 amounted to US $ 54000 million. Some of the losses are assumed by the agro-industrial corporate interests that control part of the fleet, which then leave profit-making for the processing and marketing links of their chains. But most of it is being financed through massive subsidies from governments of rich and poor countries alike which maintain over-capacity in an effort to protect employment in the shipyards and in the fishing industries, and to promote export. The European Union's support for fisheries rose from $ 80 million in 1983 to $500 million in 1990, much of it for the construction of new vessels, or for "exit grants" to get rid of the old ones.

As a whole, fishing fleets are a drain on the tax-payers' money in the industrialized countries. At the same time, the export of surplus fishing vessels to developing countries, be it direct or through joint ventures, turns them into dumping sites for fishing to over-capacity. In the pursuit of the development of their own industrial fisheries, many Southern governments are either unaware of or unwilling to take account of the fact that when a Northern fishing authority subsidises the export of fishing vessels, it subsidises the exportation of debt. Fishing industries from rich countries also benefit from another kind of subsidy: their governments put pressure on coastal non-industrialized countries in urgent need of hard currency to provide cheap access to their fishing resources.

FISHING OUT AQUATIC DIVERSITY

There is a whole series of human activities that threaten aquatic biodiversity. Uncontrolled dumping of toxic waste, unsustainable tourist development, dam construction, nutrient discharges from intensive agriculture and population concentration, are just some. However, fisheries and aquaculture are currently the biggest threats to marine biodiversity, and a serious menace to continental water ecosystems.

Due to the extension and openness of seas and oceans, the overfishing extinction of marine species very rarely occurred until recent times. Whales were an exception, due to the fact that their hunting used to be and still is profitable. However, many fish species are known to have been brought to the verge of extinction by fishing activities. Long-living and slow reproductive species are particularly sensitive to fishing activities. The living fossil *Coelacanth* is now threatened because of the impact of small-scale fishing activities, an indirect result of a EU Fisheries Development Programme. Commercial fishing has brought common stake to the verge of extenuation, and it is also believed that several species of shark may soon be endangered if current exploitation levels are not reduced. Some sessile species, such as giant clams, have also been decimated by fishing.

Overfishing affects fish populations in different ways. If a fishery targets a high value species, the fleets may reduce the fish stocks to a level that leads to depletion and collapse. At these low levels, the populations are more sensitive to environmental changes (in water temperature or salinity). Examples of such depletion are not infrequent. Fisheries-induced collapse of a marine population can have two consequences for biodiversity. First, the population may not recover and re-colonise its ecological niche. Secondly, rare genes can be lost as a result of a drastic decrease in population numbers. As in agriculture, fish genetic diversity is the foundation on which the capacity to react to adverse situations rests.

But then, indiscriminate fishing can have a disastrous impact on non-target species as well. Recent studies indicate that anything between one quarter and one third of all caught fish in commercial fisheries has been thrown back into the water because they are considered undesirable; the wrong species, the wrong size, etc. These "by-catches" do not enter official statistics. It is thought that survival of most discarded species is low. In a sense, "by-catches" is a typical problem associated with large industrial fishing. Small-scale fisheries often cater for local markets with a demand for a wide variety of fish species and sizes. The definition of "wanted" for industrialized fisheries however is much more limited as they are often catering to the specialized cannery or other processing industries. Tropical shrimp - trawling fisheries (where a sack shaped net is dragged over the shallow sea bottom shrimp habitats) are the most unselective in the world, with a ratio between discarded fish and targeted shrimp as high as 20 to 1, and even 30 to 1. Marine mammal, turtle and birds populations are also harmed by fisheries, due to their long life-span and low fecundity. For example, the vaquita is the most endangered marine mammal. It gets entangled in the illegal gillnets targeting totoaba, which is also an endangered species. In the Western Mediterranean Sea, the illegal Italian swardfish driftnet-fishing very seriously threatens the stripped local dolphin population.

Fisheries also have an impact on biodiversity through the degradation of marine habitats. Dyanmite-fishing is widespread, and when it is practised in coral reefs, one of the most diverse ecosystems in the world, it not only kills fish but also damages and degrades the reef. Another example is trawling in shallow waters, a common practice in many areas of the world. Shallow waters host the most complex and diverse marine ecosystems thanks to the availability of both nutrients and sunlight. The destruction of sea grasses of *Posidonia oceanica* in the Mediterranean Sea - a refuge for juveniles of fish species—is a clear example of habitat degradation. Shrimp trawling in shallow waters—mentioned above —also erodes the sea bed.

INTRODUCING EXOTIC SPECIES : DESTROYING DIVERSITY

The problems are not confined to the open seas. Overfishing in closed systems- such as rivers or lakes has possibly a larger impact on genetic diversity than in the open seas. In every continental water system, populations have evolved in relative isolation, in a permanent process of adaptation to their environment. This has led to the selection of particular combinations of genes which result in a maximum adaptation for a given environment. With the decreasing number of individuals of the same species, a lot of that genetic diversity is getting lost... without the possibility for natural refreshment and diverse genetic input from elsewhere. One could argue that a helping human hand introducing foreign specimens of the same species would be the solution. But that is highly questionable as those specimen are not likely to be adapted to the specific micro environment into which they are introduced. It could result in a broader gene pool, but not necessarily the one needed.

What normally occurs is the human introduction of new species foreign to local ecosystems. The introduction of new species in closed lacustrine systems— for aquaculture or fishery enhancement—has been the cause of huge losses of biodiversity. One classic example : in the 1950s, the Nile perch was introduced in Lake Victoria for sport fishing. Its voracity and large size has led to the extinction of many smaller indigenous species : estimates are that 200-300 fish species may have been lost. The impact of introduced species can be even more important if it results in the introduction of new parasites or diseases. Although the Lake Victoria region has now based its fisheries on the new perch and has become one of the most productive in the world, the people around the lake who tended to rely on the extinct fish species, have suffered. The new fishery industry produces more for export than for local consumption.

FISHING OUT COMMUNITIES

The results of overfishing and depletion of resources take their toll not only on biodiversity and marine ecosystems but also on the peoples' livelihoods. The Canadians in Newfoundland fishing communities know this too well. Northern cod in the Northern West Atlantic, off Canada, is commercially extinct. In 1992, Canada closed northern cod fisheries and they have not been reopened since then. Over 20,000 people lost their jobs. The biomass of the stock is estimated to have gone from 400000 ta in 1990 to only 2700 ta by the end of 1994. In Canada and New England (USA) other groundfish fisheries have also been closed. Bad news for the 50000 people out of work in the North West Atlantic fisheries sector; and also bad news for the tax-payers who must foot the bill for the urgent corrective measures that Canada has had to apply to alleviate this difficult situation. The Canada Fisheries Minister seemed to believe that in order to make fisheries sustainable again, a dramatic decrease in fishing will be necessary.... in the inshore fishing fleet, exploited by relatively small family enterprises. Newfoundland communities, who have relied upon cod fisheries for centuries, are now excluded from them.

Small-scale fishermen and fishing communities in the South are hit even harder by similar marginalisation from control over the fishery resources they have traditionally depended on. At least 10 million people are traditional full-time fishermen and fisherwomen in developing countries, with a further 10 million as part-timers. They are among the poorest social groups. It is estimated that 100 million of the world's poorest depend on fishing for all or part of their livelihoods. Small-scale fisheries have played a capital role in supplying internal markets in developing countries with fish protein, traditionally a food of the poor. Approximately 60% of the people in the Third World obtain 40% or more of their animal protein from fish.

9

Is Aquaculture the Solution?

Ismael Serageldin, the Chairperson of the CGIAR is on the record (1995) as saying "On the land we have learned to produce food by cultivation. But in the sea we still act as hunters and gatherers". He continues stressing that aquaculture—the domestication of fishing—should be the next great leap in producing food. It seems logical. We are overexploiting the wild resources to meet a growing demand, so why not grow it under controlled conditions? The move from backward "gatherers" to sophisticated "growers", just as the world's farmers started doing 12000 years ago. This is not a wild cry in the emptiness. A recurrent theme in documentation from official institutions such as the FAO and the European Commission, dealing with fisheries has been the urgent need to develop aquaculture, given declining fish stocks, expanding population and increasing demand for fishery products. Intensive, high-tech aquaculture has been indicated for high valued species in the Northern countries, where consumers will be able to pay high prices. On the other hand extensive aquaculture is recommended in order to meet nutritional needs of the poor in the South.

Nevertheless, the projection of aquaculture as another means to get more fish products to the consumer—poor and rich—hides a number of important problems. **First**, one of the less published aspects of this proposed solution to the depletion of marine fish stocks is the fact that intensive aquaculture itself involves the consumption of huge amounts of protein. Most high-value species are predators which need top-quality fish protein. About 30% of world fish catches are converted into fish meal and oils, which are used essentially for animal feeds in agriculture and aquaculture. Carnivorous aquaculture—which comprises about a quarter of all aquaculture—consumed about 15% of the world fish supply in 1995.

Second, fishing wild fish to feed domesticated fish. Thailand, which has witnessed a spectacular 400% rise in shrimp farming, can serve as an example of this approach. Over the past decade this country has increased its forage fishing by 25%. Part of this increase has been possible through the development of biomass fishing : the sea bed is indiscriminately dragged not for shrimps and prawns as it used to be, but for anything that can be turned into fish meal for shrimp. An environmental and socio-economic danger, given not only the physical impact of these activities, but also the importance of some of these "trash species" in the diets of local communities.

Third, intensive shrimp aquaculture also has a heavy and direct impact on marine diversity. It has resulted into the loss of extensive coastal mangrove forests in order to build ponds : Thailand lost 100000 hectares of mangrove forests, and Ecuador over 120,000 hectares. Half of the world's mangrove forests have now been cut down, with aquaculture being the main cause. In Guatemala, Costa Rica and other countries of Central America, larvae fisheries use chemicals that kill any other species in the mangrove forests, including the mangroves themselves. **Fourth,** damaging effects of shrimp farming include the discharge of nutrients and chemicals into the environment and **Fifth,** the increase of salinity in surface and ground water.

Sixth, intensive aquaculture suffers from the same problem as intensive agricultural (monocultural) production : an uncontrollable spread of pests and diseases that had never been a problem before. In Taiwan aquaculture production rose to 95000 ta in 1987, before collapsing to 20000 ta due to virus outbreaks. In 1993, Chinese farmed prawn production declined by two-thirds due to algae blooms. In the same year, Ecuadorian prawn production fell to 40% of its peak because of similar factors. When government officials push outmoded "fish gatherers" into domestication and intensification, they seem to forget the implications of "Green Revolution" in agriculture from which we are still recovering.

Seventh, genetic diversity is suffering as well. Most intensive aquaculture is based on highly uniform population, and breeding has focused mostly on short-term yield concerns and nothing else. Only in recent years- through the Intenational Centre for Living Aquatic Resources Management (ICLARM) - has an aquacultural development programme taken into account the role of genetic resources, both to obtain improved performance and to avoid genetic resource erosion. In most other cases, however, experimental genetic management technologies such as hybridization, ploidy, gynogenesis and gene transfer have been used as shortcuts to obtain higher yielding fish.

In this context, biotechnology is presented as the great promise for the culture. Research has focused on genetic engineering and oriented to obtain fast-growing fish for higher yields (i.e., carp, salmon and super tilapia), show growing fish for higher quality flesh (i.e. salmon), stress-resistant fish (i.e., low temperature resistant salmon), and disease-resistant fish. The result at the moment seems to be irregular, as in the case of fast-growing Biogrowl Atlantic Salmon, developed by the Canadian subsidiary of Boston A/F Protein. After one year, the engineered fish and the control group had the same average weight and size, but the genetically engineered group contained individuals that were 11 times heavier than the control group, and one was 37 times larger than the average of the control group. Even with such irregular results, the company, which is to receive a CAN $ 265000 grant from the Canadian government, has already filed worldwide patents on the gene and transformation method involved in increasing growth rates, with licensing under negotiations in New Zealand, Scotland, Canada, the US, Chile, and possibly other countries. A/F Protein also intends to develop fast-growing tilapia and catfish.

The problems of wild fish genetic pollution through escape and inter-breeding with cultivated fish—and even aquaculturists' problems due to small parental stocks—may be increased by the spreading use of biotechnology. Some research is being done in order to obtain fish which can only reproduce in captivity, but the efficiency of such alternatives remains to be seen. And neither A/F Protein nor other companies are waiting for the results of such research efforts before embarking on commercial production.

10

Human Genetic Diversity

The one final "resource" which has not gone unnoticed by gene hunters is the diversity of the human genome itself. As part of the project to map the Human Genome (HUGO) anthropologists and geneticists have developed a small re-marked programme to preserve, *ex situ*, the variety of indigenous humanity. Working on the assumption that endangered peoples are vanishing from the face of the earth, these scientists have taken it on themselves to mount an urgent programme, akin to the *salvage ethnography* advocated in the 1970s, to collect samples of their DNA for cold storage and study. The preliminary programme has aim to collect some 10000-15000 human specimens from 722 identified human populations-referred to as "Isolates of Historic Interest".

Indigenous Communities Targeted for DNA Collection (RAFI)			
Africa	165	South America	114
Asia	212	North America	107
Oceania	101	Europe	23
		Total	722

Consulting anthropologists have thus set about identifying peoples threatened with extinction and sending teams out to make collections of hair follicles and squamous tissue from inside people's cheeks. Once these collections are made and viable cell lines are established, the peoples are referred to as having been "immortalized". Needless to say, indigenous groups that have become aware of this practice have been indignant in their denunciations. Victoria Tauli-Corpouz of the Asia Indigenous Women's Network asks : Why don't they address the cause of our being endangered, instead of spending millions to collect and keep us in cold storage?.

The offense stems as much from the priorities of those involved who, hiding behind a supposed scientific objectivity, feel justified in collecting human samples in the name of "human welfare", while doing nothing to counter the forces that are driving these peoples to extinction. Underlying these priorities are unrecognized prejudices that consider indigenous peoples to be "our contem-porary ancestors", natural curiosities that have survived beyond their time and which are doomed to disappear once the modern world catches up with them, the idea that indigenous societies are vital, viable and no less modern alternative ways of living is implicitly foreign to salvage ethnographers and geneticists.

The concept of the genome applies both to the genetic complement which is unique to the individual as well as that which is unique to the species. The genome of every individual is a version of the species genome which is distinguishable from the genomes of other members of the same species, the degree of similarity being an index of relatedness, with identical twins having identical genomes. Genomic variation, both within and between populations, is of great interest as a historical narrative of human activity. The Human Genome Diversity Project (HGDP) specifically addresses genetic variation, albeit in a form which by implication conceives of genetic difference as being of more significance between races than within them. Since many genetic disorders have a much higher incidence in particular ethnic groups, sampling the DNA of these populations for such disorders can aid the development of genetic screening tests, and ultimately the development of gene therapy. The HGDP, masterminded by Luigi Luca Cavelli-Sforza, a population geneticist at Stanford University in the US, is supposed to cost US $ 20 million provided for by international donors—to collect large amounts of gene samples from genetically distinct human populations. Researchers have already collected genetic data from many peoples including the *San* peoples of South Africa, *Penans* of Malaysia, the Australian *Aborigines*, peoples from the Sahara, Latin American *Indians*, the *Soamis* of Northern Norway and Sweden and the *Hagahai* people of Papua New Guinea.

Indigenous peoples possessing a valuable genetic diversity are yet not valued because of themselves. Their value lies primarily in their extracted genes. For example, health workers collected blood samples from 24 members of the *Hagahai* people and these were sent to the gene bank of the US NIH. When seven people were found to have a particular virus, HTLV-I in their genetic make-up, a virus that would help fight leukaemia, in 1993 the US Department of Commerce applied for a patent on the *Hagahai* people's DNA sequence and its product. It seems likely, therefore, that, in time, health products will be developed which would not have been possible without the cooperation of indigenous peoples, such as the *Hagahai*, but which they themselves cannot possibly afford to purchase, and from which they are unlikely to benefit. Cognizant of the injustice of such outcomes a Working Group of UNESCO's International Bioethics Committee (IBC) recently criticized the HGDP and recommended UN organizations not to endorse projects under this programme.

HUMAN GENOME RESEARCH

The objective of human genome research are to construct genetic and physical genome maps, identify the function of specific DNA sequences, and in particular to determine the DNA sequence of active genes. Although not a unitary research endeavour, the sum of all the human genome research programme worldwide is called the Human Genome Project. The Human Genome Diversity Project, specifically addresses genetic variation within and between populations.

Notable as an international collaboration led by scientists rather than their governments, the HGP was first formalised by the USA in 1988 and commenced officially on 1 October 1990. Research goals, strategies and resources vary but the overall objective is to gain an understanding of the genetic basis of the species *Homo sapiens*. The DNA molecule is composed of four units, known as nucleotide bases and there are believed to be 3.2 billion base pairs in the human genome. From 1988 to 1999, the funding for the US human genome project totalled over US$ 2.2 billion, of which two third was provided by the NIH and one third by the DOE. During the course of the project, technological developments and increasing experience with large-scale sequencing have led to an adjustment of the schedule. For instance, over the last four years the time to sequence DNA has dropped by a factor of over 100, while the cost has decreased from several US dollars to determine a single base pair to US$ 1 per 500 base pairs. In September 1999, international leaders of the HGP confirmed to execute the plan to complete a rough draft of the human genome by June 2000, a year ahead of earlier announcements. This draft provides a framework of sequence across about 90 per cent of the human genome. Remaining gaps will be closed and accuracy improved over the following years to achieve a complete, accurate human DNA reference sequence by 2003, 2 years sooner than previously predicted. NIH and DOE expect to contribute 60 to 70 per cent of this sequence, with the remainder coming from the efforts of the Sanger Centre (UK) and other international partners. As a first milestone, the DNA sequence of the chromosome 22, the smallest chromosome (47 million base pairs) apart from the male Y chromosome, was published in December 1999. It has now been revealed that human physiology is governed by about 40,000 genes (originally thought to be 100,000) which however may in all kinds of combinations and permutations, produce more than 100,000 functional proteins. It appears as though *Homo sapiens* carries just as many genes as do the mouse and the basic difference in genetic information between individuals might be zeroed in on to about a 1000 or so nucleotide bases.

PUBLIC AND PRIVATE SEQUENCING COMPETITION

Public research effort was challenged by Craig Venter; a former NIH researcher who set up his own, privately funded genomics company, *The Institute for Genomic Research* (TIGR, USA) in 1992. In May 1998, TIGR announced to co-operate with the analytical tool manufacturer Perkin-Elmer (USA) on joint venture called *Celera Genomics*. *Celera* was established to sequence the entire human genome in only three years for US$200 million, a fraction of the expenses of the public research efforts. To meet this ambitious goal, *Celera* employed a 'shot gun approach', which involves randomly sequencing fragments from a genome that has been broken into short stretches. This strategy is based on pure sequencing power provided by high-speed automated sequencers in combination with elaborate bioinformatics tools. Critics contend that when the data are assembled into a sequence it contains gaps and is not very accurate. In contrast, the HGP has a map-based approach and systematically sequences libraries of ordered bacterial artificial chromosomes. Yet also the HGP's new goal of a working draft by early 2000 was to be attained using a shotgun style approach. The remaining gaps are to be filled during the more labour-intensive second phase.

PROPERTY RIGHTS OF THE HUMAN GENOME

The competition between *Celera* and the HGP is only in part driven by these scientific arguments. More important is the question regarding the proprietary status of the data generated, and in this sense *Celera's* shotgun approach becomes more rational. It aims at the detection of expressed sequence tags (ESTs) to identify genes that have the potential for further drug development, and only if they do further sequencing will be applied. As such, it tries to pick the 'crown jewels' out of the genome. Venter, who left TIGR to head *Celera*, explained that his new sequencing company would patent no more than 300 human genes, while the rest of the data would be made freely available in the public domain. But in October 1999, it turned out that *Celera* had in fact filed preliminary patent applications on about 6,500 gene sequences, fuelling the fear that the future of medical research will be hampered by an individual company's claim. Since 1995, US patent law has allowed 'provisional applications that establish the date of a discovery and give inventors the possibility to submit a detailed and more expensive application within one year. *Celera* announced that it would continue to file provisional patent applications, possibly totaling 30,000 by the time all genes are mapped. However, Venter states that most of these will be abandoned if it turns out that a sequence is of no medical use. As a result, full patent applications would indeed be filed for only a few hundred sequences, he says.

Another strategy of *Celera* to commercially exploit its genomics knowledge is to grant pharmaceutical companies licenses to use the sequencing databases. For instance, in November 1999, *Pfizer* (USA) subscribed to all of *Celera's* databases to have access to a large number of novel drug target genes derived from *Celera's* sequencing of the human genome. While it seems that *Celera* is becoming the focal point of public discontent on the issue of privatization of human genetic information, other companies are by no means less active in this field. Another company that pursues an aggressive strategy towards IPR on the human genome is the US company *Human Genome Sciences Inc.* (HGSI). As of October 1999, HGSI has filed patents for over 6,450 full-length human gene sequences, complete with information on protein expression, biological activity and potential medical use. Concern arose that decoding the human genome will not render full medical benefit if genetic information can be exploited by private companies for profit. This has led to negotiations between UK and US government officials on an agreement to prevent patenting of the human genome. At present, patent systems both in the USA and Europe in principle allow for such patents and the US PTO has already granted over 1,500 patents of human DNA.

LINKING GENOTYPE AND PHENOTYPE
In contrast to the efforts of the HGP to sequence a Euro-American set of chromosomes, the HGDP claimed to offer a broader view on the variations of the human genome worldwide. The initial idea was to collect DNA samples from over 700 genetically distinct populations. With data on specific DNA sequences and their distribution over the world, it should also be possible to answer questions about the migration of early humans. In deed it has been now revealed that the present-day Europeans were fathered by just 10 males who wandered from the Middle - East / Siberia some 40000 years ago. In the early 1990s the HGDP was initially estimated to carry out its work for 5 years and to cost about US$ 25 million worldwide. It was supposed to be funded independently for each region, mostly by public institutions. In 1995, a US patent was granted to the NIH on a cell line containing unmodified DNA of an indigenous man of the *Hagahai* people. The subsequent worldwide protests forced the NIH to drop the patent claim, but the damage to the project's image was severe. As a result, even though the HGDP and the NIH have developed a 'model ethical protocol', funds have not so far been granted to the Project's North American committee. Due to these funding restrictions, the HGDP research activities have mostly come to a halt.

Another project on disease - related genes is currently being carried out in Iceland. In December 1998, the parliament approved a bill by which the Icelandic company *deCODE genetics* gained a license for the next twelve years to build up and exclusively use a national database. This database will include not only the genetic data of all 270,000 Icelanders, but also their medical records. The bill provides that medical data are automatically transferred to the central database after every treatment as along as the patient does not declare dissent. Furthermore, the database contains medical information on deceased persons as well as genealogical data on some 700,000 Icelanders. The combination of a small isolated population with a high standard of technology and large-scale medical as well as genealogical data makes Iceland an ideal place for such research. The value of the database for drug development attracted the Swiss pharmaceutical company *Hoffman - LaRoche* to sign a contract with *deCODE genetics*. The Swiss pharma giant agreed to pay up to US$ 200 million for information *deCODE genetics* will provide on the genetic causes of twelve common diseases, such as diabetes and Alzheimer's diseases. Drugs derived thereof will be given to the Icelandic population free of charge.

GENOMICS AND THE FUTURE
As the finalization of the first complete sequence of a human genome has already come within reach, questions about the use of such scientific progress become more urgent. Of course, not even the most pronounced advocates of genomics would claim that the causes of disease are all in our genes. The interaction of genetic and environmental effects is widely acknowledged. It seems today that in the industrialized world pharmaceutical research and development has fully embraced a drug development approach based on genomics. If this is successful, the pharmaceutical industry would increasingly shift from selling substances

towards selling information. Drugs would no longer be based on the biology of an average patient, but tailor-made towards the individual's genetic preconditions. Genomics progress could also lead to an improvement of general medicines, making them more effective for a larger part of the population. With the increase in added value by genetic information the distinction between drug development for industrialized and for developing countries will widen. Genomics research in industrialized countries will continue to focus on diseases in affluent societies. Genomic research certainly will have an impact on humanity, however, for the largest part of the world population it is not any genetic predisposition that decides their fate but the access to food, land, water and basic medical care.

SHADOW OF EUGENICS

Historically, the study of human genetics is associated with eugenics, the science which deals with all the influences that improve the inborn qualities of humankind. In the early part of this century genetic science focused attention on the determination of the biological basis of traits that were supposed to account for certain sorts of anti-social behaviour and social degeneracy. However, there was a reaction to such eugenics-oriented research, and anti-eugenicists argued successfully for a human genetics free of racial and class bias. However, the eugenics history of human genetics casts a long shadow and there are those who argue that even the contemporary emphasis of such human genome research is implicitly eugenic.

BIG SCIENCE IN A SMALL WAY

The HGP originated largely from initiatives taken in the mid-1980s in the USA, notably by the molecular biologists Robert Sinsheimer, and Charles DeLisi, Director of the US Office of Health and Environment at the Department of Energy (DOE). However, prominent US biomedical scientists insisted that the NIH should take principal control of the HGP rather than the DOE and were successful in persuading the head of the NIH to support the genome project. By 1988, Britain, France, Italy, West Germany, The Netherlands, Denmark and Russia all had initiated some genome research and in that year the European Commission proposed its own genome project : *Preventive Medicine : Human Genome Analysis.* Initially rejected by the European Parliament on the grounds that its preventive aims were unacceptably eugenic, a revised proposal subsequently passed the European Parliament and was adopted by the Council. Earlier in 1987, the Japanese government, a late-comer to molecular biology and human genome research, established its *Human Frontiers Scientific Programme,* an international enterprise of cooperative basic research into neurobiology and molecular biology.

THE TECHNIQUES

The knowledge produced by human genome research has great potential to further the development of genetic screening tests for the identification of carriers of genes implicated in genetic disorders, and to enhance the techniques for DNA finger printing. Genetic screening encompasses a range of techniques used to diagnose phenotypic traits which have or are believed to have a genetic basis. In medical ethics it is necessary to obtain informed consent before a competent individual. Concerns have been expressed about the lack of informed consent. DNA fingerprinting is another technique which uses gene probes to generate personal genetic profiles which are as specific to individuals as conventional finger prints are. It is used to analyse evidence in criminal cases and paternity disputes. The proliferation of DNA data bases recording the genetic profiles of individuals challenges the individual's right of privacy. The majority of countries do not have statutes that recognise the confidentiality of public health information; and with regard to criminal justice systems the lack of data security is a serious concern.

To enable information gained from the HGP and the HGDP to be recorded and made accessible, a new information technology has been developed, known as bioinformatics, to computerize nucleic acid sequence information. Human genome data are credited with providing information about the past, present and future of individuals and species, biomedical genetic constitutions and intelligence, antisocial behaviour, mental illness, heritable diseases and workplace disorders. Since genetic screening might be used to shift responsibility of work-related disease or unhealthy working conditions onto the workers, there has been an increasing call for limiting discrimination based on genotype and the imbalance which exists in all health systems throughout the world.

A brief outline of the techniques used to study the human genome is given below :

Bacterial artificial chromosomes (BACs) are large segments of DNA, between 100,000 and 200,000 bases long, cloned from another species into bacterial DNA. Once the foreign DNA has been cloned into the host bacteria, many copies of it can be made, and the BACs can then be stored in order in libraries.

Bioinformatics is the application of information technology to analyse and manage large data sets resulting from gene sequencing and related techniques.

Complementary - DNA (cDNA) is a sequence acquired by copying a messenger RNA (mRNA) molecule back into DNA. In contrast to the original DNA, mRNA codes for an expressed protein without noncoding DNA sequences ('introns'). Therefore, a cDNA probe can also be used to find the specific gene in a complex DNA sample (genomic DNA) from another organism with different non-coding sequences.

Expressed sequence tags (ESTs) are short sections of cDNA, which are long enough to identify a new cDNA uniquely.

Functional genomics tries to convert the molecular information represented by DNA into an understanding of gene functions and effects : how and why genes behave in certain species and under specific conditions. To address gene function and expression specifically, the recovery and identification of mutant and over-expressed phenotypes can be employed. Functional genomics also entails research on the protein function ('proteomics') or, even more broadly, the whole metabolism ('metabolomics') of an organism.

Genomics is the study of how genes and genetic information are organized within the genome, and how this organization determines their function. This science was given an impetus by the Human Genome Project which stimulated the development of efficient and cheap sequencing techniques. A number of microbial genomes have already been sequenced, followed closely by simple eukaryotic genomes like yeast and the nematode *Caenorhabditis elegans*.

Gene chips or *Microarrays*. Identified expressed gene sequences of an organism can, as ESTs or synthesized oligonucleotides, be placed on a matrix. If a sample containing DNA or RNA is added, those molecules that are complementary in sequence will hybridize. By making the added molecules fluorescent, it is possible to detect whether the sample contains the DNA or RNA of the respective genetic sequence initially mounted on the matrix.

High throughput (**HTP**) *screening* makes use of techniques that allow for a fast and simple test on the presence or absence of a desirable structure, such as specific DNA sequence. HTP screening often uses DNA chips or microarrays and automated data processing for the large-scale screening, for instance to identify new targets for drug development.

Insertion mutants are mutants of genes that are obtained by inserting DNA, for instance through mobile DNA sequences, 'transposons'. Furthermore, in plant research the capacity of the bacterium *Agrobacterium* to introduce DNA into the plant genome is employed to induce mutants. In both cases, mutations lead to lacking or changing gene functions which are revealed by aberrant phenotypes. Insertion mutant isolation, and subsequent identification and analysis are employed in model plants such as *Arabidopsis* and in crop plants such as maize and rice.

Pharmacogenetics investigates the different reactions of human beings to drugs and the underlying genetic predispositions. The differences in reaction are mainly caused by mutations in certain enzymes and/or receptors responsible for drug metabolization. As a result, the degradation of the active substance can lead to harmful by-products, or the drug might have no effect at all.

Pharmacogenomics is a new field of science. Instead of starting from existing drugs, it tries to make use of information on human DNA sequences for the development of new drugs. The expectations are two-fold; first that pharmacogenomics will render the search for new potent substances more effective and second that it will help to find more molecular targets for drugs in the human body. It is estimated that between 1940 and 1995 the entire pharmaceutical production was based on only 400 to 500 molecular targets. With the increasing knowledge of the human DNA sequence, databases of individual drug development companies now easily contain several tens of thousands of potential targets for drug actions.

Shotgun genome sequencing is a sequencing strategy for which parts of DNA are randomly sequenced. The sequences obtained have a considerable overlap and by using appropriate computer software it is possible to compare sequences and align them to build larger units of genetic information. This sequencing strategy can be automated and leads to rapid sequencing information, but it is less precise than a systematic sequencing approach.

Single nucleotide polymorphisms (**SNPs**) are the most common type of genetic variation. SNPs are stable mutations consisting of a change at a single base in a DNA molecule. SNPs can be detected by HTP analyses, for instance with DNA chips, and they are then mapped by DNA sequencing.

CONCLUSIONS

The HGP is double-faced : on the one side, it is providing new knowledge of human molecular biology of importance for the development of diagnostic tests for the presence of those genes which are implicated in diseases and disorders, and for the development of gene therapies. However, on the other side, genetic discrimination in employment, personal insurance, and possible violations of individual privacy including the individual's right not to know about the genetic profile have become serious ethical issues. We also share the concern of those who are critical of the potentially exploitative aspects of the HGDP: In particular, the issues surrounding informed consent, individual autonomy, the quality of genetic counselling, and the injustice done when patented genes derive from indigenous people who will clearly not benefit from such applications.

To address these concerns, the US National Centre for Human Genome Research, the NIH and DOE's Human Genome Program have established the Joint Working Group on the Ethical, Legal and Social Issues assisted with mapping and sequencing the human genome. UNESCO is preparing a declaration on the *Protection of the Human Genome* and the Council of Europe a draft *Convention for the Protection of Human Rights and the Dignity of the Human Being with regard to the application of Biology and Medicine*. We await with great interest the deliberations of these bodies on the important issues.Meanwhile, following the Iceland model, Estomia and Tonga have pledged their precious gene pool to private MNCs in order to develop drugs in return for large sums of money into the national exchequer.

11

The Convention on Biological Diversity

The UNCED's Convention on Biological Diversity is the culmination of two decades of arduous international efforts and negotiation. Its entry into force on 29 December 1993, just 18 months after its signing in June 1992 at the UN Conference on Environment and Development, Rio de Janeiro, will be recorded in modern history as a major step taken by humanity towards sustainable development. Elizabeth Dowdeswell, the Executive Director of UNEP, described the Convention as 'one of the most significant recent developments in international law and in international relations relating to environment and development.

The Convention signed by 154 countries represents a major global initiative. The Convention provides a broad legal framework for conserving and utilizing biodiversity. It came into force when ratified by 30 countries. Protocols related to it covered issues such as technology transfer, funding mechanisms, property rights and access to genetic material are now being considered. At the UNCED, governments reached consensus on a global plan of action to promote sustainable development known as Agenda 21. Both Agenda 21 and the Convention stress the importance of developing and strengthening the capacity of countries to benefit fully from their biological resources. Access to new technologies and their managed use and to training, information and financial resources, will enable developing countries to conserve and utilize their biodiversity strengthening, in the process, their capacity to reduce hunger and poverty.

WHAT IS SPECIAL IN CBD?

The Convention is an important achievement, offers possibilities to firmly entrench agricultural diversity conservation and management as a major concern and objective of the international community. But it can only do so if it takes into account the specific actors, recognises agricultural biodiversity's central importance, addresses the threats and devises special mechanisms to deal with it all. The major pitfalls of CBD are 1. weak language, 2. bilateral bias, 3. non representation of indigenous and local communities 4. Patent push and 5. blurred focus.

JUSTICE AND EQUITY

The Convention is the first instrument of its kind: global in nature and comprehensive in scope. Thus, for the first time, the conservation of biological diversity is being recognized as a common concern of humankind and is considered an integral part of the development process. If we take into consideration its scope and its objectives, the Convention is more than just 'another' legal agreement to add to the 170 which now exist in the sphere of the environment. The Convention introduces a novel approach which would reconcile the need for conservation with the concerns for development based on justice and equity. It demonstrates that environment and development are not incompatible, as the latter cannot be conceived of without the sustainable use of resources. Owing to this approach, conservation of biological diversity has ceased to be viewed merely in terms of threatened species to be protected against extinction; it has now emerged as a fundamental, multisectoral issue for the achievement and sustaining of economic and social progress.

This novel approach is symbolized in the **three objectives** enshrined in the Convention. These objectives are, in their very essence, interlinked and inter-dependent. They are (i) the **conservation** of biological diversity, (ii) the **sustainable use** of its components and (iii) the fair and **equitable sharing** of the benefits arising out of the utilization of genetic resources. Thus, the Convention is a code of conduct for nations to sustain the primary resource base of our planet, recognizing the need for fair and equitable sharing of the benefits arising out of the utilization of genetic resources as a means to that end.

A CATALYST FOR COOPERATION

The Convention is a framework for a dynamic, evolving process for cooperation among nations; it is a catalyst for involvement of entire societies; it is a point of reference for all agents involved in the process of development. The international community demonstrated a sense of urgency about this Convention when it established an *ad hoc* institutional mechanism—a preparatory Intergovern-mental Committee (IGC)—to expedite its application. In the two meetings this Committee has held, it had prepared the basis for the formal operation of the Convention. Its recommendations were considered at the First Meeting of the Conference of the Parties—the governing body of the Convention—held from 28 November to 9 December 1994. But beyond the decisions the parties must take about financing, institutional and administrative matters, priority areas to develop under the Convention and its relationship with other instruments and initiatives concerned with sustainable development, Governments will be faced with the challenge of stimulating the nations they represent to become committed to and involved in working towards the goals of the Convention.

Biological resources constitute the basis of life on Earth; their destruction by us all continues in silence far from the televised 'hot spots'. It is important to create a new mentality in which the adoption of preventive actions and precautionary measures will be as natural as our reactions to emergency situations and to catastrophes. This is the most basic challenge that has to be faced in preparing to implement the Convention. The CBD partly resolved the developing countries' concern regarding national sovereignty over their genetic resources. But many questions remain unanswered. Who controls genetic resources, on what terms should access be granted, and who receives the benefits? Until the CBD came into force in 1992, the world's genetic resources were considered to be the common heritage of humankind, i.e., open to access without restriction. However, most developing countries, were opposed to the principle of common heritage to genetic resources. They questioned the fairness of developed countries obtaining genetic resources from developing countries, protecting the products through patents and plant breeders' rights and selling these protected products at high prices to the country where the material was collected. In the negotiations for the Convention, developing countries successfully argued for national sovereignty over their genetic resources.

Article 3 of the Convention affirms that states have the sovereign right to exploit their own resources pursuant to their own environmental policies. *Article 15* of the Convention addresses access to genetic resources rests within the national governments and is subject to national legislation. This is elaborated as follows :

- States shall facilitate access to genetic resources for environmentally sound use.
- The access shall be subject to prior informed consent and based on mutually agreed terms.
- The Convention provides for the sharing of benefits derived from genetic resources between the country of origin or the country providing such resources, and the users.

Unless developing countries, particularly the local communities in these countries, benefit from these resources, the political will to invest in conservation will be less than might otherwise be the case. Countries need to develop registers of biological resources, harmonize their national laws with the provisions of the Convention and create specific institutions to enforce the regulatory measures. Additionally, indigenous knowledge, innovations and practices should be recognized and protected. Although the Convention provides that contracting parties should be subject to national legislation (*Article 8*), it is premised on the understanding that the indigenous and local communities traditionally managed biological resource within their boundaries with great care, in recognition of the fact that their very survival depends on these gifts of nature.

SHARING BENEFITS : LOCAL LEVEL

Based on this understanding, an issue which is gaining recognition in international debates, is how to share the benefits of biological resources with indigenous and local communities. This is especially important when it is realized that these groups over the centuries have played an important role in the selection and propagation of current genetic resources. However, there are no established institutions that safeguard the rights of indigenous and local communities. Additionally, national legal regimes pertaining to biodiversity and intellectual property protection are silent about the rights of indigenous and local communities. This weakens the ability of the communities to derive benefits from the conservation of biological diversity and to assert their rights over genetic resources, knowledge and innovations.

SHARING BENEFITS : NATIONAL LEVEL

Article 15 on access to genetic resources has opened up three possibilities to the developing countries : (i) to derive actual economic gains from their biological resources; (ii) to apply this provision to restrict free access to their genetic resources by public and private sectors from the industrialized countries; and (iii) to govern access to genetic resource.

Since *article 15* requires prior informed consent, the implementation of this provision requires countries to develop policies and legislation which include the establishment of designated national agencies that serve as focal points for defining the scope of prior informed consent. The countries providing genetic resources will have to improve the protection measures that are in place so as to prevent unlawful collection of genetic resources. Furthermore, they need to put in place mechanisms for improved record-keeping, linking collections with patents, and for the regulation of transfer of collected materials to third parties. This will lead to more beneficial relationships between the owners of the genetic resources and the recipients.

LINK WITH TECHNOLOGY TRANSFER

Questions of access to genetic resources have been linked to the issue of access to and transfer of technology. During the negotiations leading to the Convention, most developing countries argued that access to genetic resources by (firms from) industrialized countries, should facilitate access for the South to products arising from the genetic resources, as well as technologies pertaining to the conservation and use of the resources. Developing countries were successful in pushing for this to a certain extent. The Convention recognizes the links between access to genetic resource and transfer of technology. *Article 1b* of the Convention offers developing countries new opportunities for building up their capabilities to conserve and sustainably utilise biodiversity. Countries providing genetic resources should "participate in research and development activities carried out on the basis of such resources and to share in a fair and equitable way the benefits arising from their commercial and/or other uttilization".

CAPACITY BUILDING

The issue is, how developing countries can best invoke or apply these provisions to build up their capacities and benefit from their genetic resources. One way is to link the supply of genetic resources to the access of those technologies which make use of the genetic resources. This involves establishing partnerships between institutions in the countries supplying genetic resources and corporations from the recipient countries. Under the partnerships, institutions or nations could bring together their genetic and technological resources in collaborative ventures. Although partnerships as such could be a useful mechanism for facilitating access to genetic resources, transfer of technology and technological capacity building in developing countries, this mechanism remains underutilized. Often the owners of the genetic resources have taken the wrong approach in the implementation of the partnerships. This is due to the following: the partnership can comprise at different levels. At the lowest, the owner of the genetic resources simply looks to acquire technical equipment, and at the highest the main concern is improvement of the technical capacities of the manpower, and the creation and improvement of existing institutions involved in biological resource utilization. Unfortunately, in the hierarchical representation, the owners of biological resources have tended to concentrate much more on the lower than on the higher levels. That is, they have tended to preoccupy themselves more with the acquisition of sophisticated equipment than with manpower and institutional development.

This preoccupation is due to the perception that technology transfer is the flow of equipment, skills and managerial competence and technical specifications from the North to the South, in relation to the production of goods. It should be noted also that the preoccupation with this technology transfer is misplaced, as many of the technologies appropriate to the developing countries are already in the public domain and as such already accessible. The problem is that developing countries have not properly recognized their needs and consequently do not realize that the information and necessary equipment can be obtained easily. The developing countries should concentrate on building technological capabilities through processes such as institutional formation and development, human resource development, scientific research, information exchange and technical co-operation.

CLEARING HOUSE

Another issue is that the partnerships will work well if there is overall control of the whole process by a single co-ordinating entity: a so-called clearing-house. The control will be necessary not only within a single country but may be required for a whole region. This is because a foreign genetic resource prospector can easily move to a new country or region where he/she feels that less stringent controls prevail. This clearing house would involve the creation or modification of an existing institution to co-ordinate all (inter-regional) activities dealing with the access to genetic resources and the sharing of benefits. If there are existing institutions already involved in such an enterprise, the clearing house could co-ordinate their activities. Additionally, a clearing house should deal with issues such as information exchange, the sharing and training of manpower, the development of institutional capacity and the encouragement of co-operation between member countries on scientific matter.

IPR AND TECHNOLOGY TRANSFER

Questions of intellectual property rights (IPR) are still controversial. So far there is no formulated ideal model of the form or shape IPR should take in both the developed and developing countries. What is needed are programmes in training, information exchange and access to the available information on patented material. There is a need to review and revise the many ambiguous patent laws existing in developing countries, which do not consider the rights of the suppliers of genetic material. In the revisions, it is important that these rights are recognized and protected. A protocol covering cultural property rights of indigenous peoples will strengthen the provision on indigenous knowledge within the Convention. The technical capacity of indigenous people also needs to be built up and national policies should incorporate this aspect.

The value of genetic raw materials can be enhanced if the material is put through a process of identification, collection and screening by the owners of the biological resources before presenting it to a potential recipient. Developing countries should establish a reputation as a reliable partner in the screening process. The National Biodiversity Institute (INBio) project in Costa Rica stands out as a good example in the effort of biodiversity prospecting as a result of a long period of reliability, and indeed developed countries have imitated the highly computerized system that the INBio project has employed. The Costa Rica example serves to show that a developing country can indeed succeed in this so called 'technology-intensive' venture with the right attitude and the right policies.

TAKING MEASURES

As it stands, the Convention addresses many important issues concerning the regulation of access to genetic resources, but falls short in actually giving concrete measures for the implementation of the provisions. It can be strengthened by :

- Considering the negotiation of a protocol on the basis of some principles already developed in instruments such as the FAO code of conduct for plant Germplasm Collecting and Transfer.
- Formulating a model law which can be used by various countries to adopt domestic laws, protect genetic resources and regulate conditions for technology transfer.

- Dealing with the issue of regulating access to genetic resources through material transfer agreements, which generally fall in the domain of trade secret law.
- Strengthening farmer's rights to ensure compensation, stimulate conservation and future local innovation.
- States recognizing individual and communal rights. Although this will be difficult to enforce, it would serve as a means of community empowerment and would help establish the legal basis for ensuring that future collection of genetic resources of local knowledge returns some benefit directly to the local community.

MORE LOSERS THAN WINNERS?

National sovereignty and intellectual property protection of genetic resources are two retrogressive steps of the same kind. Both offer short term financial gains but also imply a limited access to genetic resources whose free availability has been the main pillar of world agricultural research. The most important of the provisions of the UNCED-CBD and one which has received the greatest attention, relates to the control of an access to plant genetic resources. The convention lays down that the plant genetic resources are the national heritage of the country in whose territory they are found and has placed them under the sovereign control of individual states. Thus, access of other states to plant genetic resources will have to be negotiated on mutually agreed terms. The convention also calls for the results of research and development, and the benefits arising from the commercial and other utilization of plant genetic resources, to be shared in a fair and equitable way with the country which provided these resources in the first place.

The great movement of plant genetic resources for millennia has led to the concept that these resources are a common heritage of mankind. The FAO International Undertaking formally adopted this concept, stipulating that genetic resources should be explored, collected, conserved, evaluated, utilized and made available freely for plant breeding and other scientific purposes. Although the article on free availability was later extended with the provision excluding use 'free of charge', the norm of free availability has been instrumental in exploring the vast genetic diversity in the form of land races and local cultivars which increasingly is threatened with the advent of high-yielding varieties, within and outside the UN.

If the principle of free exchange has served mankind so well, why is the common heritage concept now being discarded in favour of the notion of sovereign control? The answer is to be found in the distrust of many developing countries arising out of recent proposals relating to intellectual property protection. Many of these countries have felt that it is not fair that private seed companies in the developed countries should have free access to their plant genetic resources, use them as raw material for evolving improved varieties, and later market them with intellectual property protection in the form of industrial patents. Patents of this kind for transgenic and other varieties would present several problems for farmers in the developing countries, especially the stipulation that they cannot save the harvested seed of the protected variety for planting the next crop.

It remains doubtful that the concept of sovereign control of plant genetic resources, their negotiated access and the proposed sharing of benefits will contribute a lot to the overall objective of the Convention, which is conservation of genetic diversity and its sustainable use. It will contribute even less to the developing of world agriculture. The motivation for conservation has to come from the realization that first and foremost it is in the interest of the country that the genetic diversity found in its territory is not eroded. Also, as world population continues to multiply, it will become increasingly important to identify new genetic variability for higher crop yields and to make the agricultural production process more efficient in terms of the energy input/output ratio. This will require a great deal of international co-operation in research, including free exchange of plant genetic resources and new technologies. No single country has the scientific and other resources to achieve these major objectives of future agriculture on its own.

As regards to patents, those who advocate them for transgenic varieties ignore the fact that biotechnologists producing such varieties often use materials and techniques created by public-funded research. Thus the recombinant DNA technology is the end product of a large number of major discoveries in biological and analytical sciences during the past 40 years. The legal criteria of 'novel' and 'hidden' could become even harder to satisfy as advances in molecular biology continue at a rapid pace. A recent editorial in *Nature* pointed out that the techniques employed in developing transgenic plants should become commonplace and routine practice within a few years. More than all these, the contribution of generations of farmers in selecting plants for higher productivity and better quality will have to be considered while reviewing applications for patents. Neither the classical nor the modern methods of plant breeding would yield many useful results in the absence of this solid foundation laid by discerning farmers following domestication of crop plants.

It would appear that the countries which favour the concept of intellectual property protection in the form of industrial patents for crop varieties have not thought about the full implications of this practice. They do not appear to recognize that the short-term gains which they would derive from grants of patents ignoring the above considerations, will be far outweighed by the loss which world agriculture would suffer through limited access to genetic resources. With the replacement of the concept of common heritage through national sovereignty and with the institution of patents of improved plant varieties, hardly any country gains. The loser will be world agriculture.

US BIODIVERSITY BILL

United States congressman Robert Torricelli introduced a bill for a new US programme to support NGO conservation of biodiversity in Latin America. The bill calls for the establishment of a Western Hemisphere Biodiversity Cooperation Programme, stepping over the US refusal to sign the global Convention on Biological Diversity. The initiative aims to make government funds availabile to facilitate cooperative agreements between local nonprofit conservation groups in Latin America and public or private sector laboratories of the US. Such agreements would ensure incentives for conservation in the South and "access to a continuing and reliable supply of biological resources" for US "competitiveness". The bill aims to strengthen US environmental technology exports, support US medical and agricultural research through access to biodiversity and protect intellectual property of materials derived from Latin America's biological resources. Conservation organizations in return get capital funding, training, technology and a share in the profits from commercial benefits arising from the use of local materials. Governments housing these organizations would receive half of these profits. If adopted, the bill would institutionalize the inequities of the CBD, which offer great returns to the pharmaceutical industry of the North and little tangible benefits to local communities in Latin America.

12

The North and South:
Need for Shared Responsibility

The funding of the CBD depends on the North's good will. Northern competitive edge in money, manpower and technology poses a great challenge to the good intentions of the CBD. The Earth Summit was born of optimism. However, the optimism only highlighted the fact, hitherto swept under the carpet, that the world had long been more fundamentally divided into the losing Southern two-third bulk, and the accumulating Northern one-third lobe. The Summit endorsed the prevailing flow of resources from South to North. There were countering stipulations that this should go in the other direction, but these were reduced to insignificance by the fact that funding depends on the good will of the North. The opposite of such good will has been prominent for over a millennium. Not long ago it became clear that it still prevailed, when all the North's economic, political and diplomatic might was used to quash the just, but naive, Southern call for a fair new international economic order. The optimism of the Summit and the UNCED was just one more ruse to sedate the South while it bled. In the CBD (an integral part of UNCED) the supposed good will is to be expressed through GEF, in which the World Bank is a partner. But the Bank, together with the IMF, is seen more in modernizing the old South-North flow of resources, than effecting a North-South flow of funds.

THE IMBALANCE

If this had not been so - and had *ex situ* collection not been excluded, and if there not been unfair intellectual property rights protection—the equation of the convention matching the rights and obligations of South and North would have been fair. The owners of biological diversity, mostly in the South, are recognized by the Convention as having sovereignty over it. The North is recognized as the owner of biotechnology and finance. Biological diversity is seen as essential for making biotechnology useful. Financial resources are seen as flowing from North to South through a fair and equitable sharing of the commercialization of Southern biological diversity, and to help Southern countries fulfil the obligation placed on them by the Convention.

Biotechnology is seen as coming from North to South in exchange for biological diversity and to help in its conservation and sustainable use under fair and most favourable terms, including on concessional and preferential terms. The biotechnology that can come from the North is genetic engineering. The view of many molecular biologists is that the seed in gene banks that has no unique genes should be destroyed. One cannot see how the genetic engineering generated by those who hold this view can help in biodiversity conservation and sustainable use. The South is obviously on a wild goose chase here. Some biotechnologies are also visualized as flowing from South to North. The North knows it needs Southern traditional biotechnologies. The South, lured by the glamour and genetic engineering, does not think much of this wealth that it has, and is giving it away by default of protective action. In exchange for its biological diversity, the South is supposed to share in the benefits of its commercialization by the North and through bilateral agreements. These will presumably be based on exchanges of biodiversity for financial resources, genetic engineering, or human resources development. Although the North does not have much biological diversity it can have access to it.

NEED FOR REDRESS

Biological diversity can be pilfered, so it cannot be possessed legally without the prior informed consent of the country of origin. In practice, a weak Southern country has no way of checking on such legality outside its borders which is where all uses of its stolen biodiversity will take place. Even if it identifies theft, it has little capacity for forcing redress. The effectiveness of this stipulation, therefore, depends on good will in the majority of the Northern countries (Denmark and other countries that have shown it, require any importation of biological material to be accompanied by a permit from its country of origin). Information on biological diversity is seen as flowing from South to North, while information on biotechnology goes the other way. But while Northern technology is to be protected as intellectual property, Southern technology is merely to be respected, preserved and maintained and given free. This legalizes a charge-free South-North flow but a heavily charged North-South flow. It is obviously aimed at continuing the prevalent South-North flow of resources.

This imbalance is only exceeded by the North's insistence on exempting existing *ex situ* collections from the Convention. This requires some explanation. The most valuable biodiversity is that of crops. The North now has huge collections of most of the biodiversity of virtually all the crops and related species from the South stored in its gene banks - and will therefore not need much more. It even has substantial *ex situ* collections of non-domesticated plant biodiversity and frozen animal genetic material. To cap it all, many developed countries augmented their collections by scouring the unaware South for genetic material before the Convention came into force. The North tried to preempt Southern claims on these collections by trying to have a substantial part of them, kept in the CGIAR system, transferred to the World Bank. For once (in a possible indication of future trends) the South acted decisively and, helped by Northern non-governmental organizations it blocked the move.

EXPERIMENTAL MONSTERS

The only article of the Convention that could have been useful without invocation of Northern goodwill is that on the possibility of developing a protocol on biosafety. This protocol could protect the South from becoming an experimental ground for the North's genetically engineered monsters. The United States says such monsters cannot be developed. Europe says such a protocol would be useless until the South has enough people trained in genetic engineering. But multinational corporations keep taking away such human resources with training which the South produces. So there will be no capacity in the South, and thus no biosafety protocol. The many likely horrors of biotechnology will therefore, no doubt, befall on the South.

If the South continues to be outsmarted, at the hands of the North's MNCs and their governments, the hurt and the pain will be unwittingly flinging its weight of chaos at the North. If the North wants stability to enjoy its wealth, it needs to show more goodwill. If there were good will in the North, this would be a good Convention. It is lacking in the Northern multinational corporations. Northern governments must guide these corporations. But the Northern public, including most of its NGOs, shows a lot of it, we are convinced that the Northern public will tune their governments to reflect its good will. And things will improve.

PART III

BIOTECHNOLOGY AND BIODIVERSITY

1

The Techniques

Biotechnology is generally considered to be any technique that uses living organisms to make or modify a product, to improve plants or animals, or to develop microorganisms for specific uses. Modern biotechnologies offer vast potential for improving the quality and increasing the productivity of agriculture, forestry and fisheries. Genes from plants, animals and microorganisms that flourish in the forests, fields and seas of the developing world are the strategic raw materials for the commercial development of new pharmaceutical, agricultural and industrial products. Whereas genetic wealth, especially in tropical areas such as rainforests was once a relatively inaccessible trust fund, it is fast becoming a highly valuable currency.

Introduction of modern biotechnologies in the developing world is frequently compared to the **Green Revolution**. While the Green Revolution is involved in introducing new varieties of primarily wheat and rice in selected areas, biotechnology has the potential to affect all crops and tree species, as well as fish and livestock. The Green Revolution was introduced to the Third World largely by international institutions, but the **"Gene Revolution"** is primarily in the hands of the private sector, with transnational corporations being the leading players. With few exceptions, scientific and technical capacity in the biosciences is centered in the industrialized world. As a consequence, biotechnology research, by and large, does not focus on the needs or interests of poor farmers in marginal areas of the world. Emerging biotehnologies have considerable potential to enhance food and agricultural production in the developing world, but they could also add to existing inequities by displacing and/or accelerating genetic erosion and introducing new environmental hazards.

Molecular biology is the most powerful tool of biotechnology. Through **genetic engineering** scientists can transfer genes between unrelated species endowing such "transgenic" plants, animals and microorganisms with properties that they could probably never have acquired in nature. As yet, only a handful of genetically engineered products are availabile commercially, but hundreds are in the pipeline. Genetic engineers can design crop varieties containing natural insecticidal genes, fish with human growth hormones, and faster growing trees. It must be stressed, However, that genetic engineering consists essentially of *mixing and matching genes* from different species. It *cannot* *create genetic material, replace lost material or eliminate the need to conserve* living resources. Molecular biology is important in characterizing and conserving biodiversity. For example, molecular markers can help establish the extent of diversity within a species and to identify genes of interest to breeders. Such techniques can also help establish priorities for conservation.

WHAT IS GENETIC ENGINEERING?

Genetic engineering, also known as genetic modification is the manipulation of DNA. Genes are made of DNA, which carries all the information living things inherit from their parents. DNA contains all the instructions needed to make the proteins and other materials which make up an organism, as well as information on its structure and the way in which it functions. In genetic engineering, genes are selected and moved from one organism to another. For example, the bacterium *Bacillus thuringiensis* uses a gene to make a poison with which it kills insects. This gene has been incorporated into the DNA of cotton plants to make them poisonous to insects.

The broader term biotechnology includes a wide range of other techniques. These include **tissue culture** (the creation of identical genetic copies or "clones" of an individual plant), **cell culture** (growth of plant cells in the laboratory which are then separated off and encouraged to grow as real plants) and **aquaculture**. In its wider sense biotechnology also includes **biological processes** used in the food industry. Some of these have been used for centuries, like yeasts to make bread and convert sugar into alcohol in brewing, and bacteria to digest sugars and add flavour in cheese making. However all these techniques use naturally occurring organisms. Genetic engineering creates viruses, bacteria, yeasts, plants and animals which have never occurred in nature.

BIOTECHNOLOGY PROTECTS BIODIVERSITY?

Biotechnology assists the conservation of plant and animal genetic resources through :

- new methods for collecting and storing genes (as seeds and tissue culture);
- detection and elimination of diseases in gene bank collections;
- identification of useful genes;
- improved techniques for long-term storage;
- safer and more efficient distribution of germplasm to users.

Tissue culture is just one example. The technique, which involves growing small pieces of plant tissue or individual cells in culture, provides a fast and efficient way of taking numerous cuttings from a single plant. In many cases entire plants can be regenerated from a single cell because each cell contains all the necessary genetic information (Totipotent). After selecting a disease-free cutting, for example, scientists can mass-produce copies that are genetically identical. This is the basis of plant cloning, or micro-propagation of plants. In gene banks tissue culture is now used routinely to preserve the genetic information of plants which seeds have that do not store well or are sterile or have poor germination rates. Plant cells maintained on a growth medium in a test-tube replace seeds or plants. Plants stored in this way include sweet potatoes, bananas and plantains, apples, cocoa and many tropical fruits.

OBSTACLE OR...

Biotechnology contributes to conservation and the sustainable use of bio-diversity, but several areas exist where modern biotechnology may hinder development or create serious hardship for rural communities. The economics of developing countries are threatened by biotechnology research that promises to eliminate or displace traditional export commodities, often a primary source of foreign exchange for Third World countries. Current research, for example, focuses on substitutes for tropical oil and fats ranging from cocoa butter to castor oil. Biosynthesis in the laboratory of high-value ingredients such as vanilla, pyrethrum and rubber could ultimately transfer production out of farmers' fields and into industrial bio-reactors. Without ample opportunity to plan and diversify, developing country farmers and their botanical exports may suffer massive displacement, wreaking havoc on already weak economies.

WAVE OF GENETIC EROSION?

Biotechnology may threaten the genetic diversity on which it depends. In the absence of conservation, commercial biotechnology may unleash a new era of genetic erosion. A commercial venture can propagate up to 10 million eucalyptus seedlings, all identical clones, in automated nurseries. Similarly, commercial semen and embryo transfer services for domestic animals raise concern about the displacement of traditional livestock breeds. Cloning could accelerate replacement or dilution of indigenous stock by imported breeds, leading to a loss of genetic diversity.

BIOSAFETY

A related concern involves the ecological risks of introducing genetically engineered plants into centres of diversity. Transgenic varieties, a good number of them resistant to herbicides, have been produced in more than 40 crop plants. Gene flow to weeds from resistant plants could have far-reaching consequences. The resulting herbicide-tolerant weed could be difficult to control, harming future crop production as well as the surrounding ecosystem. Will biotechnology firms seeking to penetrate markets in developing countries take into account the risks posed in regions where wild and weedy relatives of major food and industrial crops are found? Will the developing countries have the capacity to monitor and assess the risk?

2

The Dream and the Nightmare

Biotechnologists could dream of developing new varieties and breeds adaptable to low input agriculture or harsh conditions, or improve processing. Biotechnology may help create markets by developing new industrial, medicinal and aromatic crops. Given their richness in biodiversity, several developing countries that have the capabilities, such as Brazil, China and India could produce new high-value products based on local flora. The congenial agro-ecological setting and availability of relatively cheap labour should be conducive to large-scale production of new high-value crops, enabling such countries to maintain their comparative advantage in these commodities. The use of biotechnology to develop biofertilizers and to detect and control pests and pathogens will be particularly helpful to poor farmers.

The fundamental question posed by biotechnology remains; who will control the new technologies and benefit from them? The FAO is trying to strengthen national capacities to exploit biotechnology for sustainable, low-input agriculture, and to encourage biotechnology research on products/commodities that are important to developing nations. It is also fostering the best uses of biotechnologies to identify and conserve genetic resources. Finally, the FAO is developing a code of conduct that covers the issues raised above. Some of the leading biotechnology companies are:

Du pont (Wilmington, USA)
ICI (London, UK)
Monsanto (St. Louis, USA)
Sandoz (Basel, Switzerland)
Ciba-Geigy (Basel, Switzerland)
Rhone-Poulenc (Lyons, France)
DNA Plant Technology (Cinnaminson, USA)
Sanofi (Paris, France)
Calgene (Davis, USA)
Mycogen (San Diego, USA)
Bayer (Wuppertal, Germany)
Novo Biokontrol (Bagsvaerd, Denmark)
Biotechnica International (Overland Park, USA)
Plant Genetic Systems (Ghent, Belgium)
Agricultural Genetics (Cambridge, UK)

FACTS

The biotechnology industry in the USA produced pharmaceuticals, diagnostic tests and agricultural products worth US $ 2000 million in 1990.

- Two-thirds of all biotechnology companies have focused on therapeutic or diagnostic applications and only one in ten is applying biotechnology in food and agriculture.
- Researchers at the University of California have filed a patent for *thaumatin* extracted from a West African plant *Thaumatococcus doniellii*- which is 100000 times sweeter than cane sugar.
- US scientists have filed a patent application to use *endod* extracted from the African soap berry to control zebra mussels in the Great Lakes.
- *Chymosin*, the enzyme traditionally taken from cows and used in cheese-making, can now be made from specially engineered microorganisms.
- Goat and cow are engineered to secrete *insulin* and *interferon* in their milk.
- Mouse and pig are genetically tailor-made to become successful *organ donors* for humans.
- *Plasminogen Activator*, a vital clot dissolving protein is now extracted from engineered bacteria and goat milk.
- *Vaccines* against Hepatitis-B and AIDS-virus HIV are successfully tested in chimpanzees.
- Bio-engineers are now concentrating chiefly on commercial crops, but research should not ignore tropical food staples

BYPASSING THE BARRIERS

Recombinant DNA technology (RDT) permits scientists to bypass the natural barriers which prevent breeding between different kinds of organisms, making it possible to incorporate in a plant species, for example, the genetic traits of an organism from the animal kingdom. By altering its genetic configuration, a plant's resistance to a broad spectrum of predators or factors might be enchanced, from fungi, bacteria and insects to extreme heat or high soil salinity. A biotechnically designed tomato, the **"Flavr Savr"**, which has built-in resistance to decay (ripening) and therefore lasts longer in storage, went on the market in the United States in 1994.

Biotechnology's primary contribution to the agricultural sector will be to increase the actual amount of food that can be grown on the planet. Though there has been a significant increases in world food supply since 1991, with grain production alone rising by 4.3% to 1959 million tons, this has been achieved through conventional methods of crop improvement, in which genetic characteristics are exchanged between sexually compatible species. However, at current rates of population growth the conventional techniques may soon be insufficient if farming is to keep pace with the scale of increases required in the 21st century. Genetic engineering will not only provide varieties with higher yields, shorter maturity periods and broader resistance characteristics, it will also greatly reduce the time needed to evolve and screen them.

The implantation of an alien gene into a plant's genetic signature can also influence the amount of fat, protein or carbohydrate a food contains enabling scientists to modify or altogether change its nutritional value to meet, perhaps, the need for specialized consumer groups. Recently, there has been growing commercial interest in using plants as vehicles for synthesizing the enzymes used in the food industry, industrial oils and polymers. Rice, wheat, potato, cotton, alfalfa, asparagus, carrot, pumpkin, petunia, lentil, lettuce, pear, pea, sunflower, canola and poplar are among some 50 species that have been biotechnically "transformed" since the first successful gene manipulation experiment was conducted in 1986.

While these brave new technologies have caused great excitement in scientific and commercial circles in the industrialized West, they are viewed with distinct suspicion in the developing world, where entire economies and classes of people are dependent upon maintaining the existing genetic configuration of the crops they plant. The fear that biotechnical substitutes may supplant vanilla, cocoa butter or a host of pharmaceutical ingredients, fragrances, colourants and spices, is not entirely without substance, although it must be stressed that the high cost of engineering genetic replacements and society's general preference for natural products will perhaps inhibit their commercialization. Biotechnology may even strengthen the market share of developing country exporters. One example is vanilla, where very simple laboratory techniques, such as tissue culture for cloning more disease-resistant and higher-yielding specimens, could offer a strategy to prevent the replacement of the natural flavouring by synthetic substitutes.

However, the path of this still-emerging science is oriented almost exclusively towards Third World crops of commercial importance, such as wheat, rice, soyabean and cotton. Foods like sweet potato, cassava and plantain, which have an enormous value in developing countries but comparatively little in the international markets, do not figure high among the priorities of leading biotechnology companies. If research is to take place on crops that are relevant to developing country needs—particularly those with recurrent food shortage—there must be a strategy to ensure they have access to biogenetic technologies.

MUTUAL DEPENDENCE

Biodiversity and biotechnology are deeply dependent on each other. From time immemorial mankind could not and still cannot live with one without the other. Biotechnololgy, since it utilizes the capabilities of living organisms, relies on biodiversity. The vast, but rapidly diminishing, array of Earth's biota contains genetic resources that fuel biotechnology, and also provide opportunities for the future. This is fundamental to providing security for future generations, a major goal of sustainable development. The question is whether this wide genetic base can or will be sustained for future technological progress. South and Southeast Asia together, for example, are reckoned to have lost over two thirds of their original wildlife habitat. The very close symbiotic relationship between biodiversity and biotechnology is prominently reflected in article after article of the CBD.

Biodiversity is seen, portrayed and acknowledged as the foundation—the firm genetic base—from which biotechnology develops and upon which the industry is strongly anchored. Similarly, biotechnology is acknowledged to have much to offer to the conservation and sustainable use of biodiversity. Biotechnology has a potential role in helping to maintain biodiversity for the survival of and evolution of species, in enhancing or restoring the resilience of ecosystems, and in rehabilitating degraded lands. It is also important to improve biodiversity through the genetic engineering of living organisms (or parts of them) into novel forms, varieties of breeds, with desired environmental, physiological, behavioural or other traits and characteristics.

FOOD AND AGRICULTURE

THERE IS PROMISE OF:
- Crops with inherent protection from insect pests and resistance to viral and fungal disease.
- Better nutritional value of food crops.
- Crops with enhanced temperature, salinity and drought tolerance.
- Wider genetic diversity in plant and animal disease.
- Improved animal breeding techniques.

ENVIRONMENT

SIGNIFICANT HELP IS EXPECTED IN:
- Resource recovery and recycling
- Improved waste water purification
- Better waste management
- Biodegradable plastics and packaging.
- Reducing agricultural waste.

HUMAN HEALTH AND WELFARE

PROMOTION OF INDIVIDUAL HEALTH THROUGH:
- Human growth hormones to treat nutritional deficiencies.
- Human insulin to treat diabetes
- Tissue plasminogen activator (TPA) to treat blood clots and heart attacks
- Interferons to treat leukemia, viral diseases and cancer.
- Factor VII to treat haemophilia-A while preventing AIDS contamination.
- Vaccines for hepatitis-B, HIV and other diseases.

The Nightmare

They really have been created— corn with firefly genes that glows in the dark, tobacco with mouse genes that sequesters heavy metals and salmon with flounder genes that can survive freezing ocean temperatures that would kill most fish. Such experiments highlight the difference between modern genetic engineering and the more traditional methods of selective breeding used by humans in the past to modify plants, animals, and other organisms. With traditional selective breeding, humans can cross one crop variety, of potatoes, with another potato variety, and in some cases with related wild potatoes. However traditional breeders cannot add viral, insect, or animal genes to potatoes all of which have been added to plants via use of "recombinant DNA" and related genetic engineering techniques.

Scientists can now take virtually any genetically encoded trait from one organism and add it to any other, no matter how unrelated. By removing the traditional limits of cross breeding, genetic engineering techniques appear to be a boon to scientists engaged in the business of modifying organisms for human purposes. On the other hand, genetic engineering also raises ethical, social and environmental issues. For those concerned about the environment, the prominent issue has been the possibility that scientists will inadvertently create "transgenic" organisms that work ecological or other types of havoc, particularly if these organisms are intended for deliberate release into the environment.

Engineered organisms, could create ecological disasters when released into the environment. There are just as many unknown factors associated with their environmental impacts as there are with global warming, if not more. There is a difference, however, the control of global warming is mainly a reactive response to an environmental change of potentially immense proportions that is probably already underway. This situation need not necessarily arise with biotechnology. Society has the opportunity to control it in a proactive way through national and international legislation. Yet there is an inertia and an apparent reticence to take such defensive action.

LIMITATIONS OF BIOTECHNOLOGY

The following conditions are indispensable :
- .an adequate number of scientists skilled in biotechnological operations.
- access to up-to-date scientists skilled in information.
- sufficient economic resources for infrastructure and maintenance costs.
- a national biotechnology program, alongside its conventional plant improvement programs, which designates priorities and enjoys political support.
- a policy of technology transfer linking biotechnologists, agronomists, agriculturalists and the productive sector.

'THE FLY' 'THE SPECIES', AND 'THE BLOB'.

Concerns about genetic engineering date to the early 1970s, shortly after Californian scientists discovered how to make recombinant DNA molecules by using "restriction enzymes" to cut and paste DNA. Considerable debate in the next few years over the risks of RDT research led to the establishment in a number of countries of guidelines covering the research.

The more recent issues surrounding deliberate "releases" or "introductions" of genetically engineered organisms to the environment are, however, quite different from the issues surrounding laboratory RDT. The concern in the 1970s was that microorganisms modified in the course of laboratory research would inadvertently be given characteristics that would allow them to survive outside the laboratory and cause harm. Now genetically engineered organisms are being asked to survive in conventional agriculture, forestry, fisheries, and waste treatment applications. Once introduced outdoors engineered organisms may reproduce and further adapt to their environment via natural selection. Moreover, some genetically engineered organisms will be given traits, such as pest resistance, specifically to improve their health, survival or reproductive capacity. Some scientists concerned about deliberate releases of genetically engineered organisms have pointed out the consequences of introductions of "exotic" species, those brought intentionally or unintentionally from one geographic area to another. Many introductions of exotic species—such as agricultural crops and livestock—have had tremendous benefits.

Nevertheless, a small pecentage of species introductions have caused economic and environmental disaster. The Nile perch for example, was introduced in 1960s to Africa's Lake Victoria where it spread rapidly. This large, predatory fish decimated populations of almost all the indigenous fish species of commercial importance. As a result, it now feeds primarily on small shrimp and its own young. Such experiences with introduced species clearly demonstrate that introductions of organisms made with little ecological forethought can have disastrous consequences. It should be recognized, however, that introductions of exotic species are not truly analogous to introductions of transgenic organisms. Introducing an organism to a new environment is not the same as introducing a few genes to an organism. It is commonly argued that introduced organisms tend to become pests because they are freed of their native predators, pathogens and parasites. This argument generally should not hold for a genetically engineered organism reintroduced to the same environment where its parent non-engineered organism lives unless the organism is engineered to resist its natural enemies.

Could genetically engineered organisms invade and disrupt agricultural or natural ecosystems? Some proponents of biotechnology have argued that organisms and the natural communities they live in are so highly perfected by millions of years of evolution that it is virtually impossible to engineer an organism to have an ecological advantage so that it causes damage. However the argument is weak; nature tolerates a lot of slack. Although the notion of a balance of nature is deeply rooted in Western culture, modern ecological research indicates that ecological communities are not generally at an equilibrium. External factors such as climate change and internal factors such as genetic and physiological constraints may limit the ability of organisms to become optimally adapted to their environments.

In some instances, it is easy to envision traits engineered into organisms as conferring a selective advantage. Acquired characteristics that allow genetically engineered organisms to expand their range (such as cold-tolerance or salt tolerance) use new resources (such as the ability to metabolize a new substrate like antibiotics) or resist natural enemies (such as disease-resistance or insect resistance) all have the potential to increase the "fitness of genetically engineered organisms relative to non-engineered organisms. Salmon, engineered to express an antifreeze protein gene, for example, could expand their range, displacing other wild fish in cold waters. In such a situation, our disastrous experiences with exotic species could be all too relevant.

Nevertheless, for two reasons, most transgenic organisms probably will not have undesirable effects. **First**, we know that the genetic changes that have resulted from selective breeding of agricultural organisms have commonly reduced the ability of organisms to survive on their own. It is reasonable to expect that genetic engineering will often have similar effects. Many economically valuable genetically engineered traits, such as altered amino acid content of potatoes, blue flowers for roses and carnations, and pharmaceutical production in goat's milk, are highly unlikely to provide a selective environmental advantage to the engineered organisms. **Second**, a large fraction of the organisms that humans want to engineer are domesticated and have already been debilitated by selective breeding. Without assistance from humans, the survival and reproductive rates of many domesticated organisms are low. It is difficult to imagine that the addition of just about any engineered trait could turn such major agricultural crops or livestock as corn, cow and cotton, into new pests (Of course, not all domesticated organisms are extremely debilitated. Races of some crops, including sorghum and millet, can be weeds).

CROP PLANTS PREDOMINATE

Not surprisingly, that the nature of the risks presented by genetically engineered organisms will vary with the type of organism being released. Crop plants are by far the predominant type of organisms being engineered for agricultural use. As of May 1994, the US government had approved approximately 850 field tests of genetically engineered crop plants, versus about 50 field tests of genetically engineered microorganisms and two outdoor experiments with genetically engineered fish. Crop plants similarly dominate the field tests in many other countries.

ENVIRONMENTAL RISK

The most significant ecological risk of releases of transgenic crops is that they may transfer via pollination their acquired genes to related wild plants. Such gene transfer is likely when transgenic crops are grown in the crop's geographical centre of origin, so that the crop's wild ancestors grow nearby, or in areas where wild weedy relatives of a crop have been introduced along with the crop. A large fraction of the world's major crops originated in what are now developing countries than developed ones. Since genes will be transferred to close relatives of crop plants, gene transfer will disproportionately affect the gene pools of wild plants potentially valuable for crop breeding rather than other plants.

Of course, gene transfer from crop to wild relative can only have significant consequences if the transferred gene affords an advantage and therefore spreads through the wild population via natural selection. For example, in a highly controversial decision, the US Department of Agriculture (USDA) in December 1994 allowed Asgrow Seed Company to sell squash genetically engineered to resist two plant viruses. The engineered squash will undoubtedly transfer its two acquired virus-resistance genes to wild squash (*Cucurbita pepo*) which is native to the southern US, where it is an agricultural weed. If the virus-resistance genes spread, new disease-resistant wild squash could become a hardier, a more abundant weed. Moreover because the US is a centre of origin for squash, ensuing changes in the genetic make-up of wild squash could conceivably lessen its value to squash breeders.

There are other potentially significant ecological risks of transgenic crop plants besides gene transfer. Acquisition of advantageous genetically engineered traits could cause crops themselves to become weeds (or even superweeds) of natural or agricultural ecosystems. Although this risk should be very low for highly domesticated crops it could be significant for such crops as forage grasses, blackberries, and grain *Amaranthus*, which retain many wild characteristics and can survive with little assistance from humans.

Some plant pathologists have raised the possibility that the development of virus-resistant crops could sometimes allow viruses to infect new hosts or even lead to the creation of new strains of viruses. Plant viruses are simply pieces of genetic material encapsuled by a "coat protein". Plants are typically engineered to resist a particular virus by the addition of a gene encoding part of the virus coat protein which is then produced in the plant's cells. If such virus resistant plants are simultaneously infected by another virus, the engineered coat protein may once in a while become the coat for the naturally infecting virus. As the coat is vital for the natural infection by virus, the coat proteins can determine which hosts a virus infects, such "transencapsidation" may allow viruses to infect new hosts. It is also possible that introduced viral coat protein genes may exchange genetic material, or "recombine" "with infection viruses, leading on rare occasions to the evolution of a new viral strain".

FISH ARE THE RISKIEST

Fish arguably pose the greatest risks of any class of animals now being genetically engineered. Over a dozen fish species have now been engineered for the most part with growth hormone genes that are intended to make the fish grow faster or larger. Most transgenic fish will likely be used for aquaculture, although some may be used for stocking natural bodies of water or for the aquarium trade. Because it is difficult to prevent the occasional escape of fish from aquaculture facilities (artificial ponds and raceways) into natural watersheds, all but the most tightly controlled outdoor uses of transgenic fish should be considered as releases into the environment.

Most fish are not highly domesticated and can readily survive and breed with natural fish populations. If fish are genetically engineered to have traits that confer an advantage in the wild (large size is a possible example), these traits could spread in wild populations via natural selection. Having acquired a new advantageous trait, fish could then affect populations of other aquatic organisms for example by having a higher reproductive rate or being more voracious predators. These sorts of ecological effects are of particular concern because experience with exotic species of fish like the Nile perch has shown that natural fish communities are easily destroyed.

ENGINEERED MICROBES

The issues associated with introduction of genetically engineered microorganisms are for several reasons more difficult than those associated with genetically engineered crop plants and animals. **First** very little is known about microorganisms, and it is difficult to make specific ecological predictions about the impacts of introductions of many genetically engineered microorganisms. A rule of thumb is that a microbiologist is doing well if he can culture 10% of the bacteria in a soil sample let alone identify or understand the function of those microbes.

Second, although life depends on microbial communities that degrade organic matter, cycle nitrogen, and so on, most people have little conservation ethics for the microbes that make up these communities. Consistent with this attitude, people typically do not worry about the effects of introducing microorganisms to the geographic areas. Microorganisms are continually transported around the world in the gastrointestinal tracts of travellers, on the surface of agricultural products, and so on. It would be inconsistent to worry about currently immeasurable local shifts in populations of microorganisms resulting from introductions of genetically engineered organisms and still permit current practices of travel and commerce.

Nevertheless the direct effects of microorganisms, such as pathogens and nitrogen-fixers, on higher organisms have traditionally concerned humans greatly, concern about genetically engineered microorganisms should be similarly focused. Most genetically engineered microorganisms currently under development are intended to directly affect higher organisms, to control agricultural pests, to vaccinate humans and livestock and to fix nitrogen for plants. The effects of such microorganisms on target and non-target organisms bear careful scrutiny. Such scrutiny is especially vital because, more than any other class of organisms, microorganisms cannot be recalled once released.

Finally, microorganisms can transfer their genes among different species, genera, and even kingdoms of microorganisms—although the extent of such gene transfers are better documented in the laboratory than in nature. Engineered genes that confer a selective advantage could theoretically spread throughout the microbial world, making it difficult to access to long-term impact of introduction of a particular genetically engineered microorganism. A cautionary note comes from the spread of antibiotic resistance genes, some of which have become exceedingly common in populations of pathogenic and nonpathogenic bacteria since the widespread adoption of antibiotics.

3

The Cases

Herbicide Tolerance

Eight of the world's top 10 seed companies are now owned by organizations which manufacture agrochemicals. These firms have a strong incentive to develop seeds which depend on chemicals manufactured by the same firm, such as seeds bred to tolerate a particular herbicide. Herbicides have the biggest share of the agrochemicals market (about US $ 10.000 million a year worldwide). As market growth has slowed recently, so anything which allows farmers to use more herbicides without harming the crop would be a welcome boost to the industry.

The first genetically-modified crops in wide use will probably be maize, cotton, tobacco and potato resistant to herbicides, including glyphosate (marketed as Roundup), atrazine, the sulphonyl ureas (such as Glean and Oust) and 2,4-D. Some herbicides kill only selected classes of plants. For instance, a weedkiller selective for broad-leafed plants kills weeds but grain crops like wheat and maize remain untouched. Unfortunately, weedkillers are not perfectly selective. As many linger in the soil, they make it hard to rotate crops. A broad-leafed weedkiller would also kill a crop of soybeans or potatoes grown in the same field next season. But if the soybeans and potatoes were genetically modified so the herbicide did not harm them, the field could be sprayed and only the weeds would die. Seed sales of herbicide-resistant crops could exceed US $ 160 million a year by the turn of the century and herbicide sales are likely to soar.

DRAWBACKS OF HERBICIDE-RESISTANT CROPS

The promotion of such crops will permit increased use of pesticides even though there is widespread concern that these toxic chemicals are already over-used. Herbicide spraying can lead to genetic erosion of "weed" plants, which have important, though non-commercial uses. Increasing herbicide use poses a particular danger to farm workers in the South, where warnings may not be printed in a language workers can read and there is frequently no safety advice and equipment. The population as a whole is also at risk, from increased use of toxic pesticides, for example via contamination of drinking water; 2,4-D is suspected of causing cancer and birth defects; atrazine and simazine have recently been banned in Britain. A herbicide tolerant crop which remains in a field could become a serious pest, as it would be harder to kill with weedkiller.

Commodity Substitution

The UN FAO warns, "biotechnology research does not focus on the needs or interests of developing countries". Indeed, researchers are working to develop new products and processes that could replace some of the developing countries' most valuable exports, such as tropical oils, vanilla, pyrethrum, and rubber. Genetic engineering may allow Northern farmers to grow what have traditionally been Southern or tropical crops, or make it possible to produce substitute raw materials from Northern crops. Research is under way to modify or replace coffee, tobacco, sugar, cocoa, coconut, palm oil, gum arabic, vanilla, opium, ginseng and the cancer drug vincristine.

In some cases these could wipe out export markets altogether. Products in developing countries are often much cheaper than those in the industrialized world, so it may not be profitable to grow many of these crops in the North. However, the existence of such alternatives makes it impossible for producer countries to raise prices. This has already occurred with sugar, earlier forms of biotechnology allowed maize to be converted into sweeteners, and sugar's share of the US sweetener market fell from 75% in 1965 to less than 50% in 1985. US imports of cane sugar from the Philippines, India and the Caribbean fell dramatically.

Oils are a subject of intense research as they are currently imported by the North not just as food but for the enormous Northern soap, detergent and cosmetics industries (estimated at US $ 35,000 million a year). Southeast Asia is currently the world's leading producer of vegetable oil. Research is geared to replacing the more expensive oils like coconut, cocoa and olive with substitutes engineered from the cheaper palm oils. Northern oilseed rape is being engineered to imitate tropical crops.

Genetic engineering may also enable crops which currently thrive in tropical or sub-tropical climates to grow in a wider range of conditions. High-value products are the most likely targets for import substitution of research—pharmaceuticals, dyes, flavourings and fragrances. A process has already been designed which converts raw beans into chocolate. This means cheap, lower-quality cocoa from plantations in Brazil, Indonesia and Malaysia could replace higher-quality beans from all holdings in West Africa. US government scientists have synthesised something quite like cocoa butter from cotton seed oil and sunflower oil.

SUPERWEEDS AND SUPERBUGS

Once living organisms are released, they reproduce and become hard to control. Many naturally-occuring plants and animals have become serious pests when introduced into new habitats. Genetically engineered plants may be an even bigger nuisance. The genetically-engineered traits could even escape from crop plants into their wild relatives. As most crop plants originated in the tropics, it is in these countries that crops are most likely to be growing near wild relatives with which they can interbreed, and the risk for "superweeds" is greatest here.

Plants inedible to insects would have tremendous competitive advantage, especially if they were also engineered to grow well under other difficulties such as drought. According to *Nature* (17 June 1993) insect-inedible crops are among the likelier candidates to become invasive weeds, along with many wild plants which acquire insect resistance through interbreeding. The loss of their food source could wipe out populations of insects, threatening in turn the existence of birds or animals which depend on eating the insects. Genetic engineering can only transfer one, or at most a few resistance genes into a crop plant. This resistance is more easily beaten than resistance arising from more traditional forms of plant breeding. If the plant has only one trick, to beat the pest, the pest is quite likely to learn a competing trick of its own.

Engineered Bt

Bacillus thuringiensis (in short, Bt) is a bacterium which normally lives in the soil. It produces a crystal protein that has the ability to disintegrate the gut wall of many insects but is innocuous for most other living organisms. Due to these properties, Bt has been used as a biological pesticide by organic farmers since the early 1960s. It has been the environmental friendliness of Bt that has caught the eyes and investments of large agrochemical companies that increasingly face both regulatory and consumer constraints for the expansion of their conventional chemical pesticides. Also many of the smaller and specialised biotech companies have thrown their weight behind Bt research, hoping to corner part of the expected benefits. So, what is new if organic farmers have been spraying this biopesticide for many decades? It is that genetic engineering allows to pull the genes out of the bacteria and insert them into the crops. Many alternatives exist for the use of bacteria, viruses, and fungi as bioinsecticides. Bacterial agents include a variety of *Bacillus* species, primarily *B. thuringiensis*.

MICROBIAL GROUP:
MAJOR ORGANISMS AND APPLICATIONS

BACTERIA
B. thuringiensis and *B. popilliae* are the two major organisms of interest. *B. thuringiensis* is used on a wide variety of vegetables and field crops, fruits, shade trees and ornamentals. Both bacteria are considered harmless to humans. *Pseudomonas fluorescens*, which contains the toxin-producing gene from *B. thuringiensis*, is also used.

VIRUSES

Three major virus groups that do not appear to replicate in warm-blooded animals are used: *nuclear polyhedrosis virus* (NPV), *granulosis virus* (GV), and *cytoplasmic polyhedrosis virus* (CPV). These occluded viruses are more protected in the environment.

FUNGI

Over 500 different fungi are associated with insects. Infection and disease occur primarily through the insect cuticle. Four major genera have been used. *Beauveria bassiana, Meharhizium anisopliae, Verticillium lecanii* and *Entomophthora* spp. Hosts for *B. thuringiensis* are all insects other than Lepidoptera.

Work on the molecular biology of *B. thuringiensis* is progressing rapidly. The *parasporal crystal,* after exposure to alkaline conditions in the hindgut, fragments to release the protoxin. When the protoxin reacts with a *protease* enzyme, the *active toxin* is released. Six of the active toxin units integrate into the midgut membrane to form a hexagonal-shaped pore through the midgut cell. This leads to the loss of osmotic balance and ATP, and finally to insect cell lysis. The parasporal body will be expressed in *B. thuringiensis* only if a specialized plasmid is present. These parasporal bodies have been found to vary in their geometry, and it appears that the shape is related to host range and toxin effectiveness.

The most recent advances in our understanding of *B. thuringiensis* have involved the creation of pest-resistant plants. The first step is to insert the toxin gene (Bt) into *E. coli* plasmid. This major scientific advance was followed in 1987 by the production of tomato plants that contained the Bt (*A . tumefaciens -* mediated). Additional types of transgenic plants have been produced. A synthetic toxin gene was created in which natural AT-rich regions were replaced with more normal GC sequences to minimize degradation of mRNA in the plant. After successful insertion of this modified artificial gene into the plant, over 0.2% of the transgenic plant weight was the active toxin protein. Efforts are underway to make such transgenic plant modifications more cost-effective for routine production of commercial crops. Questions of stability and development of resistance by the target pest are some concerns.

B. thuringiensis can be grown in fermenters. When the cells lyse, the spores and crystals are released into the medium. The medium is then centrifuged and made up as a dust or wettable powder for application onto plants. It should be noted that *B. thuringiensis* has been found to be active against a wide range of target organisms among insects. The development of biopesticides is progressing rapidly. One of the most exciting advances involves the use of *Baculoviruses* that have been genetically modified to produce a potent scorpion toxin active against insect larvae. After ingestion by the larvae, viruses are dissolved in the midgut and are released.

SINGLE SOLUTION APPROACHES

In a world where the dangers and real price of chemical pesticides are increasingly being acknowledged, large agrochemical companies are striving to adopt to (and control) the new situation. The stakes are high; 10% of all pesticides will be biologically-based by this year, representing some US $ 3 billion in world sales, compared to the US $ 130-140 million market for biopesticides some years ago. Bt continues to concentrate over one-third of all research on micro-biological control agents. The conclusion is that out of the thousands of possible approaches to biological control of crop pests, well over 95% of all biotech research on microbial control agents focuses on two single genera; *Bacillus* and *Pseudomonas*.

The "miracle gene" is being built into virtually any crop of significance. At the last count no less than 14 crops and trees had been field-tested in the USA. Corn is target number one for most companies as it is a widely planted crop and the first money maker of the seeds industry. But then, corn is not the only focus. Monsanto's Bt potatoes and cotton have already been granted commercial approval. The IRRI is developing rice varieties resistant to yellow stem borer from genetically engineered rice containing a synthetic Bt gene patented by Ciba-Geigy. Other crops are soya, wheat, tomato, brassica, white spruce and hybrid poplar tree. However, for most of these strategic crops, the use of Bt in the form of bioinsecticides seems to be the prevailing approach. With so many differnt plants being inoculated with the same medicine (Bt gene), the question is indeed, as the Union of Concerned Scientists (USA) puts it, too much of a Good thing?

CONCENTRATING CONTROL....... AND PROFITS

By March 1995 there were no less than 440 either granted or pending patents related to little Bt bacteria, according to Derwent's World Patent Index. Such an impressive amount of monopoly titles related to this single organism already indicates the struggle going on amongst the industrial giants to control the benefits originating from it. The possibility of Bt affecting beneficial insects and other life forms - some of them as important for agriculture as earthworms, the transfer of Bt genes from engineered plants and microbes to weeds and even the dangers of its use for human health (the genus *Bacillus* includes highly pathogenic species) remain potential and unaddressed risks.

One of the means proposed by the industry in order to halt or delay resistance was to use different Bt strains in the expectation that insects with resistance to one toxin would still be stopped by another. Biotech companies have bioprospected for different Bt strains. However in 1992, it was found out that insects that developed resistance to one type of Bt toxin are often also resistant to other types of the toxin to which they have not been exposed. How exactly the insects manage this is beyond the scientists' understanding, but the appearance of this type of "cross resistance" would mean that the recommended strategy to mix different Bt strains and toxins is rendered useless. Varying the sprayed toxins (or the engineered plants) may actually increase the evolutionary pressure on the pests to develop general resistance mechanisms. Another approach which at first sight seems to be more promising is using Bt selectively in the framework of an Integrated Pest Management (IPM) scheme.

BIOTECHNOLOGICAL APPLICATIONS OF Bt

1. *As a bioinsecticide*: Plants are sprayed with Bt spores containing the toxic protein. The efficiency of this classical Bt use has been increased by two means:
* Use of Bt genetically engineered in order to produce more toxin.
* Incorporation of the gene into yeasts in order to obtain large quantities of the toxin through fermentation which can be incorporated into the sprays.

2. *Bioencapsulation*: Insertion of the Bt gene in *Pseudomonas* that are subsequently killed in a process that "fixes" the Bt protein inside the dead bacteria. This protects the protein from UV radiation and enlarges its active life.

3. *Insertion* : The Bt gene is ***inserted*** in microorganisms that are closely associated to the crops:
* *Epiphytes:* Insertion of the Bt gene into root-colonising bacteria (*Pseudomonas*) thus protecting the root crops against soil-dwelling insects.
* *Endophytes:* Insertion of the Bt gene into bacteria that live inside the plant tissue (*Clavibacter xyli*) which are then inoculated into the seeds.

4. *Transgenic plants*: The Bt gene is modified in order to insert it into a plant's genome; the transgenic plant then produces the toxin as if it were just another of its natural proteins.

5. *Future RDT leading to producing plants* :
* Where the Bt gene would express only in some organs.
* That would only synthesise Bt toxin after receiving a chemical signal from the insect (........ chewing, saliva, etc.).
* Where the Bt gene would be inserted in organelles, such as chloroplasts, allowing for its production at very high concentration.

Bt HAS BEEN PATENTED

In the continuing saga of corporations claiming broad monopoly rights over new developments in biotechnology, the Belgian firm Plants Genetics Systems (PGS) has just been awarded a US patent on any crop that is engineered to contain Bt genes. Transfering Bt genes into crops so that they become natural pesticides against their predators is one of the test pursuits of the biotech industry today.

The Bt is extremely popular in the development of insect-resistant crops. Bt toxin genes have already been engineered into maize and cotton, to protect against corn borers and boll worm. Research is also underway to incorporate the gene into other commercially important crops, including rice and coffee. An environmentally friendly insecticide for use as a spray, Bt has been widely hailed as a great improvement on toxic chemical insecticides such as DDT, dieldrin and lindane, even though it is more expensive. However the "headlong rush" to incoroprate Bt genes into crop plants will mean insects being continuously exposed to the toxin, instead of just to intermittent sprays when an infestation becomes troublesome. This will make it much easier for insects to evolve a way to fight back. In laboratory and field tests, insect pests have been shown to develop resistance to this toxin within 10 to 20 generations.

CROP LOSSES MAY NOT BE CUT EFFECTIVELY

Genetic engineering is likely to encourage the same uniform cropping patterns which have led to more and more crops being destroyed by pests and diseases over the past 50 years, and will not bring more than temporary relief to farmers. Research by the ILO shows the percentages of crops lost to pests and diseases doubled to 13% in the 30 years up to 1974. By 1985 according to the FAO losses had soared to 20% - 50% despite vast increases in the range and quantities of pesticides applied. In contrast multigene resistance is more robust. While a pest can temporarily get the upper hand, the crop may fight back without the need for more investment.

GENETIC ENGINEERING THREATENS BIODIVERSITY

Genetic engineering is being promoted as the way to make money out of biodiversity and to pay for biodiversity conservation. However, genetic engineering may in fact destroy the very diversity on which it depends on for its "raw materials". While the green revolution wiped out a lot of genetic diversity in irrigated lowlands, more diversity remains in high, steep, rocky or dry areas and those otherwise unsuitable for intensive high input agriculture. This will change if breeders and biotechnologists make a headway in breeding for marginal environments. For instance, tree botanists are seeking to find a cold - tolerance gene to incorporate in eucalyptus. This would extend the range over which eucalyptus plantations were visible, threatening as yet unexploited highland areas with loss of wildlife habitat and diversity.

COMMERCIAL EXPLOITATION MAY
DESTROY GENETIC RESOURCES

The US WRI has warned that controls are needed to stop "biodiversity prospectors" from plundering the genetic wealth of "gene-rich, technology-poor nations, leaving communities devastated and resources exhausted in their wake". According to *New Scientist* (19 June 1993) WRI lawyers have written a report advising countries to draw up contracts and regulations to restrict access to their genetic resources, to secure fees in return for the right even to prospect, and to establish local industries in order to retain the wealth generated from valuable resources.

If countries aimed to prospect, develop and manufacture products from local resources themselves, rather than allowing in outsiders, they could increase their share of the royalties 15 fold, says the WRI. If outside firms are allowed in, some payment should be sought up-front, as profitable plants may not be discovered, in which case royalties may not materialise later on. Giving commercial value to a plant variety can directly threaten its existence. The Himalayan plant *Taxus baccata* yields the substance *taxol*, a possible cancer drug. Middlemen are paying Himalayan hill peasants for the plant, which is then sold on to city-based exporting firms. Uncontrolled collecting has meant the plant reportedly already disappearing from large areas.

BIOTECHNOLOGY ALONE WILL NOT PROTECT BIODIVERSITY

Many agencies argue that biotechnology is needed for biodiversity conservation, both to carry it out and to pay for it. It is agreed that effective conservation of genetic resources must become self-supporting by producing income. However, it would be a mistake to rely on profits from biotechnology to save the world's genetic resources. Only those genes which would quickly become profitable would be selected for saving, the remainder being dismissed as "redundant to crop production or protection" and therefore lost forever.

4

Release of GMOs into the Environment

Genetic modification techniques allow scientific institutions and companies to change the characteristics of micro-organisms, plants and animals. Many of these modifications will have uses in agriculture and food processing: strawberries altered to be more resistant to insect pests; tomatoes with a longer shelf life and potatoes that make better crisps. Genetic modification also has applications in medicine and potentially in pollution clean-up. The use of many of these modifications, particularly in agriculture, involves **deliberate release** to the environment, a term that covers everything from planting modified crops in a field to spraying a biological pesticide. Since the first releases in the mid 1980s, questions have been asked about environment safety. This section outlines some of the main concerns raised by environmental groups. We should identify those who are, or should be responsible for answering the questions. Those developing the technology, selling it, buying it, regulating it, or commenting on it from a public interest standpoint, should not act in isolation from each other.

Environmental Groups are Concerned that
1. Genes inserted into microorganisms, plants and animals, that could not have got there by conventional breeding, will over time be spread to other organisms.
2. We do not know enough about ecological interactions to be able to accurately predict what the long-term consequences will be of the presence of these introduced genes in the environment.
3. Changes to the environment may not be noticed early.
4. The regulatory system controlling releases to the environment has not taken on board the concept of "genetic pollution": in other words, the spread of genes in the environment, when they could not have got there by natural means, is not seen as environmental damage in itself.
5. Work with viruses poses particular risks.
6. Genetic modification may not further the development of more "sustainable" agriculture.

7. The development of herbicide-resistant plants could cause changes in the patterns of herbicides used in agriculture in ways that will be more environmentally damaging than at present.
8. Efforts to engineer top predators such as fish could lead to serious ecological disruption.
9. Liability for damage caused by GMOs needs special provision.
10. The regulatory system does not give enough scope for consultation with the public.

The main reason for the current wave of public interest in genetic engineering is the prospect of commercial production of a broad range of genetically engineered organisms. Each of these developments represents a choice, not an inevitability. Environmentalists have joined the debate to control risks and to bring an environmental perspective to these choices.

THE BACULOVIRUSES

Baculoviruses are a group of viruses which primarily infect insects and each virus is restricted to a range of particular insect hosts. They appear unable to infect non-arthropod hosts, and as such are considered a useful alternative to chemical control for insect pests, an alternative that will not do damage to other species or leave chemical residues. Baculoviruses have been used in their natural state as a biological control for decades, particularly in Brazil where over 1 million hectares of crops are sprayed annually with the *Anticarsia gemmatalis* NPV virus. However, in their natural state the baculoviruses do not kill insects quickly enough to prevent damage to most crops, so genetic engineering techniques have been used to improve their effectiveness. These have included inserting a gene from a species of scorpion into the *Autographa california* NPV virus so that it expresses a lethal poison as it is multiplying in the insect.

The biggest anxiety associated with the use of genetically modified baculoviruses is that they might be able to attack insects other than their natural targets, for instance attacking not just the caterpillars that are pests in crops, but also the caterpillars of rare or valued butterflies. Since the viruses have been engineered to kill their hosts more quickly, the effects on a non-target species could be dramatic. Only one extensive European study has been carried out on the specificity of this particular baculovirus, and that involved only 100 out of the total of 2,500 UK-recorded species of lepidoptera (butterflies and moths). Around 10% of those tested so far may be susceptible to the virus. It is not yet clear which genes control the ability of a particular baculovirus to infect particular hosts, and whether this could be inadvertently altered by genetic manipulation, or by recombination with another baculovirus. If a genetically modified baculovirus which has been released into the environment does attack an insect other than its target, it will be important to know how long the virus can persist in the soil, whether it can be reintroduced into the insect population and therefore how long it might be a problem in that particular area. So far, experiments suggest that survival in the soil could be indefinite, albeit at low levels.

THE RELEASE AND THE RISKS

Although many field trials for risk assessment have been conducted (Figure 10), small-scale trials do not necessarily provide the information needed for assessing safety at a commercial scale. There are three categories of environmental risks.

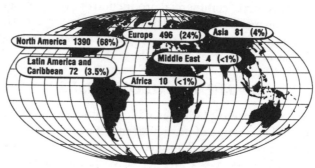

Region/Country	Total	Region/Country	Total
Latin America and Caribbean		**Europe**	
Argentina	20	Belgium	81
Belize	4	Denmark	11
Bolivia	4	Finland	10
Chile	13	France	168
Costa Rica	5	Germany	6
Cuba	9	Hungary	4
Dominican Republic	1	Italy	14
Guatemala	1	Netherlands	84
Mexico	15	Norway	1
Asia		Portugal	4
Australia	26	Spain	16
China	30	Sweden	17
Japan	8	Switzerland	2
New Zealand	15	United Kingdom	78
Thailand	2	**North America**	
Africa		Canada	359
Egypt	1	United States	1031
South Africa	9		
Middle East		**WORLD TOTAL**	**2053**
Israel	4		

Fig. 10 World-wide field trials of transgenic plants: 1986-1994.

First, the newly introduced traits may enable transgenic plants to become weeds in agricultural ecosystems, or to move out of the field to disturb unmanaged ecosystems.

Second, the transfer of the transgenes to crop relatives. An example is the transfer of a gene for salt-tolerance to a wild rice relative. The newly salt-tolerant relative might then be able to invade a salt marsh habitat, thereby displacing native plants. If the displaced plants offered a better habitat for nesting birds, the harmful effect could ripple beyond the marsh.

A **third** category of risks is the possibility that virus-resistant transgenic crops could produce new viruses or alter the host-range of existing viruses.

Weediness potential can be predicted, although imperfectly, by comparing the field behaviour of the transgenic plant with its non-engineered parent. The possibility of transgene flow can be assessed primarily on the basis of information about the distribution of sexually compatible wild and weedy relatives in the region where the crop is grown. If no wild and weedy relatives are in the vicinity, for example, there is no risk of gene transfer. An important point is made about the international implications. Approval of the transgenic crop in one country does not assure its safety in another country, because the risks associated with a particular crop depend, among others, upon the environment in which it is planted. For example, engineered cold-tolerant potatoes may be approved for commercialization in the United States. By contrast, the presence of landraces and sexually compatible wild relatives in Peru (the center of diversity of potato) means that transgenes are likely to move from the engineered crop to nearby relatives.

THREATS FROM THE TEST-TUBES

The new biotechnologies have been heralded as the definite solution to many of the world's problems. However, they have also been associated with a number of serious negative impacts and potential dangers. These impacts are both of socio-economic and environmental nature, and should be dealt with. Here are some alarming cases of how the new biotechnologies affect livelihoods of local communities in the Third World, and how developing countries are turning into uncontrolled testing grounds for potentially dangerous biotechnology products.

Many are worried about socio-economic implications as new products developed through biotechnology in the North replace traditional export crops —and millions of jobs—of developing countries. Yet others are concerned that the advent of the new biotechnologies will bring with it a tremendous wave of privatisation of the biological resources that previously were in the public domain. In its 1993 World Food Day Brochure, FAO puts it politely, but still bluntly enough "several areas exist where modern biotechnologies may hinder development or create serious hardship for rural communities".

Still, whatever the opinion about the implications of biotechnology, there are a few factors to take into account when considering its potential to promote sustainable development world-wide. One is that current biotechnological research is almost entirely carried out in the North. Another is that this research is to a large extent controlled by the private sector, mostly large transnational corporations with their main interest in agrochemicals, pharmaceuticals or food processing and trade. Corporations by definition, exist to produce as much profit as possible for their shareholders.

The consequence of this biased situation is that much of current biotech research is directed towards the agriculture and health situation in the North. The relevance of that research to the resource-poor consumers and farmers of the developing countries is highly questionable. Its impact, however, can be substantial. **One concern** relates to the question of the erosion of biodiversity as a consequence of the push for the highly uniform biotech crop cultivars emerging from the corporate laboratories. The cloning of individual high yielding and extremely uniform plants is already commercially possible for a number of species, and forms a tremendous threat to the diversity still available in the field. **Another aspect** of biotechnology development has to do with the direction of the research itself. Despite promises to help replace agrochemicals through the production of pest and disease-resistant plants, an enormous amount of research is going into efforts to do the opposite: create plants that tolerate higher doses of weedkillers.

Another concern relates to the replacement of traditional Third World export crops with laboratory-designed substitutes. This affects millions of small farmers and landless plantation workers in the South. The substitution of sugar by biotechnologically produced substitutes in the North illustrates what is at stake. Other examples that are now emerging—or are likely to emerge—from the biotechnology laboratories include substitutes for such important export crops as cocoa, vanilla, pyrethrum and a whole range of vegetable oil crops. If these developments come through, they would spell disaster for those developing countries depending on such exports, but especially for the farmers and local communities depending on them.

Yet another possible impact relates to the environmental danger of the release of genetically engineered organisms (GMOs) into the environment. Field experiments with GMOs are being conducted, mainly in the North, but increasingly also in developing countries. The last count is over one thousand field tests for genetically engineered plants alone. Yet many questions are unanswered on the safety of releases of GMOs, even in the most industrialized countries. The US *Union for Concerned Scientists* warns that among other dangers transgenic crops may become persistent weeds, genetically engineered genes could transfer to valuable wild relatives, and control over genetically engineered virus resistance genes could break down creating even greater pest control problems.

For developing countries without the scientific and regulatory infrastructure to carefully monitor the impacts of such releases and greater biodiversity at stake, the situation is even more precarious.

There is a definite risk that the Third World is used as a cheap testing ground for experiments thought to be dangerous in the North. The case of the testing in Argentina of a genetically engineered rabies vaccine without the consent of the national government has been widely published. Many more such examples exist. In the late 1980s, importation into the Philippines of a potentially dangerous rice disease for research by IRRI was only stopped after concerned citizens started protesting and the Philippines senate blocked it. In 1986, medical researchers from Paris vaccinated 12 volunteers in Zaire with a genetically engineered AIDs vaccine. Between 1991 and 1992 Monsanto conducted field tests of genetically engineered soybean coding for herbicide resistance in at least five Latin American countries, with other North American companies doing the same with other crops. In 1998, Monsanto was alleged to have clandestinely started testing of the *Terminator and Traitor* technology in many Indian states under technology-transfer. In all cases, it is highly unclear whether the national authorities have had knowledge about such releases, let alone whether they had the chance to assess the risks related to them.

5

Biosafety

THE NEED

We are being asked to enter the new age of biotechnology and especially the world of genetic engineering. Using the new technology the genetic make-up of all organisms on Earth can be changed. Trees, fish, many other animals, all other food and fibre crops, bacteria and viruses are already being genetically manipulated to fit our next version of the 'Brave New World'. Many of these organisms have received genetic material from unrelated species. Often they have been engineered to improve their ability to survive under new environmental or climatic conditions. Clearly, these genetically engineered organisms have the potential to replace natural, indigenous species and further erode biological diversity.

Some of the additional environmental risks that genetically modified crops alone can pose are the following. Crops engineered to produce toxic substance such as drugs or pesticides may present dangers to other organisms like birds feeding from the crops as well as to humans. Crops engineered to tolerate harmful pesticides may increase the use of these chemicals, further polluting water and poisoning wild plant species and the land. Genetically engineered organisms threaten the integrity of nature, as nature's final barriers (species boundaries against the intrusion of man) are breached. A new form of biological pollution threatens the environment. Genetically manipulated organisms can change, mutate, multiply and spread, but they cannot be removed from the environment once they have been released.

Precautionary action must, therefore, be taken. Many countries, particularly those at the forefront of genetic engineering, such as the United States and the European Union, have established regulations in an attempt to minimize environmental harm. Most developing countries, however, do not have even these most basic precautions. The international transfer, trade and use of genetically engineered organisms is not regulated in a legally binding manner. This may lead to the misuse of less developed countries as testing sites for genetically modified organisms, especially very risky ones.

EXISTING SAFEGUARDS

Concern has been expressed about the need for international protocols for the testing and shipment of genetically modified organisms. An existing international mechanism in a few countries is effectively dealing with potential safety issues connected with genetic engineering. Since the mid-1980s the member governments of the OECD have been developing common concepts for assessing risks. OECD reports have provided guidelines and principles that have been widely accepted. In some cases, they have served as the model for National Regulatory System. By the end of 1993, more than 1,500 field tests of plants modified by genetic engineering had been conducted on a worldwide basis. Virtually every major crop plant—65 in all has been modified in one way or another to carry traits beneficial to farmers, processors or consumers. During 1994, another 1700 field tests were scheduled to be conducted. Most of these tests have been conducted in the developing world. However active research is going on in the developed world, where crops including potatoes, cotton, rice tomatoes, and papaya are currently on or near field testing.

RELEASING OR GAMBLING?

The US Department of Agriculture has recently published guidelines for the deregulation of transgenic crops—crops with genes from other species. Deregulation will be necessary before a crop can be sold to farmers. The 350 US field trials so far (1995) of transgenic crops have been carried out under containment — trial crops must be grown away from unmodified relatives and all the material is destroyed as soon as the trial is completed. But designing trials which really could give evidence on whether crops or genes might "escape" quickly enough to keep up with the advances in biotechnology is no small challenge. In countries without even the protection of the US system, safety of commercial genetically modified crop releases will be even harder to guarantee.

SAFETY AND REGULATION

Field trials of genetically modified crops are occurring in countries with inadequate safety regulation or not a regulation at all. Attempts to establish internationally agreed safety standards have failed and remain a low priority. Most regulations so far have been introduced in Northern countries, where there is a battle between environmentalists wanting strict controls and manufacturers wanting freedom to test and market their products. In industrialized countries there is growing pressure to relax safety rules, as the biotechnology industry complains research is being "strangled" by excessive safety regulations. New rules in Britain have done away with precautionary measures and make it easier to gain permission for the release of genetically modified organisms.

NORTHERN PUBLIC DOUBTFUL

The image of genetic engineering in the eyes of the general public in the North remains poor. In Britain (1993), a government study found that four out of five people did not trust the biotechnology industry to tell them the truth about genetic engineering. The *New Scientist* (19 June 1993) said people who actually worked in the biotechnology industry felt exactly the same. In the Netherlands, a panel of 15 people representing the ordinary public was "extensively briefed by experts" before they spent three days debating genetic engineering of animals. The *New Scientist* reported the panel's conclusion that not enough was yet known to allow commercial exploitation of genetically-engineered animals, and that this should be stopped to allow more research and discussion to take place. However the recent turmoils over genetically engineered food products in Britain (1999) is a welcome departure.

RELEASE IN THE SOUTH

Resistance to the release of GMOs in the North increases pressure on the South to permit tests there. There are also agronomic reasons—climate, land and labour costs—for transnationals to field-test their products in the South. But the risks are greater in the South. Few developing countries have formal regulations on genetically-modified organisms, although many permit them to be released, which means trials can be conducted without adequate safety precautions. It is very difficult to find out what organisms have been released where. However it is certain that there have been large-scale trials of genetically-modified crops in the Third World where guidelines are still to come into force. In 1992 Monsanto approached the Brazilian Ministry of Agriculture for land to test transgenetic cotton. Unaware of possible hazards from cross-pollination, the ministry was proposing to allow the trial in the middle of a cotton-growing area. Only a chance discovery by geneticist Maria Jose Sampio interrupted the trial (International Affairs, 1993). Dr Sampio believes such unregulated trials will become "a fact of life" in Brazil. There is no comprehensive list held by the Brazilian government of proposed releases of GMOs to the environment. Meanwhile local firms are pressing on with the development of genetically modified products.

Pressure is growing on Southern governments to introduce permissive safety rules to allow companies to test their products. US anxiety to secure markets for biotechnology products increases pressure on "recipient" countries to permit trials of bioengineered organisms, often in return for some technology transfer, according to Calestous Juma of the Africa Centre for Technology Studies in Kenya. US firms are increasingly anxious to get their products tested overseas, in time to prevent the Japanese from winning the market. An expert panel on biosafety was set up by the UN Environment Programme. Most of the panel members argued that a legally binding biosafety protocol should be included in the Biodiversity Convention, but panel members from the US and OECD opposed this. An FAO-organized expert consultation on Sustainable Agriculture and Rural Development in Asia, called for the FAO to set up a mechanism to "ensure that there not be the transfer of hazardous genetic engineering experiments, research and products, which are deemed to be hazardous in the Northern countries, to developing countries".

FIRST BIOTECH ACCIDENT IN EUROPE?
In what may be the first accident occurring at a biotechnology plant in the European Community, a leakage of genetically engineered microbes recently entered the sewers of Gentofle, Denmark. The accident took place at the production plant of Novo Nordisk, Denmark's top biotechnology firm. According to Novo, about 100 liters of liquid containing genetically engineered bacteria and yeast cells were discharged into the public sewage system recently. The company has assured the public that the liquid did not contain *E. coli*, the bacteria widely used by biotechnology researchers. The accident was caused by a storage tank overflow in a facility for heat treatment of fermentation liquid.

NOVEL FOODS OR STALE TRICKS?

After years of research and investment, the agrobiotech industry has started to bring its genetically modified products to the market, and many more are waiting in the wings for regulatory approval. To smooth their path, the industry is concentrating its lobbying efforts in two main areas: deregulating the use and release of GMOs and minimizing the labelling of its products. Relaxation of such legislation has serious implications for consumers and the environment.

Tomatoes have been in the news recently. Not just any old tomatoes, but tomatoes that have been refashioned to express characteristics that nature never could. In 1994, Calgene's rot-resistant, *Flavr Savr* tomato was the first genetically engineered crop to reach the supermarket shelves. Since then, Seneca's tomato paste and Monsanto's slow ripening tomatoes have been approved in the UK and the US. Many other products have also been approved for commercial use: Ciba-Geigy's Bt-corn, Plant Genetic System's rapeseed resistant to a Hoechsts chemical herbicide, and Monsanto's soybeans resistant to the companys' herbicide, Roundup. The list of crops that are tried out and targetted is ever-increasing, all for the interests of the corporate sector.

The negative impacts are often ignored, dismissed or exaggerated beyond credibility, while the industry loudly reassures the public that biosafety legislation will contain any risks that may exist. Meanwhile, behind the scenes, the industry is doing its best to dismantle that very legislation, which is perceived as the main obstacle to the steady expansion of their products and profits. The second obstacle is consumer concerns about the health and environmental impacts of genetically modified food. With respect to the second, pressure is being directed towards preventing people from knowing the truth about the consumed foods which are the products of genetic engineering.

The world's genetech giants are adopting a messianic position on the importance of genetic engineering in agriculture to feed the world's growing population. Those against genetically modified food are portrayed as being traitors of the poor and hungry, while the industry is painted as the benevolent farmers' friend. But the industry cannot live upto its bold claims of providing large quantities of healthy food in an eco-friendly manner. Genetically engineered crops are likeiy to make the world a hungrier place. The claim that genetically engineered food grown in the North will help to feed the hungry in the South ignores the dynamics of the global trade in foodstuffs. Subsidised food dumping is clearly connected to the creation of food dependence in sub-Saharan Africa, which was once self-sufficient in basic food staples. Since the 1970s, wheat imports have increased by over 200%. Net food staple imports have risen three-fold from 3 m to 9 m ta. Food dumping has played a key role in this surge in import demand. South - East Asia too is sized up—and cultivated —as a dependent market for US food exporters.

NOVEL FOODS: KEEPING THE PUBLIC IN THE DARK?

The new biotechnologies are creating a whole range of new foods. These novel foods include foods produced by the modification of existing foods, foods modified by genetically engineered microorganisms, plants and animals. Novel foods that have already reached the supermarket shelves (or are about to do it) include cheddar cheese containing a genetically engineered form of the enzyme chymosin, beer with a high alcohol content conferred by a genetically modified yeast, oil derived from herbicide-resistant genetically modified oilseed rape and soybean, pest-resistant corn, and a genetically engineered tomato which ripens more slowly than normal ones. Although genetically modified crops are only just beginning to reach the market, other novel foods made with the assistance of genetically engineered enzymes, hormones and other chemicals have already established a market niche. The public is often unaware of the methods used to create these products. The emergence of these novel foods has required new legislation to regulate their use. In theory this offers an opportunity to create a framework to make the activities of the biotechnology industry more transparent and accountable to the public. However it may do the opposite. The industry is working hard to ensure that the legislation creates a tool for it to conceal the real nature of its products. Among the most controversial aspects of novel foods regulation is the issue of *labelling*. Consumer organizations world-wide (including the European Consumers' Organization and Consumers International) have been demanding the compulsory labelling of all products of genetic engineering.

IN ORDER TO OPEN IT FOR SOYBEANS

In 1995, the US requested permission to export to Europe Monsanto's Roundup-Ready Soybean (RRS) which is genetically engineered to resist the company's own herbicide Roundup. The application was for all kind of uses as a product, but not for planting. Its approval was delayed because Denmark, Sweden and Austria insisted on labelling the soybeans as "genetically modified". This prompted a very strong reaction from US trade representatives, who argued that before long it would be impossible to distinguish RRS from ordinary soybeans, as they would end up in the same bags or containers. Since they expect RRS soon to be approved in other countries such as Argentina, by which time "all soybean shipments, from the US or anywhere else, can be assumed to include RRS'.

BIOCOLONIALISM?

The best documented case of all illegal GMO test took place in Argentina (Table 1). In 1986 the national authorities learned that a field experiment to test a rabies vaccine recombinant virus had been performed, involving domestic livestock. The new vaccine was smuggled into the country. National health agencies were not notified. No Argentinean experts were consulted, the experimental protocols and the actual trials were not evaluated or coordinated by local authorities. The press was not informed. The new vaccine was released without any kind of containment in the richest and most populated region of Argentina. The trial took place in secret in an experimental station of an international organization. Workers were not informed about the risks involved.

Table 1 Third World Countries targetted for GMO release

Countries Surveyed	Confirmed Releases	Total Releases
Argentina	43	43
Belize	—	4
Bolivia	1	5
Chile	9	17
Costa Rica	6	8
Dominican Republic	1	13
Egypt	1	1
Guatamala	2	1
India	2	3
Mexico	20	20
Peru	2	2
Puerto Rico	21	21
Republic South-Africa	17	17
Thailand	1	1
Total	**139**	**156**

BIOTECHNOLOGY SUGAR BLUES

Sugarcane was once known as the "Golden Crop" due to the huge amounts of money that was made from it. Then came the maize-derived *High Fructose Corn Syrup* (HFCS), which thanks to new biotechnological extraction processes can deliver sweeteners at 30% less cost than sugarcane or beets. Used especially in the USA, this substance has been directly responsible for severe cuts into US imports of sugarcane from the Third World. Then the market was hit by *Aspartame*, a non-caloric sweetener (200 times cane sugar) construed, combined and recombined in chemical laboratories. However the transnational food industry, never able to satisfy its "sweet cravings", has taken to bioprospecting in the savannas, tropical forests and deserts in search of plants and indigenous knowledge that can produce even cheaper sweeteners. They already found "Kaṭemfe" in the hummed zones of West and Central Africa. This plant has a gene that produces proteins which are 2500 times sweeter than sugar. They also found a wild berry in West Africa, 3000 times sweeter than sugar, and the very sweet *Stevia rebandiana* from Paraguay. There are plans to insert these sweet genes into micro-organisms that would then produce the desired sweeteners, or incorporate them directly into Northern food crops. In both cases the market for sugar cane will further collapse as a consequence of these substitutes, rendering millions of cane-dependent Third World farmers economically extinct.

The US company *Escagenetics* is working on genetically altered coffee, to change the flavour, reduce the caffeine content and to increase the proportion of solids which can be extracted to make soluble, "instant" coffee. Another US firm Sungene, is working to develop sunflowers whose oil is high in oleic acid and believed to protect against heart disease. Many genetically-modified crops are currently awaiting approval. Those already field-tested in the US which are now waiting for commercial permits include: alfalfa, maize, cotton, tobacco, potato and soybean modified to tolerate herbicide; apple, oilseed rape, maize, cotton, potato, rice, strawberry, tobacco, tomato and walnut modified to resist insect pests; alfalfa, melon, maize, cucumber, papaya, potato, rice, squash, tobacco and tomato modified to resist virus infections; and oilseed rape, maize, tomatoes, rice, potatoes, soybeans and others (Table 2).

WAR OF LABELLING ON HOT POTATO

The "humble" potato earned quite a place in the history books for its role in the Irish potato famine and the subsequent mass migration of Irish citizens to the US. Now it has done it again: this time catalysing one of the biggest public outcries against GM foods and shaking the UK government. Some modest experiments undertaken in Scotland's Rowett Research Institute by Dr. Arpad Pusztai have led to all kinds of scandals in the world of GM food, with revelations about the suppression of scientists and scientific research, the serious inadequacy of safety testing for GM foods and the government's lack of interest in addressing this, and the ever-increasing power of the genetech industry in pulling the strings of governments.

Rowett director Professor Philip James initially praised Dr Pusztai, then reversed track, announcing that an emergency audit of his work would be undertaken and apologized for Pusztai's release of "misleading information". James issued false information about the experiments that were undertaken, discrediting Pusztai's work. The world authority on lectin research was told that his contract with Rowett would not be renewed and he was issued with

Table 2 Some Transgenic Crops of Twisted Fate and Function, Released Since 1986.

S.No	Product	Company	Altered Trait	Purpose
1.	Canola (oilseed rape)	Calgene	High lauric acid	Expand use in soap and food
2.	Corn	Ciba-Geigy	Bt toxin	Control insect
3.	Corn	Mycogen	Bt toxin	Control insect
4.	Cotton	Calgene Rhone Poulenc	Herbicide resistance	Control weeds
5.	Cotton	Monsanto	Bt toxin	Control insect
6.	Potato	Monsanto	Bt toxin	Control insect
7.	Soybean	Monsanto	Herbicide resistance	Control weeds
8.	Squash	Asgrow	Virus resistance	Control virus
9.	Tomato	Calgene	Delayed ripening	Enhance market value
10.	Tomato	DNA plant Technology	Delayed ripening	Enhance market value
11.	Tomato	Monsanto	Delayed ripening	Enchance market value
12.	Tomato	Zeneca/Peto Seed	Thicker skin. altered pectin	Enhance processing value
13.	*Pseudomonas fluorescens*[3]	Rhone Merieux	Immunity to rabies	Control rabies epidemics
14.	Vaccinia virus vaccine	Rhone Merieux	Immunity to rabies	Control rabies epidemics
15.	Canola	Monsanto	Herbicide1 resistance	Control weeds
16.	Corn	Dekalb	Herbicide resistance	Control weeds
17.	Corn	Hoechst/AgrEvo	Herbicide resistance	Control weeds
18.	Corn	Plant Genetic Systems	Male Sterility	Facilitate breeding
19.	Corn	Mansanto	Bt toxin	Control insect
20.	Corn	Sandoz/Northurp King	Bt toxin	Control insect
21.	Cotton	Dupont	Herbicide resistance	Control weeds
22.	Cotton	Mansanto	Herbicide resistance	Control weeds
23.	Tomato	Agritope	Altered ripening	NA
24.	*Rhizobium*	Research Seeds	Enhance N_2 fixation	Increase yield
25.	Cotton	D &PL and USDA	Terminator & Traitor	2nd generation seed abortion, Detecting IPR violations.

NA : Information not available

a "gagging order", preventing him from defending his work. The innocuous potato became too hot to handle which then provided the political flashpoint for the now famous war on the GM foods and the need for labelling in the UK. Today the war has become trans-atlantic, with a new bill being introduced in the US Congress : *GM Foods—The Right to Know Act, 1999*. In 1998 itself GM crops were cultivated in the USA over an area equivalent to the size of the entire UK. Starting from UK, the political debate over labelling and the acceptance of the GM foods and organisms is looming large over the entire Western Europe and the USA. The *Montreal Biosafety Protocol 2000* was an attempt by the UN to put in place an international agreement on limiting imports of GMOs and GM foods. After intense debate, the US could not persuade the EU and the developing countries to agree on the terms that qualify the GMOs and GM foods "harmful to the people and enviroment".

"SUBSTANTIAL EQUIVALENCE" AND SAFETY TESTING

One of the key findings of Pusztai's study was that the genetically-engineered potatoes used in his experiments were not "substantially equivalent" to the parent lines. This finding is particularly important because substantial equivalence is the key to safety testing for GM crops in the US and Europe. The genetech industry has long argued that the actual process of genetic engineering doesn't affect safety—only the traits that are spliced are of significance. Before field testing, genetech companies are required to demonstrate that their products are substantially equivalent to non-GM varieties in terms of their composition, i.e. that they contain the same amounts of proteins, carbohydrates, fats and so on.

However evidence is accumulating that many GM crops are not substantially equivalent to non-GM crops. In addition, it is becoming blindingly obvious that substantial equivalence is only part of the equation that needs to be examined when considering biosafety. GM plants can have wide-ranging and unpredictable effects on the environment, upsetting the ecological balance. In 1998, the Scottish Crop Research Institute found that ladybirds-fed aphids reared on transgenic potatoes experienced reproductive problems and failed to live as long as those fed aphids from ordinary potatoes. The engineered potatoes contained the snowdrop lectin gene—just like Pusztai's. Scientists from the University of Chicago recently reported work in wild mustard plants that demonstrated that the process of genetic engineering can cause dramatic changes in the transgenic plants. They made the stunning observation that genetically-engineered herbicide-resistant plants were 20 times more likely to outcross (interbreed with relatives) than herbicide-resistant plants produced by traditional breeding. Standard tests for *substantial equivalence* only require testing for compositional differences, whereas the real indicators should be much wider-reaching, including ecological effects such as these.

Recent research from New York University provides as an example of the kinds of impacts that *"substantial equivalence"* testing does not highlight and field testing is unlikely to demonstrate. Typically, toxins in naturally-occurring *Bacillus thuringiensis*, and sprays made from them, exist in an inactive form, which becomes activated once ingested by the target insect. By contrast, the toxins in many Bt crops are already in the active form. The researchers found that unlike natural Bt, these active toxins do not disappear when added to soil, but become rapidly bound to the soil particles, and are not broken down by soil microbes. The researchers contend that engineered Bt toxins could build up in the soil, killing Bt-sensitive soil organisms and increasing selection pressure for resistance to develop. In addition, a broader range of organisms is likely to be susceptible to the active, engineered toxins, since some organisms lack the enzymes to activate the inactive form when they ingest it, but are still sensitive to the active form.

Another example of how GMO releases might cause widespread ecological damage is illustrated by work on the *Klebsiella planticola* bacterium. The addition of a genetically-engineered bacterium to a small microcosm consisting of wheat plants and sandy soils killed the plants, while the addition of the non-engineered parent did not. These, and an increasing number of other examples, make a mockery of the mantra *"substantial equivalence"* that regulators love to repeat over and over. A myriad of different kinds of tests on GM crops, examining the whole range of their primary and secondary impacts on the environment, are also needed to establish their safety.

THE IMPACT OF TRANSGENICS ON NATURE

An increasing number of transgenic crops are deliberately released into centres of biodiversity, which are mostly found in the developing countries. Since these centres are important for the future of the world's major food crops, there is great concern about the potential ecological impact of the releases of GMOs. Information and knowledge about the ecological impact are, however, still marginal. This section focuses on the hypothetical risks, with potato serving as an example.

Traditional farming or the release of transgenic crops may each affect the stability and diversity of an ecosystem. A generalized prediction on the behaviour of transgenic crops is not possible. Consequently, only a few studies address the potential impact of the release of (transgenic) crops, of which most are theoretical in nature. This is surprising, since an ecological impact is not restricted to recombinant DNA or transgenic plants. In particular the behaviour of released exotic species in the past, provided the respective difference between "exotic" and "transgenic" if considered, may serve as a useful empirical model for the release of transgenic crops. The following **three general scenarios** describe how transgenic crops may influence the composition and stability of natural ecosystems.

    (1)   The transgenic plant itself becomes a weed, because of its added characteristic. It will leave the area under cultivation and displace wild species.

The crop "escapes". It should be noted, that the transgenic crop may also escape because of minor genetic changes which are not related to the transferred DNA. Transgenic plants of highly domesticated species will have a lower probability of escaping compared to low-input crops like pasture legumes, sorghum or cowpea, since the former usually cannot compete with other plants outside the farmers' fields.

(2) The introduced DNA is sexually transmitted into the wild population and may confer weediness if expressed in the progeny of a cross between the respective crop and its compatible wild relative (a hybrid). This can be regarded as a probable event, especially in centres of biodiversity.

A hybrid may invade the area only if the stressor (e.g. a virus) represents an important pressure outside the area under cultivation. Usually, however, stressors relevant in agricultural areas are irrelevant in wild populations. Assuming that the spread of this dominant and single trait into the wild population is faster compared to "natural" recessive and multigenic traits. On the other hand, "natural" recessive and multigenic traits might not be subject to immediate selection and may stay "latent" in a population and thus may not be subject to immediate selection and remain for a longer time as part of the crop's gene pool.

(3) The introduced DNA is transmitted asexually to species of other kingdoms, such as bacteria, viruses and animals. Although there is no experimental proof to show that this can happen, this horizontal gene transfer does occur in nature. In fact, the horizontal gene transfer mediated by the bacterial plant pathogen *Agrobacterium tumefaciens* has become the most successful tool in genetic engineering of plants. This poorly understood dynamic gene flow between species might represent a driving force behind evolution. In this respect, the under-estimated role of DNA and micro-organisms of unknown function and distribution deserves more attention.

Assuming that a transgenic crop or hybrid has become a weed, this may result in the loss of indigenous species because of competition. Notably, the number of species in an ecosystem does not sufficiently describe biodiversity. The genetic variability within a species, which allows the adaptation to a variable environment, is probably of equal importance. In addition, the establishment of a transgenic crop or the introduced DNA in the natural environment depends on the number of plants, i.e., the size of the founder population. Also the number of introduced genes may influence the potential weediness. The principle, the more novel characteristics introduced into the system, the higher the probability of finding a respective ecological niche within the system which perfectly fits into the introduced pattern of characteristics.

The whole discussion on the impact on biodiversity of transgenic crops concentrates on the potential weediness of the new crop (scenarios 1 and 2). Surprisingly, the important question as to whether or to what extent engineered or conventionally acquired resistances against bacteria and fungi do affect the associated soil-borne microflora and endophytic micro-organisms (scenario 3) is usually neglected.

DEVELOPING COUNTRIES

Biosafety regulation in most developing countries is still in its infancy. The ecological and economic importance of such regulation, however, is undoubted. Appropriate biosafety regulations are one of the prerequisites for a successful transfer of biotechnology to and among developing countries. Major issues in the debate on biotechnology regulation are up-scaling of field trials, harmonization of regulations, and capacity building in developing countries.

The overwhelming majority of developing countries, however, do not have regulatory or monitoring procedures in place, mainly because of lack of monetary and enticement systems, and often inadequate institutional capacity. The notable exceptions are India and the Philippines, which established regulations and incorporated them in national laws. Others, such as Argentina, Bolivia, Brazil, China, Colombia, Costa Rica, Cuba, Indonesia, Malaysia, Thailand and Zimbabwe, have *ad hoc* committees that are generally set up to review field trial applications for transgenic plants. Although the number of field trials conducted in the Third World does not come near the ones in the OECD area, it is increasing steadily. In Latin America alone, over 60 field trails have been conducted in the last three to four years.

CO-ORDINATION AND CAPACITY BUILDING

Most developing countries are still in a process of designing and implementing safety regulations. This stage offers opportunities for international co-ordination of national approaches. Therefore, capacity building means (1) the training of those nationals who will be developing and implementing biosafety regulatory mechanisms, and (2) the sharing of experience with agencies that are already for many years involved in developing and implementing such regulations. This can be done, for example, through small but intensive workshops that would enable participants to receive hands-on experience relevant to the procedures and issues.

For transnational biotech companies there is also a clear interest in establishing and harmonizing biosafety regulation in developing countries. **Firstly,** if a regulatory system is in place, companies can share responsibility with regulatory authorities, in case something goes wrong. **Secondly**, supporting regulation may provide a chance to influence the content of the regulation. And **thirdly**, implementing and harmonizing regulation can avoid unfair competition from companies located in countries without strict safety regulation.

RISKS VERSUS BENEFITS

The procedures for risk assessment of transgenic plants should provide scientific information about the chance of an adverse effect to occur. Field trials are the main method for gathering this information. However there is always the next phase of weighing the outcome of these trials. This is the phase of balancing risks against benefits. In this balancing, ecological effects are only one of many items to be evaluated. Acceptance of risk depends on many factors, such as the expected benefits, the kind of products involved, the possibility of the agency providing information on risks and benefits.

The evaluation of potential risks against expected benefits may vary between different countries. When application of biotechnology for food production is involved, industrialized countries can more easily afford to place higher priority on health and environmental quality, whereas developing countries have to be more concerned with the production and distribution of food. Thus, developing countries may be more inclined to accept certain ecological risks associated with biotechnology, if the application of this technology results in enhanced food supplies.

More often the dichotomy is not between 'North' and 'South', but between different groups of actors within industrialized and developing countries: between entrepreneurs and consumers, and between biotechnologists and ecologists. As entrepreneurship is inherently a risk-taking activity, entrepreneurs may be more inclined to accept certain risks than the consumers. Consumers can 'wait and see'; if their risk perception of certain product is too high, they can decide not to buy that product. Biotechnologists focus on the genes of an individual plant, and stress that genetic engineering has opened a large range of options for improvement of plant production. Ecologists can focus on the effect of transgenics on the ecosystem.

PART IV

BIODIVERSITY PROSPECTING

1

The Problems

"Biodiversity prospecting" is being tooted as a new and viable framework to merge conservation of biological diversity with sustainable development. Third World countries may not generate economic benefit from their ecological treasures unless they learn how to market the goods. However marketing national biological resources—once considered a global heritage of mankind —also means marketing indigenous peoples' knowledge about them. There are some fundamental problems underlying this new push to commodify and commercialize the planet's biological and ethnobotanical treasure chest.

The past few years have witnessed an incredible upsurge in talk about "biodiversity prospecting" and intellectual property rights (IPR). For indigenous people, governments, pharmaceutical companies, non governmental organizations, conservationists, lawyers, ethnobotanists, and indigenous rights activists— it seems that everyone today who is interested in genetic resources conservation and development is buzzing with talk of making money from the rainforest and ensuring the local people with a share in the benefits. The bioresources—micro-organisms, insects, plants and animals—of the "gene-rich" South are of tremendous value to the food and pharmaceutical industries of the "gene-poor" North. Already lots of money has been made over the backs of the local people that maintain these resources. What is new is the emerging, belief that together, the custodians of biological diversity in the Third World and those who want to make money out of it in the North can do it in collusion now, through "equitable and just" partnerships. While the thinking behind this drive to strike fair deals in the historically inequitable "gene drain" of the South may be well-motivated, many proponents of the new bioprospecting mode of conservation and product development seem to be skirmishing over some of the fundamental issues.

WHAT IS DONE BEHIND BIOPROSPECTING?

Bioprospecting entails the search for economically valuable genetic and biochemical resources from nature traits such as pest resistance and improved crop yields found in the genes of wild species that could be introduced into other species, through breeding programmes or genetic engineering. Certain chemical compounds discovered by the systematic exploration of plants, animals and microorganisms, act on other biological systems such as human cells, and can be developed into products drawn straight from nature or man-made after nature's inspiration. Some examples are medicines, insecticides, enzymes for the food industry, and microorganisms to process industrial wastes. These and many other applications are the fruits of bioprospecting, but the term is most commonly associated with the hunt for novel molecules of medical potential.

In a sense, "biodiversity prospecting" dates back to colonial times. One modern definition describes it as *"the exploration of biodiversity for commercially valuable genetic and biochemical resources"* which is exactly what the colonial powers started doing in their search for spices, dyes, flavourings and other plant products many centuries ago. They found pepper, rubber, coffee, indigo, coco, sugarcane, oil palm and hundreds of other plants that lay the foundation of a world order built around the extraction of those biological resources from the South to serve the accumulation of wealth in the North.

Over the centuries, the methods of "bio-extraction" might have changed but the principles are still the same. With a better understanding of the plant breeding, some scientists started looking for genetic combinations of local plant materials in the South to cross them into the crops that had become the basis of the North. Other scientists started scavenging forests and coral reefs of the tropics searching for chemically useful plants and animals, and the medicinal knowledge of indigenous people, only to study them in their laboratories and turn them into commercially marketable drugs. In the end, all of this has resulted in a food system in the industrialized countries that heavily relies on genetic infusions from the South, and a health system that is to a large extent extracted from the intellectual and biological resources of the local people in developing countries. While there is still some bickering over the exact dollar value, the importance of genetic resources from the South to today's world economy goes undisputed. As the North American sociologist Jack Kloppenburg puts it simply, "Indigenous people have in effect been engaged in a massive programme of foreign aid to the urban populations of the industrialized North."

"Biodiversity prospecting" could be seen as just a new name for this old extractive process. However it carries a twist this time. Without doubt, the future of world food production and health care will for the foreseeable future, continue to depend on the availability of biological diversity in the South, since that is where most of the planet's ecological wealth is to be found. Scientists cannot invent DNA - the genetic blue print of life. They can synthesise or copy it, but they need a recipe first. The problem is that those recipes (the diversity of plants and animals) and the master chefs behind them (indigenous and local people) are disappearing under the guise of "development". International recognition that the loss of biological and cultural diversity is one of the most serious threats to our future has galvanised people to rethink the link between conservation and development. "Prospecting", as an enlightened version of "extracting", is being forwarded as a way to make consumer product development work and pay for conservation.

In a wide sense, biodiversity prospecting entails or supposes four types of activities :(1) **protection** of biodiversity (2) **collection** and **taxonomic identification** of biotic samples, (3) pharmaceutical **research and development** and (4) **sustainable** development. The first activity is mostly carried out by local communities and natural parks personnel in the South—sample hunting and classification is normally the remit of locally-based collectors, whether their sponsors are national or foreign, while taxonomists are often specialists from the North. Collection strategies are either random (samples of anything around), targeted to certain species, or solely directed to local peoples' pharmacopoeia (medicinal knowledge systems). As for pharmaceutical R and D, the third activity, it is almost exclusively carried out in the industrialized countries. Over the past 30 years, over 90% of all the new pharmaceuticals on the health market were developed in the OECD countries.

DOING IT BETTER?

What is new in the flurry of interest and enthusiasm about bioprospecting is that it is being forwarded as a pragmatic tool to get some of the profits made on biodiversity by the industries in the North back to the countries in the South. There are basically three ways in which biodiversity prospecting is supposed to radically differ from the old mode of plundering and extraction : the corporations who want access to the South's biodiversity will now assign a monetary value and pay for it; the money will be used for conservation, not profit; and compensation will now be provided to local communities. The main mechanisms proposed to achieve all of this are formal contracts between the countries having the biological resources within their boundaries on the one hand and the companies interested in screening and exploiting them on the other. Such contracts would typically include upfront payments for collecting and taxonomic identification of samples and arrangements to share the benefits via a percentage of the royalties on new successful ones. Thus, finding a new way to put some of the money companies make from drugs and crop seeds back into the preservation of the original tropical treasure chest is the impetus behind the new bioprospecting drive. The shift is from uncontrolled collecting that only benefits the powerful, to a bilaterally negotiated approach, so that the resource base is preserved. At least, that is the picture presented by the prospecting proponents.

THE PROSPECTS

Bioprospecting holds out the possibility of new medicines, income for developing countries and an incentive to conserve biodiversity, but it is surrounded by controversy. At one extreme, bioprospecting is regarded as a form of 'biopiracy' the perpetuation of the colonial habit of plundering others' resources without fair and equitable compensation, resulting in environmental, economic and social detriment. At the other, it is seen as the means to a new 'green petroleum', capable of bringing wealth to the gene-rich, but financially poor countries of the South. In reality, bioprospecting is likely to be neither a catastrophe nor panacea. With careful management, the major risks can be avoided, and many useful results achieved.

The UN CBD places the authority and responsibility for taking appropriate measures aimed at securing fair and equitable bioprospecting activities onto governments, particularly of countries providing genetic resources, and the parties negotiating individual agreements. At the same time, it acknowledges the role of many other 'stakeholders—non-governmental organizations, academic and research institutes, indigenous peoples, local communities, business and donors—and encourages their participation in the conservation and sustainable use of biodiversity. In the past bioprospecting has been associated with serendipity. Today, while luck will inevitably continue to play some part in the discovery of new medicines, the contribution that bioprospecting will make to environmental protection and sustainable social and economic development will depend largely on the awareness and actions of these stakeholders.

Roughly 150 drugs derived from higher plants are currently on the market, and these are obtained from less than 100 species, while some quarter of a million species of higher plants are thought to exist. There is understandable optimism that new, useful medicines may be developed from chemicals yet to be found in animals, microorganisms and the vast majority of plant species that have not been examined, some two thirds of which are tropical species. This optimism is tempered by the knowledge that an unknown but alarming number of species are becoming extinct, and by the expectations of bioprospecting.

It is unrealistic to view bioprospecting as a major incentive for the conservation of biodiversity, or a guaranteed means of generating nationally significant levels of revenue. Research and development for naturally derived medicines is a risky, costly and time-consuming business. The total global budget available for sourcing natural products for pharmaceuticals, is estimated as a modest US $ 125 million per annum, and the chances of generating significant revenue from royalty agreements governing the use of biological resources supplied in this way are slim. Perhaps 1 in 10,000 samples is likely to result in a marketable drug producing sales on which royalties between 0.5% and 20% will be generated. Furthermore, it generally takes some ten years and an investment of US $500 million to bring a drug to the market.

Alternative methods of drug development poses a challenge to the future of bioprospecting, as does the political uncertainty surrounding access to genetic resources and the fact that great genetic diversity is already freely available to prospectors in *ex situ* collections around the world without the need for benefit sharing as required for access subject to the Convention. Many developing countries currently have limited capacities to supply raw materials or value-added products that meet the standards of quality control and the strict regulatory requirements for prescription and non-prescription medicines, and even for the food supplements relevant to herbal remedies.

However, bioprospecting can make a valuable contribution to sustainable development. Biological resources remain an important source of novel compounds for drug design, and of genes and cells for other approaches such as recombinant DNA technology and tissue culture. It is reasonable to assume that they will continue to be of value in the future. Bioprospecting is best seen as an opportunity to improve national capacities to add value to natural resources, and to build the skills, infrastructure and technology to develop business activities in sectors such as biotechnology and information technology, both of which can be environmentally benign and play an increasingly important part in the global economy. Bioprospecting can improve the health of the local communities and contribute to the development of new products for the global markets.

Since the fate of biodiversity depends upon its treatment at the local level, it is vital to motivate all elements of society to become involved in its conservation and sustainable use. Non-governmental organizations can play a multitude of roles in this respect, amongst which are contributing to bioprospecting agreements, managing resources and information, participating in negotiations and the development of policy, conducting scientific research, and helping to educate and build the capacity of other stakeholders. Companies can adopt, and make public, best practice policies for collecting and acquiring genetic resources and sharing benefits with suppliers, and can integrate the principles encapsulated in these policies into material transfer and bioprospecting agreement. They can endeavour to help suppliers add value to their resources and to meet national needs, and to ensure that the mechanisms are in place to secure the return of appropriate benefits to the relevant stakeholders.

THE SOLUTION?

During the last twenty years, acceptance has grown that environmental protection and social and economic development must, and indeed, can only, proceed hand in hand. At the UNCED 110 Heads of States and Governments adopted the Rio Declaration and Agenda 21, both of which accept the need for the integration of environmental and economic decision-making. The Convention with its triple objectives of the conservation and sustainable use of biodiversity, and the fair and equitable sharing of the results, reflects the belief that, under certain conditions, the non-destructive use of biodiversity can not only provide goods and services useful to mankind, but also an economic incentive to protect them.

The Convention emphasizes that States have the sovereign right to exploit their own genetic resources, and that access to them can only take place with the prior informed consent of the country providing the resources, based on terms agreed mutually between the provider and the prospective user. In a parallel development, control over intellectual property is also increasing. The Agreement on Trade and Related Aspects of Intellectual Property Rights including Trade in Counterfeit Goods (TRIPS), signed as an annexe to the Uruguay GATT Agreement on 15 April 1994, obliges signatories to extend patent or alternative intellectual property protection to certain categories. These developments in international agreements are matched by the growing number of countries introducing legislation to control access to genetic resources and review intellectual property regimes.

No country is self-sufficient in genetic resources. Since prehistoric times, mankind has exchanged genetic resources and moved them across continents. Today, countries are interdependent for the plant genetic resources that support their food production. Although similar information has not been compiled for the exchange of medicinal plants, it has been estimated that a vast majority of prescription drugs derived from higher plants are based on plant species which hail from developing countries. International exchange is vital for developments in agriculture, medicine and many other areas. It is thus essential, now that the flow of genetic resources will rely upon bilateral negotiation, that such negotiations are facilitated, and that parties can reach mutually beneficial arrangements.

2

The Mechanisms and the Economics

The Mechanism of Bioprospecting

NATURAL PRODUCTS AND DRUG DEVELOPMENT

Recent developments in screening biological samples for medicinal effects, new analytical methods and technologies for chemical separation, the elucidation of the structure of molecules and chemical synthesis, have combined to make the hunt for drugs derived from plants and micro-organisms more economically attractive. Highly sophisticated computer-aided screening techniques can automate the process of conducting a range of biochemical screening tests on a large number of samples. These throughput screens enable companies to test hundreds of thousands of samples a year, compared with only a few hundreds a few years ago. Thus the modern technology has succeeded in altering the economics of drug development and heightening the interest in screening natural products for the novel 'lead compounds' that are the building blocks of new medicines.

Natural products (NPs) are used in a number of different ways in the development of new medicines. **Occasionally** pharmaceuticals, and herbal remedies, use NPs directly. Some examples are morphine, extracted from the opium poppy and evening primrose oil. **Secondly**, a NP may be used as the building block for the production of semisynthetic drugs. The NP is used as a raw material, and its chemistry altered in the laboratory to manufacture the final product. For example, the saponin extracted from neotropical yams of the genus *Dioscerea* is chemically altered to produce the sapogenins that are the basis for the manufacture of steroids. **Thirdly**, the NP provides the template or blueprint serving as the models for a new synthetic compound. Typically, the NP is screened for biological activity, the active 'lead' compound isolated from the mixture, its structure elucidated and the active site of the compounds identified. Chemists then synthesize an analogue, or molecule with a similar structure exhibiting the same, or improved activity. Examples in this category include cocaine from the coca plant. Chemical elucidation of its structure has led to the synthesis of a number of local anaesthetics with similar structures, such as procaine. A **fourth** approach is to study the way a natural product interacts with the body, and using nature as the inspiration, to design a drug to emulate the mode of action. An example is capoten, a purely synthetic drug whose mode of action was inspired by work on a snake venom.

THE ALTERNATIVES

(1) SYNTHETIC CHEMISTRY

The same scientific and technological advances that have made NP drug development attractive have increased our knowledge of how medicines interact with human cells, and the ability to synthesise drugs from chemicals, mimicking nature, but without recourse to natural biological materials. Certain companies view recent techniques in synthetic chemistry as attractive alternatives to seeking lead compounds by screening biological samples. For example, computational chemistry studies the functional parts of molecules needed to stimulate the receptor sites in human cells. Libraries of chemicals—whether compounds from nature, or chemicals created in the laboratory by combining smaller molecules— can then be searched for molecules with characteristics likely to interact with the receptors. Some view technological development in synthetic chemistry and rational drug design as a threat to the future market for genetic resources, while others see the different approaches as complementary. Certainly, drug design based purely on chemistry remains less expensive. The cost per sample of these sources is significantly lower than for natural products and screening NPs is not the most cost effective way to find new leads.

(2) GENETIC ENGINEERING

Recombinant DNA technology, where genes coding for useful traits are identified and introduced into other species (transgenic species) offers the possibility of correcting genetic defects at source, or introducing new, desirable genetic characteristics that will stay with the subject and may be passed on to its successors. Genetic engineering, and its medical application in gene therapy represents an alternative approach to screening biological materials for their chemical activity and producing drugs to treat the symptoms of the disease.

Contemporary figures are not readily available for the proportion, and market value of drugs, derived from NPs, compared with purely synthetic chemistry. In the United States some 25% of prescriptions relate to medicines derived from natural sources, but a detailed review of this assertion is long overdue.

The Economics of Bioprospecting

The role of bioprospecting in sustainable development, its scope and magnitude, depends, at least in part, upon its economic significance. This economic significance of biodiversity itself is unquestionable. Mankind has already appropriated 40% of the product of photosynthesis, and it has been estimated that some 40% of the world market economy is based upon biological products and processes.

Global annual sales of pharmaceuticals were approximately US $ 200 billion (1995). If 25% of prescriptions relate to medicines that derive from natural sources, this would suggest a global market of US $ 50b. The annual over-the-counter market for plant-based medicines in Europe is some US $ 2b (1991). The 1985 market value for both prescription and over-the counter drugs based on plants was thought to be US $ 43b. Typical royalties are between 1-5% of net sales. A rough approximation from these figures suggests that global revenue from bioprospecting is of the order of US $ 1 b annually. Global revenues from intellectual property rights will be many hundred million dollars annually. Such royalties would be shared between the country providing the resources and the collector. To the revenues from royalties may be added the US $ 125 million estimated to be available annually for sourcing supplies. This sum would be shared between all providers of genetic resources.

MORE THAN PRESERVATION

It has become obvious that preserving biodiversity is not enough. It needs to be known and used sustainably so that it will remain for future generations. Biodiversity prospecting offers tropical countries one tangible response to the question of how a society can come to value its biodiversity enough to conserve it into perpetuity.

OPPORTUNITIES

- New medicines for the global market and inexpensive appropriate medicines for local communities.
- Incentive to conserve biodiversity, motivation for those conserving and using biodiversity sustainably by rewarding physical and intellectual contributions.
- Additional source of income for developing countries and an important lever for capacity-building and technology transfer.
- One route to the development of sustainable, value-added industries for developing countries.
- Promotes technological innovation
- Offers a mechanism to ensure fair and equitable sharing of the results of using biodiversity.

THREATS

- Undervalues and takes advantage of indigenous medicinal expertise, uses national resources of remedies available only elsewhere.
- Incentive to destroy or interfere with biodiversity, and commoditize nature; disenfranchises those not involved in bioprospecting agreements, appropriating their knowledge to others.
- Distracts from and reduces funding available for, more effective methods of securing conservation and other objectives.

- Allows for the exploitation of developing countries by Northern industry, which monopolizes the adding of value.
- Discriminates against some classes of innovations, and removes useful innovations from the public domain
- Politicizes access to genetic resources, impeding access for purely scientific, non-commercial ends.

PEOPLE, PLANTS AND HEALTH CARE

Some 7000 natural compounds are currently used in modern medicine. Most of these had been used for centuries by European, Asiatic and Amerindian healers. For example, in the former Soviet Union nearly 2500 plant species have been used for medicinal purposes. In Southeast Asia, traditional healers utilise some 6500 plants. Worldwide, more than 3000 plant species are used by indigenous people to control fertility alone—with debatable results.

- In the vegetable kingdom, fewer than 2% of higher plants have been thoroughly screened for biological activities. Of the 120 active compounds currently isolated from higher plants and used in medicine, 74% show a positive correlation between their "modern" therapeutic use and the traditional, original use of the plant.
- In other words, as in crop breeding, rural folk working with local resources provide Western scientists not with "raw material" but highly sophisticated technologies as well.
- For example, alkaloids extracts from the roots *Rauvolfia serpentina* are used as treatment notably for hypertension. Although used for centuries in India for many human ailments, it was only in the 1940s that the species came to the attention of Western scientists.
- By 1967 the root alkaloids accounted for almost 90% of the US market for antihyperactive drugs.
- In 1985 the world market value of drugs was some US$ 90b of which a full US$ 43b was provided from medicinal plants. But the North dependency on Third World sources is strong. According to the UNCTAD/GATT International Trade Centre, the total value of imports of medicinal plants of OECD countries increased from US $ 335m in 1976 to US $ 551m in 1980.

THE NATIONAL CANCER INSTITUTE (USA)

One of the largest plant screening efforts led by the US government was carried out by the National Cancer Institute (NCI). Between 1956 and 1976, NCI collected and tested 35000 plant species, from tropical and temperate countries. Of these, 10% showed potential anticancer effects. Seven anticancer compounds resulting from the study in 1997 were in the final stages of drug development. One of these is the now famous "taxol" extracted from the bark of the pacific yew. Taxol is today's most promising drug to treat various forms of cancer. Interestingly, a review of its efforts revealed that the programme's success rate in finding active ingredients would have doubled if medicinal folk knowledge had been the only information used to target species rather than the random screening practices employed. Given today's combining interest in the loss of biodiversity and local knowledge, NCI has recommended a major multi-million dollar programme to collect thousands of plant specimens and folk knowledge from tropical forests over the next five years, to try as a cure for various cancers and a prime weapon to disarm the AIDS-afflicting HIV virus.

3

Human Diversity Prospecting

On 14 March 1995 a US patent was issued to the National Institutes of Health (NIH) on a cell line containing the unmodified DNA of an indigenous man of the *Hagahai* people. The same patent application is pending in 19 other countries. *Hagahai* people number 260 persons living in the remote highlands of Papua New Guinea. They only came into contact with the outside world in 1984. According to the press communique of the Rural Advancement Foundation International (RAFI), Canada/USA, due to the patent, one of the *Hagahai* man ceased to be the owner of his own genes and as a result was the cause of deep concerns worldwide. This patent is another major step down the road to the commodification of life. In the days of colonialism, research went after indigenous people's resources and studied their social organizations and customs. But, now in biocolonial times, they are going after the people themselves says Pat Roy Mooney, executive director of RAFI. Mooney is investigating prospects to challenge the patenting of human genetic material at the International Court of Justice in The Hague (The Netherlands) as well as bringing the issue to the attention of the parties of the CBD and relevant multilateral bodies.

RAFI has been closely following the patenting of indigenous people since 1993. Pressure from RAFI and the Guyami General Congress led to the withdrawal of a patent application by the US secretary of commerce on a cell line from Guaymi indigenous women from Panama. Recent cases have demonstrated the potential economic value of human DNA from isolated populations in the diagnosis and treatment of diseases, and the development of vaccines. Blood samples from asthmatic inhabitants of the remote South Atlantic island of Tristan da Cuncha were sold by researchers to a California-based company, which in turn sold rights to its technologies for asthma treatment to the German Company Boehringer Ingelheim for US $ 70 million.

THE HUMAN GENOME BARGAINED?

The bomb under the already chaotic patent situation was placed by the US NIH when in 1991 they filed patent applications for almost 3000 fragments of genes without knowing what these fragments really do in our bodies. Together with other agencies, NIH is involved in mapping the human genome with the expectation that this research might provide useful new treatments for genetically determined human diseases. The reasoning of NIH to take the patent route is that they have to protect this material in order to be able to give waterproof monopoly licences to any company who wants to take the research further and develop something useful out of it.

NIH's move caused a wave of protest throughout the international scientific community, and even brought James D. Watson, head of the Human Genome Project to resign in outrage. The ethical question as to whether someone should be allowed to patent parts of the human body is the first one that comes to a normal person's mind. But those already enrolled in the patent game also raised other objections. Most of NIH's patent applications refer to gene fragments, parts of genes whose functions nobody knows much about. It is like saying; "I found something, I don't know what it is, but it might be useful in the future so give me a monopoly on it".

Normally three requirements have to be met to obtain a patent; the invention must be **new, useful** and **non-obvious**. In a provisional decision (1996) the US patent Office found that NIH's applications filled none of these requirements. The DNA fragments are not new, as the description of the fragments were based on existing DNA libraries, they are not necessarily useful as nobody knows what they do, and they are obvious in the sense that several of the genes the NIH had description of certain fragments that were already published elsewhere.

The Human Genome Programme (HGP) and the Human Genome Sequencing Programme (HGSP) highlight a problem. Who owns the cell lines once they have been collected and established? Today, following the success in the mapping of the human genome, tens of thousands of human DNA sequences have already been patented or under patent claim. Who will profit from their use? These serious ethical issues have been brought into focus by a legal claim by the *Guaymi Indians* of Panama who have protested at the action of two scientists from the United States, who filed for a patent on a human T-Lymphotropic Virus Type 2 derived from samples of their blood. The Guaymi have demanded the withdrawal of the application on the grounds that it was made "without consultation with our community, its traditional organizations, or its corresponding administrative authorities" (Letter from Guaymi General Congress to the US Patent and Trademark Office, 5 October 1993). In response to this case and other expressions of concern, the Human Genome Diversity Project (HGDP) has now established an ethics committee and says it has decided that it will not profit financially from the samples it collects, will protect the intellectual property of the sample populations and will "work to guarantee that in the unlikely event of those samples leading to products, financial benefits will flow back to the sampled populations" (Letter from Henry T. Greely, Stanford Law School, to RAFI, 1 November 1993).

4

Prospecting or Bargaining?

There are a number of things to keep in mind before jumping to biodiversity prospecting as the ultimate, equitable solution. Upto now, the main proponents of bioprospecting have been looking at the potential benefits to be derived from screening plants, animals and micro-organisms for pharmaceutical uses— although the value of biodiversity to other sectors is equally vast. The agricultural scene has hardly been looked at in this process, and prospecting contracts with a view to isolate useful genes for agricultural crops might be far more difficult to implement. Who can effectively control which gene was found where, once it is incorporated into a commercially successful host?. Secondly, according to pharmaceutical industry observers, most natural products research today done by major corporations involves the screening of microbial sources, rather than plants or marine sources.

One handful of dirt from a tropical forest can contain millions of micro-organisms that can be readily cultured in a laboratory without any need to return to the source. Who will trace back the origin of a single microbe when the company involved has no interest or need to go back to the original sampling site? But apart from all the practical questions, perhaps the most important point is whether the true custodians of biodiversity in the Third World—the farmers, fisherfolk, pastoralists, healers and indigenous people—will see any of the benefits of the new wave in biodiversity prospecting.

DANGEROUS EDGES

Even if the current enthusiasm on biodiversity prospecting turns to practical reality, there remains a series of very fundamental questions. The **first** one is whether the commodification of biological material and indigenous knowledge is desirable. Biodiversity prospecting tries to assign monetary value to a res-ource that has long been considered a heritage of mankind. At the local level, biodiversity is a cultural and economic heritage of the people who have cared for and lived with it for centuries. The development, management and conser-vation of that diversity by indigenous communities is a process strongly inter-woven with cultural realities, communal practices and specific world views. So the question still remains whether biological resources should be privatised. For many, this is a fundamentally ethical issue. Why should we allow one company to hold a monopoly on a gene that cures AIDS or makes crops withstand droughts, even if he or she pays back part of the royalties? How can a nearby forest or local cassava variety—cared for by many generations, utilized, nurtured and conserved— suddenly be declared someone's exclusive good and traded in the name of (whose?) economic development? Should we reduce all our values to money and simply acquiesce to the single, Western concept of property? In the end it might lead to the further destruction of the societies of those whom we only recently started acknowledging as important caretakers of biological diversity. Inevitably, the destruction of those societies would lead to a further destruction of the biological wealth they maintain.

Second, who will participate in and profit from biodiversity prospecting? Many people are complaining about the topdown model of development, with decisions taken at the top, scientists and experts leading the way, and the vast majority of local populations left alienated in the periphery to receive the benefits if they ever trickle down. Commercializing biological resources through the prospecting mode might hardly alter this skewed situation. In virtually all the cases of biodiversity prospecting upto now, the major stakeholders are the companies, nature park administrators, national scientists, and government officials. There is a considerable risk that the bulk of the funding coming out of the prospecting deals will be used to strengthen traditional "nature park" approaches to conservation. Unfortunately, as numerous cases in the past have shown, this often means the exclusion of local people from the process or worse, their physical removal from the to-be "protected" areas.

This brings us to a **third** critical issue : the question of the role and rights of local and indigenous people in marketing biodiversity and their own knowledge of it. Assuming that they would form an integral part of the prospection business, the question is how can local people exert control over the resources and their own intellectual integrity? Many NGOs and activists are currently searching for mechanisms whereby in any transaction that occurs between local people and extractive researchers (bioprospectors, anthropologists, germplasm collectors) community members can assert some form of control over the exploitation of their resources, be it indigenous knowledge or a particular plant? For some organizations, this control might be achieved through Western style ownership rights as vested in IPR. While ethically it may sound fair, in practical terms IPR is a nightmare to fight for and administer. What good is a patent if you can't pay for it, defend it, litigate and license it? The opportunities available in current bioprospecting deals include money, training, and technology transfer. It is obviously upto the local people to decide what benefits they seek to gain from sharing their resources and integrity with others. And it is evident that the local people can reap this benefit—but only if they have the whole slew of rights and resources to process and enforce their decisions.

Entering into contractual agreements or assigning intellectual property to indigenous groups (so that they can harness the goods deriving from their knowledge and resources) carries the real danger of diverting our attention from the most basic problems local groups are struggling with; the right to self-determination and land tenure security. It would be socially disastrous if the hype about making profits from the rainforest undermined this most fundamental struggle. It is in this sense that bioprospecting and all the processes linked to it, could reinforce the process of extraction that started in the colonial times, rather than support the imperative fight for empowerment of the local people and the conservation of their biological resources.

THE CASES OF PROSPECTING

(1) The Pyrethrins

Pyrethrins, the economically most important of natural insecticides, are currently derived from the pyrethrum plant. Some biotechnology companies study the possibilities of industrial production. Whether they are able to overcome the biological and technical constraints is still unclear. However, if they do so, the production of it by and the livelihoods of hundreds of thousands of pyrethrum farmers in the South will be threatened. Due to an increased resistance of pests to synthetic pesticides, stricter environmental legislation, and mounting R and D costs of chemical insecticides, interest in natural insecticides has been expanding continuously in recent years. The plant world is not only a very important source of natural insecticidal compounds but also provides core structures from which new and more effective insecticidal agents can be synthesized. Today, the most economically important natural plant compounds used as insecticides are the pyrethrins, a group of six, chemically closely related, complex esters.

The principal source of pyrethrins is pyrethrum (*Chrysanthemum cinerariae-folium*). Pyrethrum is a rufted perennial herb of temperate origin, with whiteyellow flower heads. It is cultivated mainly at higher altitudes in tropical countries such as Kenya, Tanzania, Rwanda and Ecuador. Pyrethrins are found in all above—ground parts of the pyrethrum plant, but predominantly in flower heads. The harvesting of flowers is very labour- intensive, which has resulted in a decreasing cultivation in some parts of the world. Japan, for example which used to be a large producer, has abandoned cultivation, while in India only 100 to 200 hectares are presently under cultivation.

Powder and extracts prepared from the dried flower heads have been used as insecticides for many years. The natural pyrethrins have some of the qualities of an ideal pest control agent. They are very effective against a broad range of insects, while little resistance has developed. Their rapid paralysation of insects resulting in low dosage levels, and their low toxicity to mammals and other warm-blooded animals are especially valued. Another application is as a repellent to protect foods. Pyrethrins are non-inflammable and leave no oily residue.

Inspite of their superior environmental qualities, the general instability of the natural pyrethrins has restricted their application as a multi-purpose insecticide. Since pyrethrins are useful only under conditions without extensive exposure to light and air, they are too unstable outdoors to control pests of agricultural crops and forests efficiently. However, by mixing with antioxidants or stabilizers (including the natural plant compounds tannic acid and hydroquinone) and synergists (including the natural plant compounds sesamin and mysristicin), the stability has been improved and pyrethrins have become economically viable insecticides. Today, the natural pyrethrins are used predominantly in domestic insecticide sprays.

The instability of an otherwise very powerful insecticide led to the development of pyrethrin-like synthetic compounds, called *pyrethroids*. In the late 1960s and early 1970s the first synthetic compounds were produced, and several of these compounds were registered. The greater stability means that the time the insecticide is present in the field after spraying is much longer than with the natural pyrethrins. This could cause the build up of insect resistance and increases the potential of toxic and/or carcinogenic effects on mammals, which are seen today as the major drawbacks of synthetic pyrethroids. Pyrethroids are commonly used in crop spraying.

Biotechnological alternatives
The disadvantages of the synthetic pyrethroids, together with the labour intensity of conventional pyrethrum production, the commercial importance, the high demand, and the often unstable supply of pyrethrum has stimulated research in alternative production of the natural pyrethrins. Efforts have been made by several research groups and biotechnological companies to generate pyrethrins by *in vitro* cultures of the plant (callus culture, cell suspension culture, shoot and root cultures) and more recently, bioconversions of pyrethrin precursors.

a) Bioconversion
Recently, bioconversion of readily available precursors by isolated plant enzymes or genetically engineered micro-organisms has emerged as another alternative to the conventional production of pyrethrins. In 1984 a patent was granted to McLaughlin Gormley King Co. for the enzymatic synthesis of pyrethrins. Large-scale industrial production with such a process is questionable, particularly because of possible variations in composition and enzymatic activity of a cell-free homogenate.

b) Genetic Engineering
The synthesis of precursors and/or its bioconversion to pyrethrins, could also be carried out by the use of genetically engineered micro-organism. Based on knowledge of the pyrethrin's biosynthetic pathway, certain steps can be selected as candidates for bioconversion of readily available precursors.

Commercialization and possible impact
For the successful commercialization of a biotechnological process for the production of pyrethrins, the ultimate criterion is that it must be less expensive to make pyrethrins by alternative biotechnological means than to extract it from field-grown plants. Nevertheless, there are economic potentials making research

in the biotechnological production of pyrethrins feasible. The annual world market for the natural pyrethrum insecticide has been as high as US $600 million (1994), while the conventional production of natural pyrethrins is still below global market demand. Therefore, even with a moderate capture of 10% of the world market, biotechnology pyrethrins could reach annual sales of US $ 40 million, far more than the suggested threshold for commercialisation of US $ 10 million per year.

(2) The Pesticide Tree : Neem

The powdery, dark brown neem cake is the residue left after the odorous oil is extracted from the seed of the neem tree (*Azadirachta indica*), native to India. The oil goes mainly into soap, which is sold at a premium for its germicidal effects. The farmer is taught to incorporate 200 kilograms of neem cake into each hectare of soil once a year to control tiny nematodes, which attack roots and thereby starves the crops. India is a leading exporter of cardamom, and the educated and affluent farmers of the cardamom hills, who produce the prized aromatic spice, buy more than 3000 tons of neem cake annually. Vegetable and citrus growers in South and Central India also use neem cake to control soil-borne pests, while poorer farmers and landless tenants mix a handful of neem leaves with wheat, rice and other grains to protect them from storage pests. Although the leaves are bitter, the relatively small quantities crumbled inside the container do not affect the taste of the grains. As a result of these and other medicinal and traditional uses—the twigs make handy toothbrushes—the handsome and hardy tropical trees towers above many mud-walled South Asian village huts, its dark green foliage providing shade and a striking contrast to the brown semiarid landscape.

As word of neem's effectiveness as a potent but poison-free, natural pesticide has spread to other parts of the globe, so has the tree. It is now found in virtually all the tropical countries of Asia, Africa and Latin America and in northern Australia and Hawaii, and it has come under close investigation by scientists, environmentalists and policy makers grappling with the problem of how to increase farm production in an ecologically safe manner.

What is in Neem?

Of 2400 plant species scientists have tested in recent years for their reported pest-control properties, neem has emerged as the most promising. According to the Hand book of Plants with Pest-Control Properties (M. Grainage and S. Ahmeed, John Wiley, New York, 1988):

- Neem chemicals can help control more than 200 pest species, including locusts, borers, mites and termites, nematodes and scales, bugs and beetles. Testing is being carried out to verify its effectiveness against the diamondback moth (*Plutella xylostella*) and the citrus leaf miner.
- Neem's pest-control properties are due to some 15 complex chemicals found in its leaves, seed, bark and roots. These are mainly limonoids belonging to the general class of natural products called triterpenes. The

best-known limonoids found so far are azadirachtin (aza), salannin, meli-antriol and nimbin.

- These compounds do not kill pests outright but repel them, disrupt their growing and reproductive cycles or discourage them from feeding on treated crops. Aza, structurally similar to insect hormones called ecdysones, controls the process of metamorphosis, insects pass from the larval through pupal to adult stages. Acting as an "ecdysone blocker" it prevents the adult insect from emerging from the pupa.
- Neem's active ingredient concentration varies. While aza concentration usually ranges between 2 and 4 mg per gram of kernel, neem from India generally contains more aza and other active ingredients than neem from elsewhere.
- Neem compounds are environmentally safe; neem spray does not affect beneficial insects like dragonflies and spiders or fish, frogs and other aquatic life. Far from harming human health, neem has therapeutic effects. Indians eat neem leaves to purify their blood.

Research could double or quadruple the neem seed yield, and compact neem plantings have sprung up in Belize, Guatemala, Honduras and Haiti in the Caribbean, the biggest plantation to date has nothing to do with crop protection. Some 50000 neem trees were planted over 10 square kilometeres near Mecca in Saudi Arabia 12 years ago to provide shade for Muslim pilgrims during Haj. The plantation has a marked impact on the area's microclimate, microflora, microfauna and soil properties and could serve as a field laboratory for scientists studying neem.

Synthesis of aza and other neem chemicals is eluding scientists and may never be realized commercially because of the complex chemical structures involved, according to Heinz Schmutterer (director of the Institute of Plant Pathology at the University of Giessen in Germany and a leading neem researcher and organizer of several international neem conferences). But two US companies have patented and are now marketing pesticides based on aza refined out of the neem "soap". Toxicity studies show the products to be environmentally safe and the US Environmental Protection Agency approved them initially for non-food crops and now for food crops as well. Sales are growing, but farmers complain that they are about twice as expensive as comparable synthetic pesticides.

Scientists are not entirely happy about these neem-based products either, participants in an international neem conference (East West Center, Honolulu, 1991) warned that because of the commercial neem soap, pests may develop resistance to it as they have to some synthetic pesticides. Worse, this could also trigger resistance to aza in the natural neem soap—significantly reducing neem's natural pest control effectiveness. The situation is more encouraging in India where the government recently relaxed registration requirements for pesticides based on natural neem extracts, about a dozen Indian companies are producing their own patented products, guaranteeing a certain percentage of enriched aza without excluding neem's other active chemicals.

Looking Ahead

Neem is an example of science learning from culture, and a model for a new generation of safe pesticides, meeting the requirements of sustainable agriculture and the interests of farming, forestry and industry. It can find a niche as a backyard pesticide tree or exploited at a profit by small, medium, and even large-scale industries. The FAO might consider recommending it as part of Integrated Pest Management (IPM). More research is needed not only on neem itself, but also on such issues as registration requirements for natural plant extracts, patenting and property rights and incentives to farmers and industries to use neem. However the US National Research Council has already given neem its vote of confidence by publishing a book entitled Neem : A tree for solving global problems (National Academy Press, Washington, D.C.1992).

(3) Vaccine-producing Plants

To show how simple it can be to produce vaccines in plants, researchers at Biosource Technologies and the Naval Medical Research Institute (USA) recently produced an experimental malaria vaccine by infecting tobacco plants with a genetically engineered strain of the *Tobacco mosaic virus* (TMV). The studies showed that segments of protein on the surface of the parasite stimulate a strong immune response in humans against malaria. Synthetic genes were developed that manufacture the segments of the protein, which in turn were inserted in the nucleic acid of the TMV.

The tobacco plants infected with the altered virus produce large quantities of the surface protein, which is extracted by simply grinding up the leaves. The advantages of producing a vaccine this way (instead of using the conventional method) are; (1) it is easier to store (2) it is even safer (since the TMV cannot infect humans), (3) it is cheaper since one plant may be able to produce more of the vaccine than a 300-litre fermentor. Biosource Technologies is also looking at possibilities of using edible plants to make vaccines against cholera. Researchers at other institutes are currently working on plants producing potential vaccines against hepatitis B and foot and mouth diseases. So far, these vaccines are all in the experimental and/or testing stages.

5

Intellectual Property Rights (IPR)

Intellectual property is comprised of **industrial property** (inventions, trademarks and industrial designs) and **copyrights** (primarily literary, musical, artistic, photographic and audiovisual works). Inventions may be protected by patents, inventor's certificates, utility models and industrial designs. The protection of utility models generally covers inventions in the mechanical field. Industrial-design coverage protects new ornamental or aesthetic aspects of an useful article, such as the shape, pattern or colour.

A **patent** confers the right to protection on an inventor or employer of an inventor. The holder of the patent has the exclusive right to use the invention for a term, usually 15 to 20 years. Inventor's certificates are issued instead of patents by some governments. The inventor is remunerated and the government owns the invention.

Some states require compulsory licensing of patented inventions. Patents can be part of joint ventures and technology licensing agreements which give the suppliers of process technology considerable control over the operation of the new production facilities. Patents can also be part of collaboration agreements. Patents are a compromise between the public interest and the inventor. The inventor or discoverer discloses the invention in return for an exclusive monopoly over its commercial use for a specified period of time. In general, food, health and energy developments cannot be patented, nor can processes vital to national security. Laws vary widely regarding compulsory licensing and the length of time for patents, making them flexible development tools. Many countries have withheld patenting in certain sectors to enable domestic industries to grow. For example, patenting of pharmaceuticals was permitted in France (1958), Switzerland (1972) and Japan (1976). The European Patent Convention continues to prohibit the patenting of plant and animal varieties. When Japan allowed pharmaceutical patents, it ranked second in world production of drugs and controlled 80% of its home market. In India, patentability of inventions relating to substances intended for use as food, drugs or medicines is limited to claims for the methods or processes of manufacture only (process patent); patents containing claims for the products themselves are not permitted in such cases (Indian Patents Act, 1970).

Trademarks are signs used in connection with the marketing of goods, and may consist of one or more distinctive words, symbols or devices to identify the product and distinguish it from another in the same commercial field. In most countries trademarks must be registered. The term of registration is normally five to ten years, and renewable. Service marks are trademarks for services. Association marks are for members of a group (labour-union labels) or for a certification of origin or characteristic (Roquefort). Trade names are commercial signs used to identify businesses, vocations or occupations. Finally, appellations of origin denote geographical origin and product characteristics. Copyright protects literary and artistic works, including words, music, pictures, three-dimensional objects, and combinations of them. Authors or their employers are protected for the life of the author plus a specified number of years after their death. Copyrighted words may be used only with the owner's authorization or for some personal and educational purposes ("fair use" doctrine). Intellectual property protection is extended by each country and normally is valid only within the boundaries of the granting state. However, international protection may be obtained from the World Trade Organization(WTO). The World Intellectual Property Organization (WIPO) is responsible for promoting the protection of intellectual property throughout the world.

Today, most intellectual property protection are afforded to companies, not to the individual creator or discoverer. It is common practice for enterprises, including universities, to require employees to sign waivers of rights to any discovery or new idea developed during the course of employment. Intellectual property laws also monopolize technological advances in western societies, despite the fact that the new materials and knowledge are often derived from developing countries.

In the GATT negotiations, industrialized countries sought trade-related intellectual property rights (TRIPS) in order to extend patents to all products and processes which are new, useful, and non-obvious. This will enable companies, that use biotechnology to patent genetically altered seeds, organisms and products. At the same time, naturally occurring organisms, or those previously developed, will be classified as "common heritage". The result will provide primary protection to industrialized countries processing traditional knowledge without any benefits to those traditional communities. Uniform patent standards may not be appropriate in all circumstances. Clearly there is an intellectual contribution made by local communities to new natural-products development, and their invitation to synthetic chemistry.

The GATT, IPR and TRIPS

GATT was set up in the 1960s to play the role of "police officer" in international trade, at a time when the UN Conference on Trade and Development (UNCTAD) looked too "biased" towards the interests of the South. As a non-UN institution where governments negotiate behind a black curtain, GATT has largely been viewed as a major power tool of the North, to serve the interests of the industrialized countries. The GATT agreements have done far more to strengthen the market opportunities of the rich than to inject equity into world trade. This is no rhetoric—a real problem; the North gained tremendous benefits to the detriment of the South.

IPRs AS A "TRADE" ISSUE

In the 1970s, many Third World countries began to exert pressure through the traditional international fora dealing with IPRs such as the WIPO and UNCTAD, to try to find ways of amending IPR laws to service their development needs. A range of important studies and proposals were produced, advocating in a way that protects national security interests and stimulates local innovation. For many countries this means excluding certain economic activities from patent laws (e.g. food and health), keeping patent terms reasonably low and providing mechanisms of compulsory licensing. However, for the industrialized North, what was really needed were stronger IPR regulations to protect the new emerging technologies (computer, biotechnology, electronics) from an ever-growing body of emerging competitors. So they moved the issue from the UN where each country has a vote, to GATT, which the North effectively dominates.

In 1986, when the Uruguay Round of trade "liberalization" talks began, the United States and other industrialized countries added intellectual property rights onto the agenda. IPRs have little to do with liberalisation and free markets; in fact they are a government intervention on the market to provide exclusive monopoly rights to those individuals who can prove that they invented something new and useful. The point, for the US and other Western powers, was to assure that their companies reap profits from the South where IPR laws are generally not so advantageous to corporations dealing in the food, agro-input and pharmaceutical sectors.

At the outset of the negotiations, the US International Trade Commission declared that American corporations alone could earn upto an additional US $ 61 billion a year from the Third World, if the South's IPR regimes were harmonized with those of the North. Suddenly, intellectual property laws were no longer to be seen as national tools for economic and social development, adjusted to each country's needs, but grounds for international "piracy" and "theft". Through GATT, the industrialized countries demanded uniform IPR provisions across the globe so that the South has to pay more royalties to the North. Added to the burden of servicing the accumulated external debt and the ever-falling prices paid for commodity exports, this would entail a huge increase on South-North resources transfer. Through TRIPS, the industrialized countries are betting on their technological edge to offset their lowered productivity. The failure in 1999 of the Seattle 3rd Ministerial of WTO is a case in point.

International trade agreements have become the ideal meeting place to execute policy changes that could have enormous effects on peoples' health and safety, cultural survival, economic future, genetic resources and the environment, without being subject to national public scrutiny or lobbying. The

American people, according to polls, opposed the North American Free Trade Association (NAFTA) two to one. Most governments and legislatures in the Third World lack the expertise and intergovernmental coordination necessary to deal coherently and successfully with the complex issues involved in IPR and TRIPS; nor do they usually have the political or economic clout to face upto the enormous pressures put on by the transnational corporations (TNCs) which increasingly control the world's trade.

In many cases governments in the Third World have not had to wait for GATT in order to feel the pressure to change their national IPR legislations to the demands of developed countries. In what has been described as a macro-economic shift from the development policy of import substitution to the "new economic order", emphasis has been placed on export required by the powerful western labour unions. Developing countries are forced to accept stronger IPRs if they want access to modern technology and foreign investment. Mostly under US pressure, with the European Union (EU) lending a willing hand, over forty countries, including China, Brazil, South Korea, Mexico, India, and Thailand have felt the burden. The Indians are waging a legal war in US courts to vacate the patents granted on Basmati, turmeric, neem ... and now on garlic, bitter-gourd, brinjal... all their native plants.

WHAT TRIPS MEANS FOR THE SOUTH?

The GATT agreement is a take-it-or-leave-it package. No country can choose the parts it likes and abstain from the others. Within the package, the TRIPS agreement imposes a number of new rules on developing countries. First of all, TRIPS ensures that patent protection is available for all fields of technology. This includes agriculture, energy and health care, often excluded from monopoly rights in Third World countries. Second, according to the TRIPS agreement, countries can indeed exclude certain inventions from patentability if the exploitation of the invention would be contrary to morality of the public. This provision exists in the North, but the patent offices there do not like to pass judgment on what is "moral". For example, the Harvard Mouse—(Oncomouse) has been declared patentable in Europe because it is "more moral" to carry out cancer research on the mouse than to deprive science of this research tool because some people think it is "immoral" to patent animals. The TRIPS agreement stipulates further that no country can exclude an invention from patentability simply because domestic law prohibits it. In other words, the field for exclusions is reduced to its barest minimum and it will be next to impossible for countries to adjust to their own ethics or economic needs.

Patenting life is at the heart of the agreement. TRIPS makes special provision which allows countries to exclude the patenting of plants and animals other than micro-organisms, as well as "essentially biological" processes to produce plants and animals (Techniques of biotechnology are generally considered "microbiological" and hence will be patentable). But in the case of plants, all signatories have to provide some form of intellectual property right. It may be through patents, in those countries that agree to it, or it may be through an "effective" *sui generis* system. Either way, the bulk of our food and health supply is now up for monopoly control by the corporate sector. And this is bad news, especially for biodiversity and the poor. Patenting our crops and medicinal plants is only bound to step up genetic erosion-especially if seed markets in the South become more lucrative to the North and raise the costs of food production and health care.

What is envisioned by *sui generis* systems?. The negotiators are mainly referring to Plant Breeders' Rights (PBR), a soft type of patent for crop varieties generally available in the industrialized countries. PBR provides a monopoly to the breeder, but leaves it to national discretion whether farmers can save and sow PBR-protected seeds. There are few other *sui generis* systems around. In fact the door is open for some one to quickly come up with some innovative forms of intellectual property protection on plants, especially if developing countries want to serve the interests of small-scale farmers who will be faced with new royalty payments and restrictions.

IPR FOR INDIGENOUS KNOWLEDGE

Local communities and indigenous groups have begun to claim intellectual property protection for traditional knowledge. Article 40 of the Charter of the Indigenous Tribal Peoples of the Tropical Forests (1992) states that programmes related to biodiversity must respect the collective right of such peoples to cultural and intellectual property, genetic resources, gene banks, biotechnology, and knowledge of biodiversity. This includes participation in the management of any project on indigenous territories and control of benefits that derive from them. Article 44 demands guaranteed rights to intellectual property, and control over the development and manipulation of traditional technologies.

Such claims have had little success because intellectual property laws cannot easily be applied to protect the communal and inter-generational knowledge and technologies of local communities. Intellectual property laws are based on western concepts of property and intellectual activities. They are designed to protect readily identifiable, differentiated contributions to existing, general knowledge. A principal feature of patentability is that the product or process should be new and described in a way which makes it capable of reproduction.

In contrast, traditional knowledge is generally collective, incrementally acquired over decades and centuries. Such attributes usually preclude the protection of intellectual property laws. Yet, the discoveries of modern research laboratories are protected, although they often involve the work of large teams of people, each of whom contributes to the achievements of the laboratory. If intellectual property laws could not be extended to traditional, collective knowledge, the utility and benefits of the entire system of intellectual property could be questioned. Failure to allow intellectual property rights for traditional knowledge of local communities can be said to confuse the collective knowledge of a small group with the public domain. The knowledge is valuable to western researchers and is not readily available outside the local communities. It could be protected as intellectual property and its indigenous originators compensated for sharing it with others.

Traditional knowledge about plants is the most desired. The three primary means of protecting intellectual property relating to plants and plant extracts are patents (utility and plant patents), plant variety protection certificates and copyrights. There are problems with applying any of these mechanisms to traditional knowledge or medicines. However, trade secrets laws and contractual mechanisms may provide protection or compensation to the originating state or group. The 1989 FAO decisions on the concept of Farmers' Rights recognized the contribution of traditional farms to the breeding and selection process of genetic material. Intellectual property rights could be a means of implementing the benefit-sharing provisions of human rights and environmental agreements. It could also assist in the internalization of environmental costs and the use of economic instruments to further environmental protection. Finally, it could provide an additional incentive for local communities to conserve their knowledge for future generations and to share it with others.

Other problems must be faced in applying intellectual property concepts to indigenous knowledge: Is it new? Is it innovative? What happens when plants traditionally used by indigenous groups are acquired and found to have a different, previously unknown property? Who should benefit; the individual or the group? Which group? Should money be paid or other more culturally appropriate forms of compensation to be made? Could biological conservation be considered the best form of compensation? Will intellectual property rights serve the twin goals of protecting indigenous cultures and biodiversity? The difficulties raised by these questions suggest that intellectual property law may have only a limited role in protecting the traditional knowledge and resources of local communities.

COMMUNITY INTELLECTUAL PROPERTY RIGHTS—
THE ANSWER

Patenting would worsen the one-way resource flow. US patents have recently been granted for a genetically-engineered version of an insecticide from the Indian neem tree, whose properties have been observed and used by generations of Indians. Other examples include patents issued for the shellfish-killing properties of a berry which is used in Ghana to stun fish. The special properties of these plants have been observed and developed for centuries. Useful genes are most often found in the South because the North's climatic history (ice ages) and development of industry and large-scale agriculture have already depleted much of its genetic diversity. Southern countries generally treat these genetic resources and associated knowledge as common property. Biotechnologists though have the power to effect genetic innovations, they require the genetic material before working out the innovative recombinations of the genes. They find it by going to the people who have selected, cultivated and used it over centuries.

6

The Tangled Genes: Invention or Discovery?

Patents on individual genes are an important vehicle to enable the commercial exploitation of genetic engineering. However, the extension of patents to genetic material and living organisms remains controversial. There are some fundamental questions about the definition of genes on which patents are based. The ongoing debate on patenting genes focuses on two complex issues. The **first** issue composes the ethical, social and economic consequences that result from the extension of patent protection to genetic material and living organisms. The **second** issue concerns the definition of the object to be patented. What kind of patents for what genes should be granted? Are the descriptions of the full structure, the function and the potential use of the concerned DNA sequence prerequisites for patent protection? And, can genes be patented as such, or only when they are part of an invention?

The discussion related to the second issue reflects specific problems, which are at least partially due to the ambiguities of the understanding of the gene itself. Genes are not only continuous stretches of DNA which code for a protein, but can be rather complicated structures. In eukaryotes, most coding sequences are interrupted by so-called introns, which are excised prior to translation into gene products. Furthermore, matching strands of the double helical structure of a gene can code for different products. For example, one strand of a particular region in the DNA of a rat codes for a hormone produced in the brain, while the corresponding strand codes for a gene product found in its heart. Genes are therefore often understood as "continuous stretches of one of the two opposing strands of a duplex DNA molecule which may include meaningless stretches" (which are dutifully removed). Other definitions describe the gene as a coding sequence, which may or may not include introns or regulatory sequences. These definitions take into account that genes can occur in the cell in different structures and at different stages of processing. Therefore, there is no common structure, which can unanimously be identified with "the gene".

The situation does not differ much if one tries to identify the function of a gene. Although the biochemical properties of a gene product can be described precisely as soon as it is identified and isolated, its physiological function quite often cannot. For example, the gene for a particular isomerase has been discovered in bacteria, yeasts, insects and mammals. Inspite of their almost identical structural and biochemical properties, the proteins are involved in different process in the various species. In the fruit fly, the specific isomerase is involved in vision, while in mammals it regulates the maturation of immune cells. Therefore, it is not just a gene's sequence which determines its functions in the organism, but also its location in a specific chromosomal, cellular, physiological and evolutionary context, may play a role. These findings are pointing out some of the problems of the current gene concept. Although it must be very clear that no normative conclusions can be drawn from empirical evidence, this evidence is of specific relevance to some aspects of the debate on patenting:

Firstly, any definition of the gene upon which a patent would be based is a convention, which includes or excludes specific findings and interests. **Secondly**, there can be no patent on "genes" as physical entities only, since the function of a gene is not only determined by its sequence but also by its genetic environment. When a coding sequence is transplanted from its original host into a new one, it may still be responsible for the synthesis of a protein with specific biochemical properties, but its function in the new organism may be different or missing. **Thirdly**, since "genes" cannot be defined and hence not patented as such, the question arises in which way they can be part of an invention. When a transgenic organism is manufactured, one particular coding sequence is selected and combined with other genetic elements. None of these elements (coding sequences, vectors, regulatory elements, etc.) are invented by humans, since their structure and function has been evolved over time in the context of a specific molecular and general ecology. The crucial step in constructing a biological system able to express specific traits or to produce a protein in commercially exploitable quantities, however, is to find a specific combination of existing genetic components and host cells.

Therefore, novelty or non-obviousness of an "invention" does not lie in the DNA sequence or biochemical properties of a protein, but in the new order in which these elements are combined. From this perspective, patent protection could only apply to specific combination of genetic elements and host cells used to manufacture a gene product, and not to genes, sequences, physiological processes or organisms involved. Broad patents granted to procedures of genetic intervention are questionable as well, since they do protect the obvious, and not the inventive part of a researcher's work.

PATENTS ON LIFE

An increasing number of scientists and companies are starting to experience some of the negative implications of applying the patent system to life forms. Tremendous costs for law suits and huge time delays in getting products to the markets are just some of the factors that become apparent. The most recent controversy was triggered off by the US NIH patent application for almost 3000 human gene fragments. The situation is reaching to a point where companies are starting to argue that the whole thing might work against innovation. In the meanwhile, the European Parliament—not concerned by all of this—adopted a report that basically endorses the European Commission's proposal to allow for the patenting of life forms in Europe which was later rejected by the European Parliament.

The humans, animals, micro-organisms and plants comprising *life on earth are part of the natural world* into which we were all born. The *conversion* of these life forms, their molecules or parts *into corporate property through patent monopolies is counter to the interests of the peoples of the world.* No individual, institution, or corporation should be able to claim ownership over species or varieties of living organisms. Nor should they be able to hold patents on organs, cells, genes or proteins, whether naturally occurring, genetically altered or otherwise modified. Indigenous peoples, their knowledge and resources are the primary target for the commodification of genetic resources. Responsible intellectuals call upon all individuals and organizations to recognise these peoples' sovereign rights to self-determination and territorial rights, and to support their efforts to protect themselves, their lands and genetic resources from commodification and manipulation. Life patents are not necessary for the conduct of science and technology, and may in fact retard or limit any benefits which could result from new information, treatments or products.

The Neem controversy

The ethics of patenting life and people's knowledge of our life support systems has never been so controversial as in the case of neem. The neem tree is native to India and other Asian countries, where rural communities have used its insecticidal and bactericidal properties since time immemorial. Neem is rightly part of many people's cultures, chewed as a tooth cleaner or ground and sprayed on crops to keep the insects away. The neem seed—and its pesticidal compound azadirachtin—is not patentable in any country because it is a product of nature. The knowledge that neem seeds are useful as pesticides also cannot be patented. The method of scattering ground neem is not a patentable process because it is not new. However, patents have been granted in the US for (i) extracts from pre-treated neem bark shown to be effective against certain cancers; (2) neem seed - extracted azadirachtin—derivative insecticides which have a greater stability than the naturally occurring form of the compound. Public protest has recently risen in India against Grace's monopoly over which is originally an indigenous Indian technology. The cultural and ethical bias inherent to current IPR systems will never validate the intellectual innovation of indigenous people. According to the courts, their knowledge and resources are neither, "new", nor "inventive", nor "unobvious". Yet when one person in the West takes a Third World technology and works around with it, then it becomes an "invention" of benefit to humanity and deserving a state-enforced monopoly. How can such a system be of benefit to the poor?.

PATENTED PEOPLE?

Biotechnology is surging ahead very fast and does not wait for mankind's ethical scrutiny of its consequences. The manipulation and patenting of an increasing number of life forms is growing rapidly, and includes not only plants, animals, bacteria and viruses, but human life as well. Human cell line patenting is already under way, although stealthily. Affiliated with the HGP and supported by the U.S. NIH and other agencies and governments, the HGDP has been established to collect and "immortalize" the DNA of between 10000 and 15000 indigenous individuals from approximately 722 different peoples; the specimens will be used for pharmaceutical as well as historic purposes.

According to a RAFI survey of the American Type Culture Collection, at least a third of the human cell lines stored there are under some form of patent claim. In doing this survey, RAFI learned that the US Secretary of Commerce has filed US and world patent claims on the cell line of an indigenous woman from Panama. The claim was dropped in November 1993, after protests from the World Council of Indigenous Peoples and the Guaymi Congress, which wants the cell line returned. The commercial value of such human material is underscored by a number of recent developments.

- In early 1993, it was found that members of a remote community in Limone, Italy, bore a gene that codes against many cardiovascular ailments. Swedish, Swiss and American firms are reported to be seeking patents on the genetic material collected.
- A unique group of prostitutes in Nairobi, Kenya, who by all accounts should have been infected with the AIDS virus, were found not to be infected, and it is believed they have a natural immunity to the virus.
- A Sudanese community which appears resistant to malaria has been identified.
- In 1993, the US NIH offered to fund private biotech firms to obtain genetic samples from weakened AIDS patients, to test potential vaccines and to derive materials for use in future vaccines.
- The pharmaceutical multinational Sandoz has patented and licensed a tumorous human spleen, with a potential market value of US$1000 million.

7

Why Patents Should not be Extended to Plants and Animals?

The legal theory behind patent law is quite simple. Patents are contracts between the state and the inventor in which the inventor is granted a monopoly for a limited period of time in return for full disclosure of the invention. In principle, both the inventor and the public benefit from this. However evidence suggests that an extension of patent law to higher organisms is not likely to serve the public good for several reasons:

1. There is virtually no evidence that patents actually stimulate invention. Studies suggest that patents are used to block other firms from entry into the market.

2. Patent law was designed with mechanical and chemical inventions in mind. In those areas the distinction between discovery and invention is clear: tractors and corn flakes are clearly inventions. They are nowhere to be found in nature. In contrast, biological "inventions" often lack such an inventive step. They involve only the recombination (in novel ways) of genetic material that already exists.

3. The description provided with biotechnology patents is quite useless to someone who does not have access to the genetic material it describes. As noted above, patent law is supposed to make the knowledge about how to create an invention public. But this is essentially impossible in the area of biotechnology as the ability to create new genes is still a dream.

4. While most plant varieties are replaced after just a few years, the duration of protection of utility patents generally is about 20 years. Utility patents prohibit research using patented materials. Thus, they may slow down invention or alternatively, create enormously complex cross-licensing arrangements, whereby a given plant or animal variety might be covered by dozens of patents.

5. The basic principles of biotechnology and genetic engineering were developed in the public sector. Without huge public investments in molecular biology, the biotechnology industry could never have developed at all. In a certain sense then one can argue that patents for biotechnology inventions require that the public pay twice for the necessary research. Is this fair and just?

6. There is no particular reason to privatize public goods. Public plant bre-eding has succeeded in raising yields. Moreover, public sector breeding at least in principle, is accountable to public concerns. Public breeding has managed to cover the range of agricultural commodities and to develop cultivars appropriate to a wide range of agroecological zones. Private breeding will tend to focus on the few commodity crops and areas in which most profits can be made.

7. The legal requirements of utility patents demand uniformity. Such unifo-rmity is not desired in the field, since it may well increase the susceptibility of plants and animals to pests and diseases. Development of organisms that are more genetically diverse, but have similar characteristics of interest to the user, is actively discouraged.

8. The extension of patent protection to plants and animals neglects the fact that not all the nations of the world have equal ability to make use of the patent system. In point of fact, only a handful of developing nations have the public or private capacity to enter into such competition. To do so demands both a significant public sector research base and significant private capital to develop patentable materials, to file patent applications and to protect those patents against infringement.

If we must extend IPR to living organisms, then we need a legal form designed specifically for them. Such a system might resemble the current plant variety protection system, although it too suffers from an insistence on distinctness, uniformity, and homogeneity, which are qualities that may be of little value out side the legal area. A better system would focus on agronomic characteristics, food quality, and nutritional value and permit the unrestricted use of protected material in research.

COTTON HAS BEEN PATENTED

NGOs have been warning the scientific and political community all along. Opening the doors to the patenting of life forms will result in a dangerous expanding of corporate control over crops, animals, basic breeding techniques and perhaps one day even human beings. Now, in the midst of the wrangling over whether the human or rice genomes can be someone's exclusive property, cotton as a crop has fallen victim to corporate greed. The US biotech company, Agracetus, fully owned by WR Grace, has been granted a patent on all genetically engineered transformations of the cotton plant, a transgenic cotton plant by "any method". This reasoning gives Agracetus the legal and logical right to claim ownership of any and all transgenic cotton. The news has thrown sci-entists and NGOs into a fury. Cotton, which originated in Asia, is an important crop for the Third World, both in terms of export and domestic use as a source of fibre and oil. In total, cotton represents a market of US $ 13.6 billion for Third World farmers. Agracetus' patent constitutes an enormous disincentive against transgenic cotton research to ameliorate production conditions in the South.

Although Agracetus says it is prepared to license out segments of the transgenic cotton market, nobody knows under what conditions. The first transgenic cotton is marketed by Calgene, under license to Agracetus. It is resistant to Rhone-Poulenc's bromoxynil herbicide, which inhibits photosynthesis by the weeds of cotton fields. Armed with Calgene's patented Bromotol gene, the transgenic cottons can be "safely" sprayed with the lethal chemical. Thus, the new cotton will carry at least two patents, which farmers will have to pay royalties on when buying the seed. How this may help foster sustainable agriculture in the Third World is still a mystery.

AUSTRALIA PATENTS ITSELF

On 13 April 1996 Australia changed its national legislation to ensure that the Government holds the intellectual property rights over the island's flora and fauna. The move is intended to prevent any individual, corporation or foreign country from gaining monopoly rights over the genetic treasure of Australia. Currently, a number of foreign companies are investigating the properties of various native Australian plants and animals for their medical uses. To ensure that no one can pirate the national heritage, the Government now holds the ownership rights to all genetic resources of the country. The law allows the state to demand a royalty on the sale of any commercial product derived from local resources to fill the coffers. National sovereignty, yes, but the indigenous people of Australia who nurtured that diversity would probably balk at the proposal that the Government should own it in the name of the nation.

LIFE PATENTING: THE UNITED STATES EXAMPLE

- 1980. The US Supreme Court ruled in the case of Diamond versus Chakrabarty that genetically engineered microorganisms were patentable.
- 1985. The US Patent and Trademark Office ruled that plants (previously) protected under breeder's rights were patentable subject matter under industrial patent laws.
- 1987. The US Patent and Trademark Office ruled that genetically engineered animals were patentable, granting a patent to Harvard University for a transgenic mouse (oncomouse). As of March 1993, 180 transgenic animal patent applications were pending.
- 1992. The US NIH applied for patents on thousands of human gene sequences. The patent applications, denied in 1993, were particularly controversial because the NIH had no idea how the human gene sequences could be used, or what role they played in the human body. NIH claims that it will re-apply.
- 1993. Agracetus an American biotechnology company, claims broad patent protection over all genetically engineered cotton varieties, regardless of how they were produced. The broad-based claim of patent protection over an entire species is unprecedented and likely to be challenged.

- 1999. Defending the patents it granted on Basmati, garlic, turmeric... and a host of native Indian products in courts, the US Patent and Trade Office granted two more American Companies Patents on bittergourd, brinjal and snakegourd for their antidiabetic cure.

PART V

CONSERVATION

1

The Principles and the Rationale

Our generation has inherited a rich biological legacy, but what will we pass on to the next generation: a secure biotic heritage or a genetically impoverished world? Global, national and local action to conserve and utilize biodiversity will influence the future evolution of human life and civilization on Earth. Biodiversity for human development, based on equitable and sustainable use, is the path to sustainable livelihoods today, while ensuring that future generations have the resource they will need to survive and prosper. We are confronting an episode of species extinction greater than anything the world has experienced for the past 65 million years. Unlike other global ecological problems, it is completely irreversible. The earth, our planetary home, is truly finite, economic formulas, developed over the past 200 years cannot make it any larger. Nor can they give us any more of the productive systems and commodities on which we depend. The earth remains the same. We can use it and its systems sustainably, or we will destroy them.

Our species first appeared about 500,000 years ago, at the very last instant, as it were, of the planet's 4.5 billion year history. As our hunter gatherer ancestors began to move over the face of the earth, they also began to exterminate many of the large animals and birds that they killed for food. When agriculture was invented—independently in eastern Asia, the eastern Mediterranean, Mexico and Peru—11,000 years ago, there were perhaps as few as 5 million people throughout the world. However, this population then began to grow quickly and the extensive land clearing and grazing that characterized early agriculture caused rapid extinctions. The number of people grew then steadily to an estimated 130 million 2000 years ago, 500 million by 1650, 2.5 billion by 1950 and 6.0 billion today. Over the last 40 years we have wasted about a fifth of the world's top soil; lost about an eighth of our cultivated lands to desertification, waterlogging and salinization; increased greenhouse gasses in the atmosphere by over a third, setting the world on an inexorable course to warmer climate; destroyed more than 5% of the stratospheric ozone layer; and cut or converted to simplified biological deserts about a third of the forests that existed in 1950.

THE SUPER CONSUMERS

Human beings—just one of an estimated 10 million species on the planet—are currently estimated to be consuming, wasting or diverting 40% of the net photosynthetic production on land (FAO). We are using an estimated third of the planet's available fresh water. And yet our numbers are not likely to stabilize until they have reached two or three times their present level, even with continued worldwide attention to family planning, because there is such a high proportion of young people in developing countries.

Already our impact on forests and other biologically rich communities is so intense around the world that we are losing species between 1,000 and 10,000 times the natural rate that occurred before our ancestors first appeared on Earth. Judged from the fossil record, the average lifespan of a species is about 4 million years, so if there are about 10 million species in the world, the background rate of extinction can be calculated at about four species a year. At a moderate estimate, we are now likely to lose around 50,000 species a year over the next decades. The rate will presumably accelerate as the years go by. Clearly we are in the midst of one of the great extinction spasms of geological history. If we lose two-thirds of all living species over the course of the next century, this will be more or less equivalent to the proportion which disappeared at the end of the Cretaceous period, 65 million years ago. It took more than 5 million years for the world to regain its equilibrium after that.

There are **three classes of reason** for concern. **The first** is ethical and aesthetic. As *Homo sapiens* is the dominant species on Earth, we think that people have an absolute moral responsibility to protect what are our only known living companions in the universe. Human responsibility in this respect is deep, but urgent nonetheless. The **second class** of reason is economic. We use organisms for food, medicines, chemicals, fibre, clothing, structural materials, energy and many other purposes. Only about 100 kinds of plants provide the great majority of the world's food; they are precious and their genetic diversity should be preserved and enhanced. There are also tens of thousands of other plants, especially in the tropics, that have edible parts and might be used more extensively for food, and perhaps brought into cultivation, if we knew them better. But concentration just on the 20 or so best known food plants tends to lead us to neglect the others.

Plants and other organisms are natural biochemical factories. More than 60% of the world's people depend directly on plants for their medicines; the Chinese use more than 5000 of the estimated 30000 species of plants in their country for medicinal purposes. Moreover the great majority of Western medicines owe their existence to research on the natural products that organisms produce. No chemist can "dream up" the complex bioactive molecules produced by nature, but once the natural lead compounds have been discovered then the chemists can proceed with synthetic modifications to improve on the natural lead. For example:

1. **Artemesin** is the only drug effective against all of the strains of the *Plasmodium* organisms that cause malaria, which afflicts 250 million people a year. Had the Chinese not traditionally been using an extract of natural wormwood *Artemisia annua*, to treat it, artemesin may be unknown till date.
2. **Taxol**, the only drug that shows promise against breast cancer and ovarian cancer, was initially found in the western Yew, while randomly screening plants for anti-cancer activities. This molecule is structurally unique and there is no way it could have been visualized if it had not been discovered in nature.
3. A novel compound from the African vine *Ancistrocladus korupensis*, **Michellamine** B, shows a remarkable range of anti-HIV activity. When its method of action is understood, it may well assist in the discovery of other drugs that will be effective against AIDS. Against this background, it is easy to understand why the major pharmaceutical firms are expanding their programmes of exploration for new, naturally occurring molecules with useful properties.

The third class of reason for being concerned about the loss of biodiversity centres on the array of essential services provided by natural ecosystems—including the protection of watersheds, the regulation of local climates and maintenance of soils. Ecosystems are responsible for the earth's ability to capture energy from the sun and transform it into chemical bonds to provide the energy necessary for the life processes of all species, including ourselves. Clearly, much of the quality of ecosystem services will be lost if the present episode of extinction is allowed to run unbridled for much longer. The rebuilding of these systems, in which our descendants will necessarily be engaged, is likely to be seriously impaired by our neglect.

The preservation of biodiversity can only be accomplished as part of an overall strategy to promote global stability. The first prerequisite of a sustainable world is the attainment of a stable human population. Poverty and social justice must be addressed much more effectively throughout the world. More than four-fifths of the world's resources are consumed by a tiny fraction of the global population (less than one-fourth) that lives in the industrialized countries.

Global conservation efforts began in the 1950s in response to the rapid erosion of plant and animal genetic resources. A wide range of genetic resource of interest to food and agriculture have now been safeguarded. The vast majority of current and prospective losses in genetic resources are caused directly or indirectly by the activities of humans. The need to help provide basic human needs is a vital factor in planning conservation in areas where natural resources are threatened or endangered. While local human populations may be the direct cause of forest destruction, in most cases they are only responding to outside pressures and day-to-day needs.

This chapter describes the problems that are caused now and those that will affect future generations as plant genetic resources continue to be lost. Conservation is not an end in itself, but a means of ensuring that plant and animal genetic resources are available for use by present and future generations. **The two basic approaches** to conservation, once the resources are identified and characterized, are *in situ* and *ex situ* methods. *In situ* methods maintain plants and animals in their **original habitats** whereas *ex situ* conservation maintains organisms outside their original habitats in facilities such as **gene banks, cell cultures, botanical gardens** or **zoologoical parks**. The two approaches are not mutually exclusive: different conservation systems can complement each other and ensure against the shortcomings of any one method. With the exception of the small number of varieties and breeds that are widely used, particularly in the developed world, experience shows that diversity is only secure when a variety of conservation strategies are employed.

In areas where biological resources are being depleted to meet the basic needs of local populations, *in situ* conservation must be reconciled with immediate human needs. Successful conservation depends upon meeting the needs of the local people, while ensuring sustainability of the resource. Many approaches are feasible based on scientific expertise and local knowledge and participation so that genetic resources can be used and, at the same time conserved and developed.

Focus is on the need to conserve genetic resources in their natural habitats (*in situ*). *Ex situ* conservation methods are essential for plant breeding and for protecting populations in danger of physical destruction. In other cases, however, *in situ* conservation has a number of advantages; it is especially, adapted to species that cannot be established or regenerated outside their natural habitats. For example, the reproduction of many plant species depends on the presence of a particular insect, bird or animal to pollinate it. *In situ* conservation also allows natural evolution to continue and ensures protection of associated species of no present economic value.

2

Parks vs People

Nowhere is the question of sustainability, and the hard choices it imposes on land-use planners, more acute than where the world's so-called "protected areas" are concerned. The parks, reserves and conservation regions that dot our maps with beleaguered little patches of green symbolize, in microcosm, what is at stake in the larger conflict between the needs and greed of the moment and the welfare of future generations. If the human species cannot learn to strike a balance in the wise use of these sheltered places, whose natural beauty and uniqueness are usually self-evident, then what hope is there for other, less lovely lands? If we cannot be good stewards of the nature's treasures we cannot be expected to properly manage our farms and forest plantations.

Yet more preservation— the "museum syndrome"— is a poor basis on which to build long-term viability. Museums are for artefacts, not living and evolving ecosystems. Human populations are an integral part of virtually every ecosystem on planet earth. Any plan to assure the growth and health of such systems must include the people who live in them, or it is doomed to fail. The following section shows how ordinary people—not just "professionals"— can successfully be brought into the management of protected areas. The conclusions are remarkably similar: if the earth is an ark, we are—all animals, trees and people— in it together. Whether it is logging in western North American parks, mining in Amazonian African protected areas, there is almost always pressure to allow humans to exploit land resources that have been set aside for nature preservation. There is also a tendency, when land is removed from private economic exploitation, to seek to "make it pay" in other ways.

Resentment has festered in many communities when access to an area has been cut off because it was named a park or protected area. People perceive environmentalists and governments as intent on preserving plants and animals, with little consideration for the needs of the nearby humans—even though local communities may have successfully exploited the resources of an area in a balanced way for generations. Such resentment, coupled with a real need, has often meant clandestine use of parklands for poaching, hunting, fishing, ranching and logging. Cases have been documented of deliberate destruction of resources by nearby communities, angry that park supporters seemed to care more for birds and animals than for humans living beside protected areas. In reaction to this reality, management of protected areas has evolved considerably and is putting greater emphasis on the need to include local communities in the planning and use of protected lands if those areas are to be viable. Successfully involving non-professionals in management, however, is far from a simple matter.

INTERPRETATIONS

The term "**Protected area**" can be interpreted in many ways—**national park, national reserve, game reserve, forest reserve, marine park, nature reserve, wildlife management area**—that even those working in the field can be confused. The World Conservation Union (IUCN), however, has developed the following **definition** of a protected area : "*An area of land and/or sea especially dedicated to the protection and maintenance of biological diversity, and of natural and associated cultural resources, and managed through legal or other effective means*". IUCN, through its Commission on National Parks and Protected Areas, has also identified six broad categories of protected areas ;

Category I—Strict Nature Reserve/Wilderness Area ;
Category II—National Park;
Category III—Natural Monument/Natural Landmark;
Category IV—Habitat and Species Management Area;
Category V—Protected Landscape/Seascape; and
Category VI—Managed Resource Protected Areas.

These categories are defined on the basis of management objectives for each area and are largely arranged in relation to the level of human use permitted. The categories are intended as a conceptual frame work, not as a directive to national governments. Traditional systems for protection of natural resources existed long before the modern era and traces its origin to Yellowstone National Park, established in 1872 in the United States.

Most countries have established formal systems of protected areas. There are now more than 9800 such areas convering more than eight % of the earth's surface (IUCN, 1994). Trends in the growth of protected areas indicate a rapid period of recent growth; some 38% of the space protected globally has been designated only in this decade. The areas which are more strictly protected (Categories I and III) comprise a relatively small 3% of the globe. Protected areas which incorporate varying levels of human use (categories IV to VI) represent a significant and increasing percentage of the global protected area.

THE VALUE

This rapid increase and the substantial interest of donor and other agencies in protected areas indicate the importance attached to their establishment, based on the fact that they :

(1) safeguard many of the world's outstanding areas of living richness, natural beauty and cultural significance;

(2) are a source of inspiration and an irreplaceable asset of the countries to which they belong;

(3) help maintain the diversity of ecosystems, species, genetic varieties and ecological processes (including the regulation of water flow and climate) which are vital for the support of all life on earth;

(4) protect genetic varieties and species which are vital in meeting human needs, for example in agriculture and medicine;

(5) are often home to communities of people with traditional cultures and irreplaceable knowledge of nature;

(6) have significant scientific, educational, cultural, recreational and spiritual value, and provide major direct and indirect benefits to local and national economies.

Despite their value, protected areas face unprecedented challenges as we move into the next century. Intense pressure for land, along with land degradation (often stemming from exponential population growth) is likely to increase. This and other challenges were brought into focus at the 4th World Parks Congress in Caracas (Venezuela) in 1992, which attracted some 1000 professionals from 133 countries and produced the *Caracas Action Plan*—a far-reaching document outlining recommendations for the future establishment and management of protected areas. The congress posed two key questions : 1) how can protected areas command broader support from society, and specifically, how can local communities be more effectively involved in protected area management? 2) how can protected area management be made more effective and, specifically, how can protected areas be financed at both the national and site level?

BRING IN LOCALS

Protected areas, particularly those in categories I to III have often been designed and managed to exclude human use, as detrimental to the primary definition of a national park (IUCN, 1994): "Natural area of land and/or sea, designated to: a) protect the ecological integrity of one or more ecosystems for present and future generations, b) exclude exploitation or occupation inimical to the purpose of designation of the area and c) provide a foundation for opportunities, all of which must be environmentally and culturally compatible".

Reality often falls short. In many countries protected areas have been "imposed" on local communities, and populations relocated outside the boundaries. The result is often ill feeling and local hostility toward the park or protected area. Human communities living in and around protected areas often have long-standing relationships with these areas, and should be involved in protected area management and decision-making. In the past, protected area authorities have seldom given adequate attention to local community involvement. Protected areas cannot coexist in the long term with communities which are hostile to them. Local people working with protected area managers can make an important contribution to the conservation of biological diversity. They often have significant knowledge of the resources within protected areas and the means to ensure their sustainable utilization, having depended on them for generations. Involved communities are more likely to be supportive of protected areas, leading to improved managment.

Heading into the 21st century there is in fact, no choice but to involve local communities and those responsible for protecting and management must undergo a change of attitude so that working with the local people becomes an integral part of planning.

There is a need to

- cast the "community involvement net" more widely and to seek the support of influential decision-makers in the community, i.e. people and groups who have the power to influence how protected area s are viewed by the other community members. These may include, for example, traditional chiefs, church or women's groups.
- examine structures which allow more effective management, such as locally based management boards designed to give communities a "voice" in protected area decision-making:
- build on success—singling out examples of successful community involvement in protected are as and determining why they worked (or failed), and what were the key factors of their success.

Some lessons drawn from the experiences worldwide are :

- Effective involvement of local communities in protected areas takes time, effort and resources.
- Local communities need to be involved at an early stage of the decision-making process, and cannot be an "add-on" after planning and decisions have been made.
- Economic incentives will increase the effectiveness of local participation and local support for protection areas.
- The selection of staff who are both technically competent and well respected by local communities can influence the community positively.
- Involvement will be enhanced if local communities directly invest in projects and protected area management.
- Decisions relating to conservation of species and ecosystems must be based on the best available information, both biological and social. Decisions which directly impact on local residents will need to be clearly communicated to communities.

One option with some potential, is private sector management of protected areas. Another option is greater involvement of non-governmental organizations (NGOs), which are increasingly involved in conservation in many countries. The management of protected areas by large international NGOs, such as IUCN, GRAIN, Green Peace and WWF has also proven successful in several parts of the world.

3

Conservation Outside Protected Areas

The small island parks and reserves will not be enough to conserve all the values of tropical forests. In particular, large wide-ranging animals, and those tree species that exist at very low densities, will be at great risk in small protected areas. Conservationsists have long realized that the establishment of protected areas will not by itself maintain all biodiversity. If a balance is to be achieved, conservation values must be integrated into all aspects of human activity. To this end, conservationists and environmentalists led by IUCN developed the World Conservation Strategy, which defines conservation of the environment in terms of human use rather than the preservation of wilderness (IUCN, 1991). It seeks the management of human use of organisms and ecosystems to ensure such use is sustainable. Besides sustainable use, conservation protection, maintenance, rehabilitation, restoration and enhacement of populations and ecosystems.

SUSTAINABLE LOGGING AND THE RAINFOREST HARVEST

Conservationists have also put considerable efforts into identifying other lucrative means to achieve conservation objectives. For example, in order to conserve tropical forests, IUCN and the International Institute for Environment and Development (IIED) have actually promoted tropical forest logging. The IIED has gone even further, arguing that "it is a fact that sustainable management is technically feasible" and that "the sustainable management of natural tropical forest for timber production is one of the keys to forest conservation and to the timber trade". But the amount of tropical forest under sustainable management is negligible and there are many who doubt if it is possible at all. Indeed, most tropical forest logging has been very destructive.

Farmers and rural communities have been the stewards of biodiversity since time immemorial. From our hunter-gatherer origins through the invention of agriculture, people have domesticated, diversified, nurtured, conserved and made available a wealth of valuable species and varieties. Since the past few centuries, they have increasingly been marginalized in the role. Governmental actions to promote nature parks and genebanks as the solution to the extinction of biodiversity overshadow and overtake the efforts of local people.

The long-term conservation of biological diversity especially for food and agriculture, is one of the most important tasks we have before us to ensure the livelihoods of our own and many future generations to come. How to go about it, though, is a question of strategy and choice-decisions which have important technical, political and socio-economic implications. A principal objective of the CBD is to promote the conservation and sustainable use of biological diversity. However, only two traditional approaches, *in situ* and *ex situ* conservation, are stressed by the Convention. Each of them has its rationale, merits, social consequences and costs. And both of them historically depend on the centralisation of resources and decision making. A third, more decentralized and people-oriented approach has to be given equal footing and support. The Convention does provide elements to do this, but only if specific action is taken by those who have to put the Convention to work.

The CBD is fundamentally rooted in an *in situ* conservation mindset, "on site" conservation, basically directed at preserving the dynamics of whole ecosystems (such as tropical rainforests or mangroves) and / or species. The method employed is to isolate zones of particular "natural" diversity from society, basically in the form of protected areas (national parks, nature reserves etc.). In 1985, some 2000 protected areas were registered in the world covering 4 million sq. km. In 1993, there were close to 8500 major protected areas in the world, many of them in the developing countries. Protected areas now exist in almost 170 countries, covering 7.7 million sq km. - almost the size of Egypt - or some 5.2% of the earth's land area.

The major drawback of the current *in situ* approach is that the local people who depend on access to or interaction with the diversity zone in question are pretty much left out of the scheme. Their role in conserving, managing and using wildlife is ceased or relegated to the terrain of nearby "buffer zones". A recent review of protected area conservation approaches shows that there are numerous examples of local communities being expelled from their settlement (in to-be-protected zones) without adequate provision for alternative means of work and income.

PEOPLE AS ACTORS

The CBD does include in its definition of *in situ* conservation, domesticated and cultivated species (Article 2). Both the classic protected area approach and the gene bank system face serious shortcomings in saving what is left of the diversity of both domesticated and wild species. In both systems, local people, the original stewards of the world's biodiversity, are completely left out of the action. Clearly, there is an urgent need to elaborate a third conservation strategy within the framework of the Convention, an on-farm management of genetic resource.

Rural people have been using and conserving biodiversity—domesticated and wild since time immemorial. It is the past few centuries that they are increasingly being marginalised from access to these resources and any role in managing them. Yet wild species and domesticated crop genetic diversity are fundamental to people's livelihood systems. It is often because they are being aggressively deprived of such an important resource base that people are taking action today to regain control over biodiversity in their food, farming and income generating systems.

In the past few decades, organised action to reinstate, promote and improve people-based conservation systems of agricultural biodiversity has been building up. The dynamics of on-farm conservation is centered on use; diversity is maintained not because people set up local museums, but because they use, nurture, live off/with and manage biological resources. In crop and live-stock husbandry, on-farm management often consists of recuperating diversity and reintegrating it into production systems, which includes on-farm breeding.

4

Ex Situ Conservation

Gene banks provide the principal means of storing plant genetic material. This *ex situ* approach relies on three methods of storing the material.

(1) **Seed banks** provide a controlled environment where seeds can be dried to low moisture content and stored at low temperature without losing their viability.

(2) **Field gene banks** such as **arboreta, plantations** and **botanical gardens** are useful for species that are difficult or impossible to store as seeds, including many perennials, vegetatively propagated crops and tree species.

(3) *In vitro* **methods** which conserve plant parts, tissue or cells in a nutrient medium can be used to conserve species that do not readily produce seeds, or where the seeds cannot be dried without damaging them.

Under ideal conditions, gene banks provide long-term (but not indefinite) storage. Both seeds and tissues deteriorate with age and plants must be grown periodically to generate fresh seeds and tissues for continued storage. Unfortunately, even the most sophisticated gene bank cannot always provide adequate security. Large collections of germplasm continue to be lost as a result of technical and financial shortcomings or natural disasters. Power failures, inadequate documentation and evaluation, or failure to regenerate plants can result in massive losses of stored collections. Earthquakes, floods, social and political unrest also put gene banks at a risk.

The biggest shortcoming of *ex situ* gene banks (off-farm) is that, once stored, plants are removed from the evolutionary process that they undergo in nature. There is no pressure from changing natural conditions or competition with other species. The ultimate aim of conservation is to maintain a dynamically evolving system. Therefore, while gene banks will continue to be vital to conservation, complementary systems are likely to assume greater importance in the future.

Gene banks are temperature-controlled storage units—essentially giant ice boxes—which are meant to preserve biodiversity in the form of seeds, sperms, ovules, tissue culture, pollen and even DNA. Worldwide, 131 countries currently house national *ex situ* collections of plant genetic resources for food and agriculture in one form or another. Added to this, ten International Agricultural Research Centres (IARCs) of the CGIAR maintain important collections of the world's major food crops. Altogether some 4.35 million plant samples are being stored under *ex situ* conditions today. Despite the fact that the bulk of these materials originating from the South, the CBD has been construed in order not to disturb this imbalance, to the advantage of the breeding and biotech community in the North. All of these collections can effectively be treated as the property of the governments or companies which hold them and they can also be patented. Further what happens to the "international" collections held by IARCs of the CGIAR remains in doubt. The IARCs are only "International" in an informal sense and the legal status of their gene banks is unclear.

After many years of relying almost exclusively on *ex situ* conservation of plant genetic resources, the international community is at last beginning to face the shortcomings of gene bank fridge conservation. The UN (FAO) has (June 1996) prepared a Draft Report on the State of the World's Plant Genetic Resources that analyses the progress in this field. The background report, which comes in three volumes, contains a wealth of information, statistics and assessments. The "highlights" of the report especially of its *ex situ* section shows how some of the NGO's past fears are finally being confirmed by the FAO.

Farming communities throughout the world have adopted local crops and plants to their needs. However, it has been in the tropical and subtropical belts of the planet where the largest wild biodiversity is concentrated, and thus where the farmers' process is intimately tied to local knowledge systems of plants, animals, their interactions and uses, and fosters the conservation and development of indigenous knowledge. They have had access to a wider variety of material to meet their needs. As a result, the centres of origin and most of the diversity of the 30 crops that provide 95% of human dietary energy of protein are to be found in the South. The same is true for the 120 plant species important for food and agriculture at the national level and for the 7000 plants that have been cultivated or collected by humans for food at one time or another. It is this treasure of farmer genius which has been under increasing threat for several decades now. With the modernisation of agriculture and the Green Revolution, crop varieties were promoted for one staple crop after the other, hundreds of farmer's varieties of those crops were either relegated to marginal areas or just got lost. Trying to address the symptoms rather than the cause, scientists swarmed out to collect the remaining farmer varieties of major food crops and put them into gene banks. By doing this, the local cultivars and wild relatives could be saved for a long period while still being available to breeders. This approach is the basis of *ex situ* conservation.

PROBLEM WITH THE FRIDGE SYSTEM?

During recent decades, concern is focused on three main issues; the methodology as such, the political implication and the technical constraints.

(1) THE METHODOLOGY

A conservation system that is based on gene banks relies on a crop-by-crop, fragmentary approach, which ignores the interactions of the different elements in the agroecosystem, as well as the role of farmers' knowledge. It cuts the genetic materials developed by farmers of their evolutionary process and thus forms a static approach to conservation. As far as the use of the material is concerned, it is mainly directed to official plant breeders, with farmers merely being at the receiving end of the improved varieties. In a sense, it is a band-aid approach to conservation, that does not provide solutions for the causes of genetic erosion.

(2) POLITICAL IMPLICATIONS

The main issues raised are the lack of control of accessions by those who provided the material in the first place (local communities or countries). During much of the 1970s and 1980s, the International Board on Plant Genetic Resources (IBPGR)—an institute of the CGIAR promoted a gene bank system that effectively channelled genetic resources from the South to gene banks in the North, or to the gene banks of the CGIAR itself. Other political biases were the predominance of the main commodity crops in the gene banks (and the lack of the minor crops and wild species important to subsistance farmers), the almost absolute focus on servicing breeders and the biotechnology industry, and a constant trend towards the privatisation of plant genetic resources. Some of these issues are being addressed in the current negotiations under CBD and the International Undertaking on Plant Genetic Resources.

(3) TECHNICAL QUESTIONS

Many samples in the gene banks are easy-to-access from the road collections and do not represent the full spectrum of what farmers developed. The long-term security of gene banks for conservation is questioned. Problems with power supply and consequent temperature fluctuations, seed desiccation, and poor regenerations are frequent. NGOs have suggested that genetic erosion in the gene banks may be as high as is in the field.

5

Ex Situ : UN FAO's State of the World Report

In 1996 FAO published the first (draft) Report on the State of the World's Plant Genetic Resources for Food and Agriculture. The Report is the result of an unprecedented effort to review and assess the state of the plant genetic resources in agriculture. It tries also to identify the causes of their erosion and to analyse the areas where action can be taken in order to conserve genetic resources. The report identifies the intensification of agriculture as the leading cause of genetic erosion. It formally recognizes the role of resource-poor farming communities in the conservation and development of biodiversity.

The report based on 151 country reports, 112 sub-regional meetings and the FAO's World Information and Early Warning System database, contains a lot of interesting information. It also confirms some of the fears NGOs and farmers have been expressing for a long time. Besides the political issue of who has the control over the accessions, the report talks about problems related to the security of the gene banks, available information on the accessions, the danger of deterioration due to lack of regeneration and the use of existing accessions.

EX SITU TODAY

GENE BANKS : NUMBER, SIZE AND GEOGRAPHY

By the end of the 1970s there were 54 seed keeping facilities, of which 24 had long-term storage capabilities. After a widespread but largely uncoordinated effort by both the countries and the CGIAR in the 1970s and 1980s to build up a gene bank system and to collect existing agricultural biodiversity, the world now has a total of 1308 national, regional and international germplasm collections, according to the FAO Report. Of these, 397 are maintained under long- or medium-term storage conditions, while the rest being active working collections for use by researchers and plant breeders. For the purpose of conservation, the base collections held under long- or medium-term storage conditions are the most important ones, as these supposedly contain the unique material for use sometime in the future.

According to the FAO, there are a total of about 6.1 million accessions under *ex situ* condition : 0.6 m in the CGIAR system and 5.5 in national collections and regional gene banks. Some 50% to 65% of the accessions (3-4 million) are in the base collections. About 90% are kept under cold storage, while 8% are kept in field banks and less than 1% *in vitro*. More than 80% of the accessions are held in national banks, and 45% in just twelve countries (Brazil, Canada, China, France, Germany, India, Japan, Korean Republic, Russia, Ukraine, the UK and the USA). These have secure long-term seed storage facilities, if measured according to internationally accepted criteria. To these secure national collections, one would have to add 9 of the CGIAR gene banks and 4 regional gene banks which are in a good state.

THE WORRIES

The FAO report points out with concern that one of the major gene banks in the world—the Vavilov Institute (VIR) in Russia, which holds the world's third largest wheat collection and important collections of other crops (including barley, rice, corn, cotton, lentil and sugarbeet) does not meet these criteria. The VIR has only medium-term storage facilities. The need for frequent regeneration is a strong threat to the diversity in its accessions.

In their reports many countries noted **gene bank problems**, among them:
- equipment problems, particularly in the cooling unit, lack of seed cleaning and humidity control equipment,
- irregularities in the supply of electricity and the associated temperature fluctuation,
- difficulties in seed drying, especially in the humid regions of Africa, Asia and Latin America.

In addition, the FAO notes that in many of even the few secure facilities full safety duplication is lacking, and there is often a large backlog of accessions for regeneration. So the impressive number of 1308 collections of 6.1 million samples ends up boiling down to perhaps a dozen or two truly secure, safe and up-to-date conservation facilities. Also a cursory glance at the data suggests that the genetic booty is spread fairly evenly across the world; 49.22% in southern collections and 9.6% in CGIAR gene banks, located in the South. However, both the southern origin of most genetic diversity and the continued northern control over the CGIAR bias these figures to the North's benefit.

THE DIFFICULTIES

In addition to the above mentioned technical problems with the safety of the collections, there are two additional ones; lack of regeneration and chaos in duplication. The FAO concludes that almost half of all the stored seeds world-wide now need to be regenerated. Its report also warns that some of these "may already have lost their viability or genetic integrity, or they may be from populations where recollecting may prove more cost effective than regeneration". However, for many of the accessions, recollecting may prove impossible, because of extinction in the field.

In addition, many countries do not have either the funds, facilities or staff necessary to conduct their needed regeneration activities. Although countries in the South are the most affected by this backlog, both the CGIAR gene banks and some countries in the North (such as, the USA and Japan) are also affected. Part of the problem comes from the fact that when the gene bank system was set up, nobody really took into account the needs and costs of the long-term maintenance of the accessions. One notorious example has been the spread of expensive gene banks in some Asian countries—built with Japanese aid money —several of which are now virtually empty or simply not functioning. The global picture, according to the FAO Plan of Action, is "a steady deterioration of many facilities and their ability to perform even basic conservation functions".

Duplication of the existing collections is both a problem and a need. The FAO report notes that there is a lot of uncoordinated and unknown duplication amongst the world's stored seeds. This over-duplication is a waste of money and should be minimised. On the other hand duplication of unique accessions and their storage in other gene banks is crucial to ensure their security in the face of unexpected losses (because of fire, earthquakes, war, etc). Even the IARC gene banks, with their high tech resources and funding, report high levels of duplication lacking in several crops.

The security and duplication problems in the current gene banks system lead to a situation where genetic erosion in the banks might be higher than that in the field. For example, the FAO reports that a review of the USA gene banks showed that 29% of the US collection had seed germination rates less than 65%. Furthermore, 45% of the accessions had less than 550 seeds. This means that an important part of the USA collection (one of the most sophisticated in the world) was either dead or dying, or might have too few seeds to guarantee survival of genetic diversity.

SOMETHING CONSERVED?

The high proportion of cereals (48%) reflects not only their key role in global food security, but also to Northern agriculture and to international agricultural trade. In contrast, tubers and roots, which include important crops for subsistance farmers like sweet potato, potato and cassava only account for 4% of global accessions. Banans and plantains are represented by a mere 10500 accessions. Many locally valuable crops have only just started to be collected and regional base collections are being kept by national gene banks. The FAO admits that there are very few accessions of medicinal plants. The information of the type of the accession (whether wild relatives, local varieties or breeding lines) is only available for one third of the global accessions.

Where this information is known, the proportion of each kind of accession varies according to the crops and to the gene bank system, with IARCs focusing on land races and the private sector on advanced breeding lines. Globally 48% of accessions are advanced cultivars or breeding lines, 36% are old cultivars or farmers' varieties and only 15% are wild or weedy plants of crop relatives.

THE LACUNAE

Again the picture is a biased one. When the early plant hunters went out collecting, they obviously focused on the ones they were interested in, something still reflected in gene bank holdings. Grossly lacking are crops that do not enter international trade and are only important at national or local levels. Also, species providing wild foods and other products important to local livelihood systems are notably absent. As far as the type of material is concerned, almost half of the stored seeds worldwide consist of breeder's germplasm, while only just one-third are the original farmer varieties. This poses a fundamental question on what the current gene bank system is doing—storing material ignored by the commercial breeders, or saving the original diversity developed by farmers?

INFORMATION AND USE

The information on the accessions held *ex situ* may be almost as important as the accessions themselves. This information may aid rapid identification of the required accessions and/or characteristics and may help to prevent excessive duplication of efforts, while showing where the gaps are. From a political and equity perspective, information on the origin of the accessions is also relevant. Ease of access to the information may make it easier for both breeders (as is the case) and also farmers (as it should also be) to use the materials. Yet news from the Report on what we know about the stored seeds is again not good. Although 37% of national collections and nearly all the CGIAR gene banks accessions have *passport data*, in most collections these data refer only to the country of origin. Plant breeders often develop their own collections because of the lack of information on collections in the gene banks.

The rates of characterization and evaluation are also very low. As a result the accessions of national collections are not fully utilised even by current gene bank client breeders. The only exceptions to poor characterization seem to be most countries in Europe, East Asia, North America, Ethiopia, India and the Philippines. While some gene banks have their collections fully documented, computerised and even put in the internet (as it is the case of the VIR and the USA base collections), others have not documented any of their accessions.

These factors clearly limit the use of the accessions stored in the gene banks. Nevertheless a large number of accessions are exchanged around the world. There is no doubt that *ex situ* conservation is needed and that, if the existing collections are to be saved, an improvement of the security conditions and the efficiency in the management of gene banks is needed, especially since a large part of the diversity they contain no longer exists in the field. However, the unavoidable erosion of genetic diversity in the gene banks in the long term (even under the best long-term storage conditions) question the appropriateness of this technology as a primary conservation tool for agricultural biodiversity. Diversity originated as the result of continuous interaction of plants, animals, environmental conditions and human selection. Storage of the seeds away from the fields and forests breaks this critical cycle.

CONCLUDING REMARKS

A conservation system that leaves aside farmers, peasants, pastoralists and their knowledge, and expropriates their materials—making them available as raw materials to breeders and biotechnologists who may claim intellecutal property rights over their creations—is equally perverse. Not only do farmers lose control over their heritage—the seeds—but they also lose the possibility of continuing with their sustainable and highly productive agricultural practises which build upon diversity.

Contrary to what had been assumed by most of the international scientific community, *ex situ* conservation on its own cannot ensure the conservation of precious plant genetic resources for future generations. The primary conservation effort has to focus on farmers and their fields. It should go hand-in-hand while actually making use of that diversity in the complex agroecosystems. Gene banks in the context of well-defined national genetic resources programmes can and should play an important role in facilitating the movement of germplasm between farming communities and safety backup-sites, as well as from these sites back to the farming communities. A gene bank as a dynamic partner in not only conservation, but also development of genetic resources in which not only official plant breeders but also local farming communities can participate is still a far away dream in the FAO documents. Until the FAO and the international community shift towards this perspective, NGOs and peasant organizations have to continue to do a lot of work to conserve and improve their biological resources and convince policy makers at all levels of the value of their approaches.

HOW EX SITU CONSERVATION WORKS?

Gene banks are compartmentalised cold storages in which seeds are kept in controlled conditions of temperature and humidity. The banks work on the principle that dehydrated seeds are capable of remaining viable for long periods of time in cold conditions. Seeds may be kept in **long-term storage** (–18°C), **medium-term storage** (0 to 10°C), or **short-term storage** (more than 10°C). **Orthodox seeds** (those that can be dehydrated) account for most crops, including all major cereals. The so-called **recalcitrant** seeds do not stand up to such a process, as is the case with coconut, mango and tea. The *ex situ* conservation of these crops and vegetatively propagated plants relies largely on field banks. Recently, *in vitro* conservation techniques have also been used for the conservation of recalcitrant crops. Wild crop relatives and large species (such as trees) are often conserved in botanical gardens.

For *ex situ* conservation a large number of seeds have to be collected, because even under the most stringent long-term conservation conditions seeds eventually lose viability and die. Accessions have to be regenerated regularly by planting them out in order to obtain new seeds. However, the process of regeneration also results in a loss of genetic diversity, especially if it is done in conditions different from those of the site of origin of the accession. This is because the new environment may result in a different kind of selective pressure. Information on gene bank accessions is classified in three categories:

I **Passport**: Basic data such as the sampling date and the site of origin.

II **Characterization** : Specific data on the sampling date and site.

III **Evaluation**: Data on agronomic properties of the accession closely related to the environment.

6

Conservation of Animal Diversity

Ex Situ conservation of animal genetic resources includes "cryogenic preservation techniques"—the collection and freezing in liquified nitrogen (–321°F) of semen, ova or embryos, or the preservation of DNA segments in frozen blood or other tissues. It also encompasses the **captive breeding** of wild or domesticated species in zoos or other locations away from their natural environment. *Ex situ* gene banks have similar advantages and disadvantages to those used to hold plant germplasm.

In situ conservation enables animal populations to continue to evolve and be selected for use in their natural environments. It is particularly important for species within geographical regions where cryogenic preservation is not well developed or available. *In situ* conservation can be carried out at any level, in any country, without the need for special skills or technology. Properly planned, it can incorporate farmer and industry breeding as well as continued use of the resources.

The loss of traditional breeds is an increasingly recognised threat to agriculture and people's security. Given the rapid pace of environmental degradation and the need to develop more sustainable and integrated forms of agriculture, the role of traditional herds will be crucial for the future. At the moment however, there are very few well-supported programmes in action to inventory, assess, conserve and develop animal genetic diversity important for the local people's livelihoods. In contrast to crop genetic resources, national programmes in the animal sector are few and far between. In 1992, the FAO launched a programme for the Global Conservation of Animal Genetic Resources.

If we can learn something from the plant genetic resources debate over the past decades, it is that conservation will only have a future if it is linked to sustainable utilisation. Trying to store away animal genes in deep-freezers hardly solves the immediate problem of many poor farmers' needs for improved, sustainable and adapted crop-livestock production systems based on genetic diversity. The need for decentralised and integrated farmer-based conservation and breeding programmes is glaring.

THE INITIATIVES

There is a lack of information on animal genetic diversity — predominantly in the South, and the relative weakness of conservation programmes aimed at saving and improving local breeds of "resource poor" farmers. New initiatives such as the CBD, GEF, the FAO's growing interest to play a stronger role in animal genetic resources and the expansion of CGIAR system, all open up space for new and enhanced action. However, it is not clear whether any of these programmes will support the people's participation in the conservation and breeding efforts, or promote policies that ensure clear benefits to small farmers in the South. While the CBD is a prime mechanism to get animal genetic conservation programmes going — addressing all forms: livestock, wildlife and aquatics — very little thinking or discussion has been raised on farm animals. The FAO and the CGIAR, which are both directly involved in agriculture, are likely to compete for further competence and control in the animal arena. At present, the two African-based animal centres, ILCA and ILRAD are being merged into ILRI since 1995.

Ex Situ : Cryogenic Preservation

Various techniques are available for cryogenic preservation of germplasm. The percentage of active **sperms** in high-quality semen frozen at −196°C decreases only slightly with storage. Bovine **embryos** can also be collected non-surgically, frozen and stored in liquid nitrogen for decades without major alteration. Another, not yet fully developed technique is **recovery of oocytes** (eggs) from the ovaries of slaughtered animals, maturation, fertilization *in vitro* and storage in liquid nitrogen. Eventually, it may be possible to reactivate an entire organism from the genetic information in a single cell. Collecting and freezing semen and embryos has not been very successful with some species. Research on increasing its efficiency is underway in buffalo, pigs and horses. Once fully operative, the Regional Animal Gene banks would have facilities for processing and long-term storage of germplasm, as well as for storage of blood serum for disease tests not carried out on donor animals at the time of collection. The possibility of separate storage of DNA is also being studied, which would allow banks to participate in international efforts to map genomes and the transfer of DNA.

LIMITATIONS

Despite its advantages, cryogenic storage has limitations. Techniques are not well-developed for some species, like pigs, buffalo and horses, and not available at all for others, such as elephants and camels. Populations conserved only cryogenically are also physically unavailable for cultural, historical, educational or research uses. Cryogenic storage of **semen** is relatively inexpensive for most species, but the use of semen only permits recreation of a population by the gradual upgrading of existing females, which takes at least five generations. **Embryo collection and freezing**, on the other hand, is much more expensive and requires a higher level of technical expertise. A study by the United Kingdom based Rare Breeds Survival Trust concluded that **embryo banks** were prohibitively expensive, **cloning embryos** at the 16 or 32 cell stage could cut costs, since fewer embryos would be needed to produce new clones and hence not so many would need to be stored. However, this method is still new.

In Situ : Live Animal Programmes

To compensate for the limitations of cryogenic storage, live animal programmes are needed, and several funded by governments, NGOs and private organizations are already working in Europe and North America. Government efforts include guardianship of herds and flocks in protected areas such as state or national parks, while several NGOs, like the British Nature Conservancy Council, are involved in wildlife habitat conservation and farm parks like Cotswold farm in the UK.

Not all these methods are transferable to developing countries. However, where there is a well-developed tourist industry, the idea of "living history" farm parks perhaps in conjunction with **wild game parks** could be adapted to demonstrate traditional farm skills. University research centres and veterinary institutes might be encouraged to keep indigenous breeds. Production-linked subsidies could also be paid to individual farmers in livestock programmes.

Another important facet of the global AGR programme is indigenous breed development. Since the early 1970s, the FAO and UNEP have established methodologies, conducted surveys and held training courses in breed conservation and management. An inventory of special breeds was made, including ass, buffalo, cattle, goats, horses, pigs and sheep, as well as several unmanaged populations of formerly domestic animals. Genetic improvement of selected breeds is a major programme goal, and twelve populations chosen for their regional importance and genetic uniqueness have been selected for initial research.

THE MODERN TECHNIQUES

Open Nucleus Breeding Scheme (ONBS) combined with the technique of **Multiple Ovulation Embryo Transfer** (MOET), offers potential for more progress in developing countries than traditional animal selection methods. In practice, a genetically superior nucleus flock or herd is established under controlled conditions by screening the base population for outstanding females. The "elite" females are subjected to MOET to obtain embryos, which will be superior to the base population. Resulting offspring are reared and genetically evaluated. From these, males with high breeding value are selected and used for improvement of the base population, either by natural service or **artificial insemination**. ONBS has many advantages. Due to its shorter generation interval, it yields high rates of genetic progress each year; it can be adapted to various species; it allows control of the mix of genes released to the base population, and it is flexible regarding the introduction of continually selected germplasm.

The global AGR programme will also deal with **gene technology**. **Germplasm preservation**, for instance, could be much cheaper if breeds shared a common DNA heritage. **Genome mapping** may lead to genes (traits) which could then be transferred from rabbits. Sheep, goats and pigs have been produced by **direct microinjection** of DNA from another species. Dr. Ian Wilmut's **Cloning** is a case in point for **whole genome (nuclear) transplantation**. Though already very sophisticated, **DNA transfer techniques** are only beginning to be developed. Livestock applications of advanced techniques could range from creation of disease and pest-resistant cattle breeds that thrive in harsh environments and feed on any available browse, to breeds selected for production of massive milk volumes, "tailor-graded" meat, or virtually any trait a breeder might imagine.

ANY OTHER STRATEGY?

Obviously, conservation of animal genetic resources should be part of any long-term strategy to protect the biodiversity of our planet; including plant genetic resources, aquatic resources and overall habitat preservation. Some favour grouping all genetic resource activities under a single umbrella, to reduce costs and facilitate exchanges between concerned national and international bodies.

However such a general integration of activity could have serious drawbacks. Very different technologies and economic scales are used for collecting, conserving, evaluating and using animal and plant genetic resources. Genetic variation in farm animals is largely controlled by researchers in developed countries, whereas that of plants is not. As for fisheries, not much is known yet of the effects on the genetics of fish stocks of such stresses as heavy fishing, environmental degradation or even aquaculture practices. Grouping all conservation activities together may also hamper funding, since it is harder to stimulate people's interest. At least initially, a flexible approach seems to be called for, keeping technical activities separate but retaining a single conceptual framework for global resource conservation.

Summary

IN FAVOUR OF EX SITU CONSERVATION

The arguments in favour of *ex situ* conservation of storable, non-recalcitrant seeds tend to be formulated in terms of the shortcomings of *in situ* conservation. In brief, they refer to the following:
  (a) *ex situ* conservation is most suitable for long-term conservation;
  (b) *ex situ* storage facilities can store more diversity and quantity of accessions of seeds;

(c) evaluation is easier than in *in situ* circumstances, and

(d) *ex situ* offers wider availability to breeders than do *in situ* collections.

DRAWBACKS OF LONG-TERM EX SITU CONSERVATION

(a) *differential survival* of genotypes in storage: long-term storage causes a loss in germination rate (which varies with genotype);

(b) *selection during rejuvenation*: after several cycles of rejuvenation, entries bear little resemblance to the original parent(s) collected in nature;

(c) *outcrossing* with other species: it appeared very difficult to provide adequate isolation to prevent outcrossing between different entries during regeneration;

(d) *genetic drift*: during storage, allelic frequencies can be subject to considerable changes compared with the parent populations.

(e) it is impossible to store *recalcitrant* seeds *ex situ*;

(f) *ex situ* conservation *"freezes evolution"* (or leads to evolutionary stasis); and

(g) *in vitro* storage of *ex situ* may cause loss of diversity.

IN FAVOUR OF IN SITU CONSERVATION

On the viability of *in situ* conservation, most counter-arguments have been much more practical in kind. The more important ones are:

(a) practical problems and cost of administering subsidies and monitoring the relevant areas

(b) lack of staff to supervise field sites

(c) ready availability of the material to breeders is unclear

(d) *in situ* preservation can only conserve relatively a tiny fraction of crop germplasm

(e) scientific, economic and social problems involved

(f) obsolescence of *in situ* conservation methods especially where better, non-traditional methods are available

(g) the right reserve size is unknown

(h) only a limited amount of diversity can be stored in established reserves, and

(i) there are no generally accepted methods of storing land races.

7

Fish Conservation

Clearly today's fisheries face serious problems in trying to achieve the kind of sustainability that would assure their long-range survival. Some of the solutions are obvious, but they will require widespread acceptance and a good deal of courage from both fishery officials and fishermen to be put into practice.

First, **over-capitalization** must be halted and the world **fishing fleet** reduced to lower the global loss in revenues. The FAO has estimated that the cost of correcting present day deficiencies would be on the order of US $ 7 billion to 14 billion. World Bank is now accepting that first reduction plans must be supported, while the European Community aims to cut its huge fleet by upto 40%. The supply of fish could be substantially increased if a form attractive to consumers could be found for marketing the so called **trash fish** species—a misnomer if ever there was one. Several million tons of such fish are discarded every year, even though a third of the present catch is used—ironically for making aquaculture feed. In addition, some 10% of the total food fish supplies could be conserved by eliminating careless handling, insufficient chilling, pest infestations, poor processing and spoilage.

One of the foremost barriers to sustainability could also be eliminated if open access is curtailed, or better controlled. While the Law of the Sea Convention has extended national jurisdiction, it applies mainly to foreigners fishing in a coastal state's waters, the country's own nationals still have open access. Long-distance fishing nations have access to the high seas beyond the 200 mile zones, and stocks such as sharks, tuna or the fish of the Antarctic region are overfished. Wherever access is unlimited, there will be an irresistible increase in fishing effort and corresponding decline in catch rates until maximum sustainable yield has been reached and finally surpassed. The result is further depletion of stocks and more frequent and severe conflicts between users, and the dissipation of what economists call economic rents. Extraordinarily large economic returns are currently being wasted because of the open access conditions, on the order of thousands of millions of dollars annually.

TEETERING ON THE BRINK

The ocean's most valuable commercial species are fished to capacity. Only strong action can head off ecological disaster. According to FAO's Fishery Resources and Environment Division, the whole ocean is fished to capacity... and there is nowhere else to go. At the same time, the range of species being exploited has expanded, from traditional bottom fish and large whales to small pelagic fish and temperate tuna, to tropical tuna and oceanic squid. Gradually as more marketable species become depleted, less marketable species are sought out up and down the marine food chain.

RESPONSIBLE FISHING

The International Conference on Responsible Fishing (1992) and the UN Conference on Environment and Development UNCED at Rio de Janerio (1992) both recognized that fishing must be conducted in a responsible manner, so as to ensure optimum use of resources but at the same time to minimize negative effects on the marine environment, including both target and non-target species. This realization is leading to the collaboration of a new international code of conduct for responsible fishing, formulated within the framework of the Law of the Sea and applying to all areas of fishing and fishing operations. This would include :

- specification for marking of vessels and gear to aid in monitoring and surveillance,
- reflagging of fishing vessels to curtail evasion of conservation regulations,
- development of guidelines for high sea fishing, with special attention to migratory stocks and those which straddle boundaries,
- development of guidelines on endangered species, with emphasis on special gear to exclude or protect non-target species and
- guidelines for small-scale fisheries management and development concentrating on socio economic issues

The Green Revolution with its spread of chemical use in crop farming hit hard on the traditionally associated aquatic resources—fish, frogs, shrimp, crabs and snails. Worse, perhaps, the "Blue Revolution" in aquaculture promoted by the IAR System might be based on just two species of fish; tilapia and carp. Without a strong diversification effort, the promotion of a new "superbreeds" could enhance uniformity and dependency at the expense of fostering the local people's breeding work.

8

Conservation of Marine Biodiversity

Conservation of marine biodiversity poses a certain number of problems. Some similar to those concerning terrestrial biodiversity, others specific to the marine environment which is extremely fragile, due to the large variety of elements that go to make it up and the foreign objects that can be introduced into it. Exchanges between the water and the atmoshpere, effects of atmospheric particles linked to climatic changes, the variety of substances poured into the sea via rivers, as also direct human intervention in the various forms of marine exploitation, are just a few examples of what can cause considerable modifications in the marine environment.

It has been generally acknowledged that the main threats for the marine environment come from land. Over 70% of marine contamination comes from the mainland whether due to the dumping of waste products, pesticides, hydrocarbons or toxic products. Even air pollution started on land is eventually deposited on the water surface. Pollutants from natural sources as well as those dumped into the marine environment greatly damage the biology of animal and plant species. The resulting damage can differ in degree according to the type of environment and the state of the natural evolution of the contaminated system. If the harmful effects of this contamination are mitigated in the high seas, they are magnified in specific marine environments such as closed or semi-closed seas, deltas, estuaries and lagoons. All this is cause for serious concern specially when one considers that fish alone provide 40% of animal protein for 60% of the inhabitants of the developing countries and that about 60% of the world's population lives in coastal regions with the figure rapidly increasing due to the combined effect of population growth, migration and urbanization.

Indiscriminate exploitation of the marine environment is no less a source of concern for the conservation of marine biodiversity. In fact, given the rate of increase of world population added to that of land degradation in many parts of the world, increasing demands are being made on marine resources. Human impact is largely responsible for the loss of over 50% of the world's mangroves and now it is coral reefs that are threatened. Thanks to technological advances, fishing techniques are increasingly sophisticated (Figure 11) leading to the over-exploitation of marine resources with devastating impact on important fishing grounds. It is estimated that no fewer than 9 of the world's 17 fishing grounds

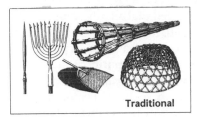

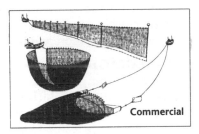

Fig. 11 Selectivity of fishing methods : Old and New

are already on the way to exhaustion. Overall fish catches since 1989 have fallen alarmingly, what is even more disturbing for marine biodiversity is that with the new fishing techniques using trawling and drift nets which capture anything indiscriminately, at times upto 70% of the catch has to be thrown away!.

HOW TO CONSERVE?

Conservation of marine biodiversity is thus an urgent, global issue as physically, oceans cannot be limited by political frontiers. It is generally accepted by the scientific community that inspite of great gaps in our knowledge of the marine environment, it is not too late to act provided that the action taken concertedly involves all concerned actors from the scientific community and political deci- sion-makers through planners, managers, economists, sociologists right down to the common man in touch with the marine environment. As in all global problems, there has to be international concentration to deal with problems relating to marine biodiversity if ways are to be found to safeguard it for the future without depriving those that currently depend upon it for their existence. The CBD and the UN Convention on the Law of the Sea are perhaps the first major step towards a worldwide, international consensus on the conservation of marine biodiversity.

MEASURES TO PRESERVE MARINE BIODIVERSITY

Any measures taken to preserve biodiversity will be successful only if the human population is kept within the capacity of the planet, even though this level is difficult to estimate due to social and technological changes.

(A) BIODIVERSITY AND GENETIC MONITORING

The FAO (1993) recommended that all development proposals that may impact aquatic habitats and aquatic organisms should incorporate due attention to aquatic genetic resources considerations. In particular, aid-funded projects in all sectors should incorporate aquatic biodiversity considerations at the planning stage. It will be necessary to take special care with the most productive areas of our marine ecosystem, such as: 1) estuaries that act as traps for nutrients entering from freshwaters, flow from land and nursery areas for many marine species; 2) upwelling areas where deep cold water rich in nutrients is brought to the surface leading to highly productive systems in neritic and pelagic environments; and 3) waters overlying the continental shelves.

(B) ADEQUATE FISHERIES MANAGEMENT

According to the FAO (1995), world fishing fleets have continuously increased, reaching a total of 3.5 million boats in 1992, of which 1.2 million were industrial vessels (over 100 gross registered tonnes). The overcapacity of this fleet is such that economic losses in the year 1992 were estimated at approximately US $ 50 billion. The reduction of this fleet is a necessary part of the urgent measures needed to preserve the world's fishery resources. However, political and social constraints have been widespread limiting factors to the adoption of adequate policies. Additionally, despite timely technical advice, catch and effort restrictions are usually imposed when resources are already overexploited and hence lead to economically inefficient fishing operations and politically delicate situations for national and international management authorities. Furthermore, the overcapacity of industrial fleets from developed and formerly centrally planned economies is increasingly being exported to the biologically diverse and more fragile ecosystems of subtropical and tropical areas. These areas, in many cases, are already heavily exploited by artisanal subsistence and commercial fisheries.

(C) IMPROVED FISHING AND PROCESSING TECHNIQUES

Bycatch has been defined as "the catch of any species, regardless of sex or size, which is unintentionally harvested and which is subsequently retained or discarded because of relatively low market value or legal requirements". A recent assessment of fishery bycatch and discards estimates that the overall average annual world levels are around 27 million ta. Bycatch and discards cover a wide taxonomic spectrum of commercial and non-commercial marine organisms, including some endangered species. Bycatch may be separated into two components. The bycatch of small individuals of the **target** species which are discarded at sea and may lead to growth and recruitment overfishing and the capture of **non-target** species may include highly vulnerable taxonomic groups, such as reptiles, birds and mammals . The best approach to reduce bycatch and discards in marine fisheries is by technological improvements and modifications of gears, as well as time and/or area restrictions on fishing activities.

(D) STOCK ENHANCEMENT AND HABITAT REHABILITATION

The first way to maintain biological diversity is to slow or stop its loss, but losses are nevertheless inevitable. For this reason it is necessary to restore depleted populations and degraded ecosystems. A variety of *in situ* and *ex situ* methods exist for recovering marine organisms. However, in the sea this is far more difficult and, even for the very few species of marine organisms that can be bred in captivity and successfully transplanted to augment existing populations or establish new ones, the costs are very high. Transplanting could also introduce harmful complications and be ineffective if the original threats are not removed. Stocking with hatchery-raised fish is a method of improving or restoring commercial or game fisheries in lakes, rivers, and certain coastal areas, and its use may soon increase in the later area.

The major goal of fisheries stock enchancement and rehabilitation should be to maintain the evolutionary potential of the population and efforts should be promoted to maintain genetic continuity of vulnerable species/populations through, for example, cryo-preservation of genetic material and the development and maintenance of aquatic reserves for natural and/or artificial propagation of species/populations prior to reintroduction. Efforts should also be made to restore and rehabilitate the vital marine habitats (the life-supporting systems) such as the seagrass beds, salt marsh, mangroves, and the coral reefs.

(E) EDUCATION

Many fishery managers are unaware or do not accept that fishing activities may disrupt the genetic diversity of target and/or nontarget species or populations. In this regard, the FAO (1993) recommended the production of a publication aimed at fishery managers and government agencies, outlining (in simple, non-technical language) the potential and documented genetic impacts of fishery and aquaculture activities.

Wild : The Hidden Harvest

Decades of official agricultural development policies have completely overlooked the importance of food harvested from wild species. This has led to the undermining of food security at local levels and the loss of biological diversity. After decades of focusing on developing a handful of commodity crops and blanketing them across the globe in the name of the Green Revolution, policy makers and agricultural scientists are being faced with a new reality. They are having to recognise that producing bushel upon bushel of rice, wheat and potatoes does not add up to food security. Infact, in many cases, increasing commodity yields has quite the opposite effect decreasing food security at the local level and increasing vulnerability.

Recent research has shown that the importance of staple crop in community food supplies has been greatly overestimated. "**Partner**" **species**—which refer to wild plants and animals, semi-domesticated and domesticated livestock and crops (other than the staple crops) - play a critical role in ensuring food and livelihood security for countless families and communities around the world. The drive towards commodity-based agriculture seriously threatens both the food and livelihood security for millions of people.

These partner species are important for achieving a nutritional balance in the diet, and are, particularly, important for ensuring food security for women, children and the poor, who rely heavily on them. In times of stress, such as famine, wild plants literally keep people alive when they would otherwise perish. In addition, many partner species have significant economic value by preventing the need for cash expenditure and providing ready sources of income to cash-poor households. Partner species also have cultural value and "existence" values associatied with wilderness areas and wild resources.

HOW MANY PLANTS FEED THE WORLD?

When researchers (of IIED, London) asked this question they came up with rather different answers from their peers. Common figures in the scientific literature quote between 7 and 30 crops that provide the vast majority of the world's food supply. Their study examined the FAO food production data of 146 countries. The findings suggest that 103 species contribute 90% of the world's plant food supply. This is much higher than previous figures, but is also considered to be "very much of an underestimate", because of the limitations of the data they had to work with. The FAO data ignores several countries, such as Ethiopia (a global biodiversity hot-spot and centre of origin for a significant number of food plants). Production in home gardens is excluded from the data; and dietary importance is measured only in terms of fat, protein and calorific content, excluding many plants which are valuable in other ways, such as being key sources of vitamins or making staples more palatable.

THE IMPORTANCE OF "WILD" FOODS

"Wild" resources harvested in agricultural and forested areas are of crucial importance. The project entitled "The Hidden Harvest" by researchers at IIED demonstrates clearly that wild resources are important over the whole range of rural livelihood systems, and are not limited to the exclusive preserve of classical "hunting and gathering" societies. The term "Wild" is misleading because it implies the absence of human influence and management. In reality, there is no clear divide between "domesticated" and "wild" species; rather, it is a continuum resulting from co-evolutionary relationships between humans and their environment. Much of "the wild" is shaped by people. Many species that have long been considered to be wild are actually carefully nurtured by people, albeit less intensively than those cultivated in fields. The unfamiliarity, seeming chaos and haphazard appearance of domestic gardens has led many Western researchers to overlook the rich complexity of these production systems. In the same way, forests and other vegetation that extend from the immediate neighbourhood of settlements have been assumed to be self-regulating "wastelands", rather than productive ecosystems which are the partial product of human design.

Within agricultural systems, the greatest diversity of resources is found in multi-layered, complex agroforestry systems and home gardens. However partner species are also important even in seemingly simple monocultural systems, such as the rice paddies that dominate South-East Asia. The irrigation canals that are home to fish, snails, frogs and other animals are important sources of protein and other nutrients for people. Pathways, field edges and erosion gullies often yield useful plants. Even plant pests, such as rodents and weeds, have important nutritional value in certain circumstances. For the *Yukpa* people of Venezuela and Columbia, ants' eggs and beetle larvae are a delicacy. They also supplement their diets with grasshoppers, beetles and caterpillars, while the stingless bee provides them with honey and wax. These dietary additions are particularly important as domestic meat is not acceptable to all *Yukpa* people.

The benefits of wildlife to local livelihoods often go unseen, yet food and income from hunting may be very significant. Contrary to popular belief, a lot of the hidden harvest of game meat is derived from small animals — rats, mice, squirrels, rabbits, hares, small buck and so on. Agricultural lands may be managed to encourage wildlife. Farmers in Thailand plant particular trees on paddy irrigation ditches to attract lizards, rats and other potential food sources. One of the advantages of wild game over domestic animals is that they sometimes have greater production efficiencies than domestic livestock. For example, a South American rodent called *acapybara* is 3.5 times more efficient at converting food to meat than cattle.

'FAMINE' FOODS AND FOOD SECURITY

Wild foods are an important component of coping strategies in times of severe food shortage. During the Sudanese famines in 1973, 84-85 and 1998, the *Berti* of Western Sudan survived off wild grass seeds and tree fruits. In Rajasthan, India, 25 famine foods have been described, including grains, fodder species and the desert locust. History demonstrates the danger of reducing access to wild resources during famine times. In Great Britain, the famine caused by the rains of 1314-16 that killed 10-15% of the population was more severe than previous famines because of the reduced availability of wild resources following agricultural expansion. Those resources that did exist were crucial—even the King ate tree bark!.

In less extreme conditions, wild foods still form an essential part of food security. They may be important to tide communities over the "hunger season" that preceeds the harvest, and to provide people with the necessary energy to harvest their fields. Famine foods may be difficult to prepare and are often less palatable than other foods, but this is not always the case. When food is short in Bhutan, farmers go into the hills to gather a mix of wild avocados, bamboo shoots, orchids, mushrooms and giant wild yams that grow upto one metre in length.

Partner species are often the food of choice for daily sustenance, not only in leaner times. Partner species may have higher fat, protein, mineral and vitamin contents than cultivated crops. For example, the *Kung* people of Southern Africa, who depend exclusively on "wild" foods have a higher per capita calorie intake than the average in Africa or Asia. The average intake of calories is 2,355 per adult, which is derived from mongongo nuts (58%) meat (30%) and wild vegetable plants (12%). This food is obtained from hunting and gathering 84 plants and 54 animal species over a working week of only 2.3 days at six hours per day. This makes them much more efficient than many farmers or Westerners who devote a much greater share of their working week to grow their food or pay the grocer. Similarly, cutting and processing a sago tree in the Molucca islands in Indonesia provides for the bulk of a family's calorific needs for about three months.

WHOSE VALUATION COUNTS?

Wild foods have different values for different people for example, in some societies, men tend to concentrate their work on agricultural plots, whereas there may be associated areas such as field edges, contour ridges and pathways that women value highly and manage intensively. These may be the areas where leafy vegetables, rodents or fruits are found and harvested. The value of these marginal areas may not be recognised by the menfolk. Women are more involved than men in wild resource management, harvesting, processing and sale, which means that they value the resources higher than men. Poor women in UP, India, derive almost half their income from plants found in the commons compared with middle-class women, for whom this figure is one-third, and men, who gain only 13% of their earnings from this source. During the 1984-85 famine in Sudan, females led men because they were more knowledgeable in the collection and preparation of wild foods.

Wild resources are more important to the poor than the wealthy. Income derived from the collection and sale of wild resources is particularly important for the rural poor as a source of cash for the purchase of other goods, for education or for emergencies. In Brazil, for example, the sale of kernels from the fruit of the babassupalm supports more than two million people, representing an average of 35% of the families' income. In some cases, the collection, home use and sale of wild resources represents a more lucrative option than wage labour or farming. The *Huottuja* Amerindians in Venezuela net 30% more through the sale of wild palm fruits than they would working as wage labourers.

In addition, the consumption of wild foods and cultivated fruits often saves money by reducing the necessity to buy food. In Thailand, households living far from forests spend three times as much money on food (excluding rice) than those living near the forest. The use of wild resources for fuel, to make household and agricultural implements, for building materials or medicines, also offers an important, low-cost alternative to the cash economy, which may be prohibitive for the poor. Children also value wild foods highly, as they are the most frequent collectors and consumers of wild fruits. Since children are particularly prone to malnutrition, their foraging activities provide them with essential supplies of fats, proteins, vitamins and minerals.

Common property resource areas (where most wild resources are found) are valued much more highly by the poor, who are reliant on them for their livelihoods. It is the poor, therefore, that are most adversely affected by changes in land use and tenure. For example, in India, common property resources provide 14-23% of the rural poor's income, rising to 42–57% in times of drought. Despite this, common property resources have shrunk by a third to a half over the past 30 years, mainly due to privatisation, which has had a disproportionate impact on the poor.

THE IMPACT OF AGRICULTURAL INTENSIFICATION

It is clear that wild resources are of great importance to communities in a number of ways. This is not reflected, however, in most modern agricultural research and practice. Policy makers, researchers and agribusinessmen remain transfixed by the goal of increasing yields of the main commodity and food crops through the application of external inputs. This approach has had serious implications for people's livelihoods and the maintenance of genetic diversity, especially the wild.

1. As cultivated areas expand and traditional agroecosystems are simplified the availability of wild resources diminishes.
2. Loss of resource diversity may also mean less available genetic diversity for future agricultural adaptation and breeding. A diverse cropping system which includes access to wild resources can provide a buffer against the vagaries of local and international markets.

ON ANIMALS

The Green Revolution with its spread of chemical use in crop farming hit hard on the traditionally associated aquatic resources of Asian agriculture: fish, frogs, shrimp, crabs and snails. Worse, perhaps, the "Blue Revolution" in aquaculture promoted by the IAR System might be based on just two species of fish; tilapia and carp. Already, the genetic base of the Nile tilapia farmed in Asia is reported as dangerously narrow. Without a strong diversification effort, the promotion of a few "superbreeds" could enhance uniformity and dependency at the expense of fostering local people's breeding work.

Long-term food security will continue to depend on wild genetic resources. Genes from wild plants and animals have been the source of agricultural innovation for centuries, and will continue to be so. A lot of the genetic diversity on which the future sustainability of agriculture depends is found in and around farmers' fields, in village woodlands and on grazing lands. Wild resources and farmer's varieties are critical to enable plants, animals and humans to adapt to ecological change. They will become more and more important as agriculture spreads further into marginal lands, such as areas of degraded soil, cleared forests and upland slopes. Global climate change may also put new pressures on existing crops, requiring their continuous adaptation.

CONSERVATION OF THE WILD

The most effective way of conserving this crucial genetic pool is *in situ* in farmer's fields, in women's home gardens, in village woodland areas and in protected areas—it is exactly what millions of people have been doing quietly, modestly, for centuries. The incorporation of indigenous crops and other native plant germplasm in the design of self-sustaining agroecosystems will ensure the maintenance of diversity. Agricultural research needs to be conducted with the custodians of this living genetic database and the genius that goes with it in their fields, gardens and forests. The few progressive initiatives taken on farm conservation with *ex situ* strategies show the benefits such an approach can have both for meeting local food production needs and conserving biodiversity for the benefit of the local and international communities.

ACCESS AND RIGHTS TO WILD RESOURCES

There is a global trend towards restricting access to communal lands, where many important wild resources reside.This undermines local peoples' traditional rights to and regulation of wild resource use, and results in unsustainable exploitation. Recent research suggests that reinstating legal access and increasing the economic value of wild resources can promote resource conservation by making sustainable use a viable option. Existing legal frameworks do not acknowledge the innovations, labour and knowledge of rural people which have shaped the wild. Local people's rights to use, access and profit from the genetic resources they have nurtured must be secured for the sake of their own livelihoods, for the conservation of biological diversity and for the sustainable management of our global resources.

POLICING THE WILD LIFE : THE AFRICAN EXAMPLE

Genetic erosion is not only affecting domesticated animals. Wildlife and aquatic resources are also being hit hard by "development" pressures and mismanagement. The case of wild animals has received a lot of publicity. Habitat destruction, change of land-use patterns and environmental degradation are the main culprits behind the high rate of extinction of wildlife. While nature parks and ecotourism are on the rise, little serious attention has been paid to the importance of wild animal resources to the livelihoods of local communities and their role in conservation programmes. Even less publicity has gone to the aquatic resources important for food and agricultue.

Along the rutted dirty roads that wind through vegetated highlands and dusty savannah of eastern, western and southern Africa, there is a steady traffic of big diesel-powered lorries plying the cross-border routes headed for South Africa. African wildlife law enforcement officials know that these lorries are hauling the elephant tusks and rhino horns that are the most prized booty in an ever increasing African trade in illegal flora and fauna. Contraband from animals poached in Zaire, Angola, Zimbabwe, Botswana, Malawi and other African nations is usually transported across boarders to South African cities (Johannesburg, Durban and Cape Town). There syndicated and other illegal traders ship the goods to the Far East.

It is simply a case of an ever increasing illegal trade in ivory. The governments in Africa and others around the world can—thanks to the recently signed Lusaka Agreement—quickly make significant inroads to halting this burgeoning illegal trade. Coordinated by UNEP's Environmental Law and Institutions Programme Activity Centre and signed by eight African nations in Zambia, the Agreement will establish a law enforcement task force that will allow joint undercover operations and other cooperative, regional efforts crucial to halting the sophisticated syndicate behind much of the illegal trade. Although the illegal trade in elephant tusks and rhino horn will be the chief targets of the Lusaka Agreement, joint enforcement efforts will also focus on tropical birds and hardwoods and other animals and plants listed under the

CITES. In the last 35 years there has been a loss of some 97% of rhinocerous species and, in many countries, more than 90% of the elephant, while the poaching for elephant tusks has been drastically reduced in Kenya nd Tanzania.

It is time for the Western governments to put into practice their policies. If they really want to see the elephant and rhino saved it is time to fund this Agreement. But it is not only governments; IUCN, NGOs such as WWF can also provide funding. If NGO groups are serious about saving the elephant and the rhino, they have a good chance by supporting this agreement. Should the Lusaka Agreement succeed, CITES Enforcement could very well serve as a blueprint for similar cooperative regional law enforcement in other parts of the world to save turtles, snakes, tigers, etc.

10

Global Programmes of Conservation

(1) THE FAO AND ANIMAL CONSERVATION

The FAO has been active in animal genetic resource conservation for decades. With the UNEP, it established Regional Animal Gene Banks in Africa, Asia and Latin America for the cryogenic storage of germplasm of endangered species and breeds. With the EAAP it also created a Global Animal Genetic Data Bank, in Hannover, Germany.

In 1989, the 10th Committee on Agriculture (COAG) urged the FAO to expand its AGR programme to develop a Global programme for AGR. An expert consultation in Rome in September 1989 recommended the establishment of "an international undertaking on animal genetic resources, to promote and coordinate international cooperation for conservation and sustainable use of AGR. Since the consultation, a five-year, US $ 15 million global programme has been developed and financed by the FAO, donor organizations and national governments. Under the programme, a global inventory of animal genetic resources, the first of its kind, would be developed and published, describing each breed, its effective population and production parameters. Based on this data, a World Watch List (WWL) of breeds at risk would be published at regular intervals. Information gathered from national data banks, such as those in India and China, as well as Eight Regional Animal Gene Banks, would be stored in the FAO/EAAP genetic data bank in Hannover.

There is already less genetic diversity in farm animals than in crop plant species and over a third of the remaining animal genetic resources is currently at risk. The FAO programme for the global conservation of AGR includes:

1. A global inventory of animal genetic resources including a database to characterize and enumerate all breeds of livestock used in agriculture.
2. Action to identify breeds at risk of extinction as well as ways of protecting them.
3. Promotion of programmes in developing countries to conserve endangered breeds in their native habitats. The aim is to enhance the attraction of indigenous breeds at risk of being substituted by imported breeds which are often brought in without considering the local conditions or sustainability.

4. Improvement of livestock breeding capacities in the developing world. In particular, new technologies will be used to identify livestock diversity and the specific genes responsible for valuable traits.

The FAO is exploring the possibility of establishing a global centre for domestic animal genetic diversity to serve as the focus for efforts to overcome the present erosion of these irreplaceable resources and to promote their effective and sustained use. Conservation of animal genetic diversity is essential to global food security and to protect our ability to meet the challenges of the future.

CLASSIFYING BREEDS

Criteria for classifying animal breeds would include population size, recent growth trends, number of herds and the relative extent of pure and crossbreeding. Following European surveys in 1982 and 1985, the EAAP's Genetic Commission set the number for "endangered" status at below 1000 cows, 500 ewes or she-goats, and 200 sows. Below these minimum numbers, avoiding genetic loss is difficult since the resulting high degree of inbreeding often saps breed vitality and leaves the animals vulnerable to disease outbreaks. Six species marked for the initial data gathering effort include 83 breeds of buffalo, 622 breeds of pigs, 265 breeds of goats, 636 breeds of sheep and 274 breeds of horses. Once a breed is identified as endangered, efforts would be made to save it, through cryogenic methods and conservation of live animals *in situ* or *ex situ* in zoos.

THE FAO AND RESPONSIBLE FISHING

In May 1992, the International Conference on Responsible Fishing at Cancun, Mexico, called upon the FAO to draft an International Code of Conduct for Responsible Fishing. The concept of "responsible fishing" embraces sustainable utilization of fishery resources in harmony with the environment, and the use of capture and aquaculture practices that do not harm ecosystems, resources or food quality. The FAO supports comprehensive programmes on fishery management, focusing on both coastal zones and high seas. It is also committed to international efforts to introduce ecologically safe fishery technologies. The FAO provides technical assistance aimed at environmentally sound aquaculture practices as well as incorporating aquaculture in rural development planning.

To conserve aquatic biodiversity, the FAO emphasizes the sustainable use of aquatic resources. Activities include genetic selection programme in aquaculture; the elaboration of codes of practices for the introduction and transfer of aquatic organisms and on access to genetic resources and biotechnology, and maintenance of a world database on introductions and transfers, as well as a database on species, strain and race identification.

(2) THE FAO AND CONSERVATION OF PGR

The farmer uses seeds as plant genetic resources since the seeds are the propagated material; they are often the input that farmers can produce for themselves. The FAO assistance includes projects for the production and use of good-quality seed, training and guidance in propagation and multiplication, quality control, processing, storage and distribution of improved seeds. The FAO provides samples and information to research centres, scientists and field projects for use in crop introduction, evaluation and breeding.

The FAO, as a sponsor of the CGIAR, supports plant breeding and other research carried out at IARCs. Many of its projects focus on traditional food crops such as roots and tubers which in some developing regions contribute upto 46% of total calories consumed. Traditional crops have yet to be explored genetically, but their potential for improvement through breeding seems promising. The FAO has pioneered the collection of plant genetic resources. An early activity was to field seed-collecting missions, particularly in centres of diversity, where modern cultivars are already displacing traditional varieties. Recently, these and related activities have been undertaken in cooperation with the IBPGR, a CGIAR centre that was established in 1974. Since 1983, the FAO has developed a global system on plant genetic resources based on the principle that plant genetic diversity is the heritage of humanity. The objective is to ensure safe conservation, sustainable use and preserve germplasm.

THE FAO AND THE GLOBAL SYSTEM FOR PGR

The FAO works on plant genetic resources, the part of biodiversity that nurtures people, in cooperation with farmers, the people who have nurtured biodiversity for millennia. The FAO's activity in plant genetic resources dates back to 1947, and the organizations's work with NGOs in this field is almost just as long-standing. The FAO and the NGOs have often collaborated on programmes and projects with a plant genetic resources component. With the intensification of interest and debate surrounding both programme and policy issues since the Twentieth FAO Conference in 1979, NGO activity has also increased. Along with their role as observers in the FAO Conferences, a notable range of NGOs have attended all five sessions of the FAO Commission on Plant Genetic Resources, offering a useful diversity of views that have helped governments in policy formulation. The following three major factors also require consideration.

    i)   The value of genetic diversity in providing the essential material for agricultural development, food security and environmental stability.

    ii)   The fact that plant genetic diversity of agricultural interest is largely concentrated in the tropical and subtropical developing regions.

    iii)   The fact that no country or region is self-sufficient in plant genetic resources. Recent studies indicate that the average level of regional dependence is more than 50% for the most important food crops.

Acting on the recommendations of its member countries, in 1983 the FAO began developing the **Global System for the Conservation and Utilization of Plant Genetic Resources** in co-operation with governmental and non-governmental organizations.

The Global System's objective is to encourage and ensure the safe conservation, availability and sustainable utilization of plant genetic resources for present and future generations. By providing a flexible framework for sharing benefits and burdens, the system is at once a forum and fulcrum for co-ordination and co-operation. It addresses the conservation (*ex situ* and *in situ*) and utilization of genes, genotypes and gene pools at molecular, population, species and ecosystem levels. Ten years after its establishment, 135 countries had formally joined the Global System. A description of the major elements of the Global System follows.

The Commission on Plant Genetic Resouces is a unique intergovernmental forum through which donors or users of germplasm, information, technology and funds can work towards consensus and co-operation on all the vital global issues and programmes pertaining to germplasm conservation and development. One of the most important tasks of the Commission is to monitor the Global system and to develop international agreements and instruments necessary to facilitate germplasm conservation and use. **The International Undertaking on Plant Genetic Resources** is a non-binding agreement assuring that resource species of present or potential economic or social importance are explored, conserved, evaluated, utilized and made available for plant breeding and other research purposes. **The International Fund for Plant Genetic Resources** is providing a channel for countries, intergovernmental, and non-governmental organizations, private industry and individuals to support conservation and promote sustainable use of plant genetic resources.

The International Code of Conduct for Plant Germplasm Collection and Transfer will be an important tool in regularizing the collection and movement of germplasm in order to ensure equitable access and utilization. **The Code of Conduct for Plant Biotechnology** as it affects conservation and the use of plant genetic resources is in a preliminary phase. An **International Network of *Ex Situ* Base Collections** is being extended under the auspices of the FAO, with the technical assistance of the **International Board for Plant Genetic Resources** (IBPGR). This network relates to a further networking of *in situ* conservation areas, emphasizing wild relatives of cultivated plants and the promotion of on-farm conservation and development of farmers' varieties.

The **World Information and Early Warning System** on Plant Genetic Resources has been established in order to collect and disseminate data and encourage information exchanges related to germplasm and relevant technologies. The Early Warming System is intended to draw international attention to hazards threatening the operation of gene banks and the safety of plant genetic diversity throughout the world. A report on the **State of the World's Plant Genetic Resources** is being developed as a periodical that will cover all aspects of the conservation and utilization of plant genetic resources as well as activities and programmes carried out by governmental organizations. **A Global Plan of Action on Plant Genetic Resources,** based on the findings of the State of the World's Plant Genetic Resources, is aimed at rationalizing and co-ordinating global and regional germplasm efforts.

The **Fourth International Technical Conference on Plant Genetic Resources,** following the UNCED and recommendations in its Agenda 21, the three International Technical Conferences on Plant Genetic Resources hosted and supported by the FAO in the past will be convened. When the FAO announced its intention to establish the **International Fund for Plant Genetic Resources,** the first contributions to that fund came from private foundations, NGOs and individuals. Since then, the FAO and NGOs have collaborated on projects to conserve and develop plant genetic resources from India to Ethiopia and the Andes.

(3) THE NGOs

NGOs have played a large and often controversial role in the debate over the conservation and use of PGRs. Among them, RAFI, WWF, IUCN and GRAIN have taken the issues not only to international fora but also to farmers' fields. The following is the summary of the collaborative contribution of these organizations. Governments and NGOs have embraced the principle of Farmers' Rights, not only as a counterpoint to Plant Breeders' Rights, but also as recognition of the innovative role that rural communities play in conserving, developing and making available PGRs. The debate has also brought new dimensions to the longstanding relationship between the FAO and NGOs devoted to sustainable rural development. Stimulated by the "bio-battles" of the 1980s, many NGOs both in the South and the North, have developed strong genetic resource programmes. By the beginning of the 1990s, it was possible to estimate that grassroots NGOs in more than 30 countries were allocating close to US $ 10 million per annum to seed conservation and development. In several cases ranging from India to the Andes and Ethiopia—these projects are the result of close collaboration between the NGOs and the FAO. While policy debates continue, practical cooperation is nevertheless growing.

National programmes lie at the centre of efforts to conserve biodiversity. However, the conservation of genetic resources is not merely a task for national governments and scientific institutions. Biodiversity will not be secure without the deployment of a variety of conservation strategies each in tune with the nature of the resource and the environment in which it exists, nor can biodiversity be adequately protected without being used. Managed use is generally the most effective way of conserving breeds and varieties. National gene banks and other conservation efforts must be regarded as a backup to the complementary system of living, evolving collections utilized by people. Only in use can agricultural genetic resources continue to evolve and thus retain their value.

Grassroots conservation movements have emerged worldwide in response to the loss of biodiversity. Individuals and NGOs are conserving, nurturing and exchanging plant and animal genetic resources at the community level. In the United States, a network of nearly 10000 dedicated farmers and amateur gardeners, known as the *Seed Savers Exchanges,* locates and conserves thousands of endangered vegetable varieties.

(4) THE CGIAR

The Consultative Group on International Agricultural Reserach is an informal coalition of donors (Governments, Intergovernmental agencies and Private foundations)—co-sponsored by the World Bank, the UN FAO and the UNDP. The self-stated mission of the CG is to raise food production in the South. When it was set up, there were 15 donors providing US $ 20 million for four IARCs (International Agric. Research Centres). Today, there are 40 donors contributing nearly US $ 500 million to 18 IARCs. The Group has a small permanent secretariat in the World Bank and a Technical Advisory Committee with a secretariat at the FAO. There are 252 Board of Trustee members governing the 18 autonomous IARCs. Over half of them are from the North (52%) and over two-thirds of them are men (69%). Of the 18 CG centres, 14 are chaired by men from the North, mainly Canada, Germany, the UK and the United States. Throughout the CG's power structures (Canada, the US, the UK and Australia) some 53% come from two cities, Washington and New York. The 18 IARCs governed by this group carry out research in the field of crop agriculture, livestock, agro-forestry and fisheries and also develop policies and strategies for national agricultural research programmes. The bulk of their work is dedicated to genetic conservation of their mandate crops and the improvement of production systems through breeding and dissemination of so-called high-yielding varieties.

THE ACCESSIONS UNDER CONTROL

The CGIAR and the FAO signed (26 October 1995 in Washington) an agreement to place the international PGR collections housed in the CGIAR gene banks under the auspices of the UN FAO. The CGIAR collection contains more than 500000 accessions, which include up to 40% of all unique samples of major food crops held by gene banks world wide.

The deal comes as a welcome conclusion to a long negotiating process started back in 1987 when the FAO asked the CG Centres to bring their gene banks officially under its auspices. During the second Session of the intergovernmental Committee for the CBD (IGCBD-2, Nairobi, 1994) many delegates became alarmed when the NGOs made public that the CGIAR's then Chairman Ismail Serageldin, also a World Bank Vice-President had suggested that the almost concluded negotiations between the IARCs and the FAO might be stalled for some time. There was concern that the World Bank might try to gain control of IARCs' valuable germplasm. Under the new agreement signed in Washington, the IARCs' germplasm will fall under the auspices of the FAO's Global System for the Conservation and Sustainable Use of Plant Genetic Resources. The IPGRI will oversee a CGIAR system-wide integrated genetic resources programme to guide policy and management of all the genetic resources units of the individual IARCs. Individual centres will hold the germplasm in trust for the benefit of the international community, under stipulated standards, but they may not claim ownership nor seek any intellectual property rights over it. The Centres also commit themselves to prevent others from patenting the material, although it is unclear how this will be legally enforced. What is also unclear is what will be the status of the crop varieties developed from materials held in trust: will the "no-patent" clause also apply to them? These and other policy questions will have to be dealt with, but at least the international community—through the FAO -now has a say in the future of these important collections.

References

Ahmed, S. 1995. Science learning from culture: The multiple uses of the pesticide tree. *Ceres, The FAO Review*. 155: 4-6

Altieri, M. 1995. Heirs of the revolution: Escaping the treadmill. *Ceres, The FAO Review*. 154: 15-23.

Bainton, J.A. 1993. Considerations for release of herbicide resistant crops *Aspects of Applied Biology*. 35:51.

Bartley, D. 1995. Ocean ranching: The solution or only a bad idea whose time has come? *Ceres, The FAO Review*. 151: 42-45.

Bell, J. 1997. Biopiracy's latest disguises. *Seedling* 14(2): 2-10

Bell, J. 1995. The hidden harvest. *Seedling* 12(3): 22-31

Bentley, J.W. 1993. What farmers don't know? Folk knowledge is filtered through a screen that reflects farmers' own values. *Ceres, The FAO Review* 141: 42-45.

Bijman, J. 1995. Strategies of US biotechnology companies. *Biotechnology and Dev. Monitor*. 24: 12-16.

Bijman, J. 1994. Biosafety regulation *Biotechnology and Dev. Monitor*. 18: 14-15.

Brush, S.B. 1989. Rethinking crop genetic resources conservation. *Conservation Biol.* 3:19-29.

Brush, S.B. 1992. Farmers' rights and genetic conservation in traditional farming systems. *World Dev*. 20: 1617-1630.

Brush, S.B. 1994. *In Situ* conservation of landraces in centres of crop diversity. *Crop Sci.* 35: 346-354.

Budiansky, S. 1992. The covenant of the wild: Why animals chose domestication? William Morrow & Company Inc., New York pp. 1-190.

Busch, L. 1995. Eight reasons why patents should not be extended to plants and animals. *Biotechnology and Dev. Monitor*. 24: 24.

Busetto, B. 1993. Conversation with the counter-revolutionaries. Just how organic is the low-external input movement? *Ceres, The FAO Review*. 144: 19-23.

Butler, L.J. 1995. Regulation of agricultural biotechnology in the USA. *Biotechnology and Dev. Monitor*. 24: 2-6.

Chaturvedi, S. 1997. Biosafety: Policy and implications in India. *Biotechnology and Dev. Monitor*. 30: 11-13.

Christy Jr, F.T. 1993. Back to school *Ceres, The FAO Review*. 142: 32-26.

Cholchester, M. 1994a. Salvaging nature: Indigenous people, protected areas and biodiversity conservation. Discussion paper. UNRISED/WRM/WWF. pp 1-29.

Colchester, M. 1994b. Towards indigenous IPRs. *Seedling* 11(4): 2-4

Collinson, M. 1995. Green evolution *Ceres, The FAO Review*. 154: 23-28.

Commandeur, P. and P.B. Joly 1996. Public debate and regulation of biotechnology in Europe. *Biotechnology and Dev. Monitor*. 26: 2-9.

Commandeur, P. 1994. Patents, genes and butterflies *Biotechnology and Dev. Monitor*. 2: 3-4.

Comte, M.C. 1993. Teetering on the brink. The ocean's most valuable commercial species are fished to capacity *Ceres, The FAO Review*. 142: 17-32.

Comte, M.C. 1991. Diversity is a survival tool. We can't afford to lose our livestock options *Ceres, The FAO Review*. 132: 15-19.

Cooper, D., R. Vellve and H. Hobblink. 1993. Growing diversity: genetic resources and local food security. Intermediate Technology Publications, London pp. 1-166.

Cordeiro, A. 1995. Diversity, a feminine noun. *Seedling* **12**(2): 17-21

Creedon, J. 1997. The Ownership of life — when patents and values clash. RAFI/CS Fund CA/HKH Found. New York. pp. 4-37.

Crowley ,M .1990. "The Ecology of genetically engineered organisms: Assessing the environmental risks. " In: *Introduction of genetically modified organisons in to the environment.* Mooney, H.A. and Bernardi, G. (eds). pp. 133-150.

Crump, A. 1991. Bounty's menace: Countering the threat of transplanted pests. *Ceres*, The FAO Review. 130: 15-20.

Dale, P.J. 1997. Unintended movement of live genetically modified organisms across national boundaries In: *Transboundary movement of living modified organisms resulting from modern biotechnology: issues and opportunities for policy-makers.* Mulongoy, K.J. (ed.) *Intl. Acad. Envir.* Geneva. pp. 195-199.

Dam, C.D. 1993. A member of the family: *Bubalus bubalus* is an integral part of rural Vietnam's past – and economic future. *Ceres*, The FAO Review 141: 39-41.

De Castro, J.A. 1997. The biotrade initiative : an incentive to conservation of biological diversity and sustainable development. In: *Transboundary movement of living modified organisms resulting from modern biotechnology: Issues and opportunities for policy-makers.* Mulongoy, K.J. (ed.) *Intl. Acad. Envir.* Geneva. pp. 13-28.

De Kathen, 1996. The impact of transgenic crop releases on biodiversity in deveoping countries. *Biotechnology and Dev. Monitor.* 28: 10-14.

DiMasi, J.A., R.W. Hansen and Grabowski. 1991. The cost of innovation in the pharmaceutical industry. *J. Health Econ.*10: 107-142.

Dixon, D. 1993. A 'sexist' approach to breeding bigger and better Tilapia *Ceres*, The FAO Review. 142: 3-4.

Dumoulin, J. 1998. Pharmaceuticals: The role of biotechnology and patents *Biotechnology and Dev. Monitor.* 35: 13-15.

Dunn, K. 1995. Patented people *Ceres*, The FAO Review 153:31.

Dunn, K. 1995. The numbers game: Playing by whose rules? *Ceres*, The FAO Review 155: 15-20.

Ekson, D. and K.S. Jayaraman. 1995. Aid groups back challenge to neem patents. *Nature* 14 Sept. 1995. p.95.

El-Ghonemy, R. 1995. Food security = social security. *Ceres*, The FAO Review 152: 17-21.

Ellstrand, N.C. 1994. Are there unique risks when testing in Centres of Diversity. *Proc. 3rd International symposium on the biosafety results of field tests of geneticaly modified plants and microorganisms.* Univ. California pp. 311-313.

FAO, 1993. Plant genetic resources. *Deep* pp. 3-13.

FAO, 1993. Harvesting nature's diversity: World Food Day Handbook. pp.1-24.

Flitner, M. and D. Leskien. 1997. Intellectual property rights and plant genetic resources: Options for a *Sui generis* system *Issues in Genetic Resources* No.6: pp. 1-14.

Gillman, H. 1994. Safe storage or safe Environment? "Ecofridge" could end the dilemma *Ceres*, The FAO Review. 149: 10-11.

Goldburg, R. 1995. Pause at the amber light *Ceres*, The FAO Review 153: 21-25.

Goldsmith, E. and H. Hildyard. 1991. World agriculture : Toward 2000, FAO'S plan to feed the world. *The Ecologist.* **21**: 81-92.

GRAIN, 1992. Patents on life : Obviously not. *Seedling.* **9**(4) : 6-9

GRAIN, 1994. Animal alarm. *Seedling* **11**(1): 3-10.

GRAIN, 1994. Agricultural biodiversity in the Convention Biobriefing 4(1): 1-4.

GRAIN, 1994. International transfer of GMOs: The need for a biosafety protocol. Paper presented at the intergovernmental committee on the convention of biological diversity Nairobi. July 1994. p. 1-7.

GRAIN, 1994. Reviving diversity in India's agriculture. *Seedling* **11**(3): 6-13.

GRAIN, 1995. The green revolution in the red. *Seedling* **12**(1): 16-18.

GRAIN, 1995. Engineered BT: From pest to market control. *Seedling* **12**(4): 2-10

GRAIN, 1996. The biotech battle over the golden crop. *Seedling* **13**(3): 23-32

GRAIN, 1997. Engineering the blue revolution. *Seedling* **14**(4): 20-30.

GRAIN, 1998. A greener than green revolution. *Seedling* **15**(4) : 8-19

GRAIN, 1998. Fields of dreams: Gene tech goes South. *Seedling* **15**(3): 22-33

GRAIN, 1999. Biodiversity: A perspective within. *Seedling* **16**(2): 24-30

GRAIN, 1999. GM foods turn political hot potato. *Seedling* **16**(1): 8-15.

GRAIN, 1999. Reclaiming diversity, restoring livelihoods. *Seedling* **16**(2): 11-23

GRAIN, 1999. Tug of war over life patents. *Seedling* **15**(2): 2-9

GRAIN/CEAT, 1994. Threats from the test tubes: *Seedling* **11**(4): 7-12

GRAIN, 2000. Potato: The new global traveller. *Seedling* **17**(4): 19-25.

Green Alliance, 1995. Why are environmental Groups concerned about release of GMOs into the environment? Briefing Document, London. pp 1-12.

Greenstein, J.L. and D.H.Sachs. 1997. The use of tolerance for transplantation across xenogeneric barriers. *Nature Biotechnology.* **15**: 235-237.

Griffin, U. 1993. It's collapsing completely *Ceres*, The FAO Review. 142: 28-31.

Grisley, W. 1993. Strength through flexibility: Farmer's own experiments may lead the way to eventual food security. *Ceres*, The FAO Review 144: 28-30.

Habbard, R. 1995. Genomania and health. *American Scientist* **83**: 8-10.

Hahn, N D. 1993. Victims of the Green Revolution *Ceres*, The FAO Review 140: 41-42.

Hardon, J. 1996. National sovereignty and access to genetic resources. *Biotechnology and Dev. Monitor.* 27: 24.

Hawkes, J.G. 1991. International workshop on dynamic *In Situ* conservation of wild relatives of major cultivated plants: Summary of final discussion and recommendations. *Israel J. Bot.* **40**: 529-536.

Hendry, P. 1994. Poison-proof plants *Ceres*, The FAO Review 149: 30-34.

Herbert, J. 1993. A mail-order catalogue of Indigenous knowledge:From databases to news-letters, a vast network of information is available, and growing *Ceres*, The FAO Review 143: 33-34.

Ho, M W. 1997. The unholy alliance, In: *Genetic engineering Dreams or nightmares? The brave new world of bad science and big business.* RFSTE/TWN pp.1-12.

House of Commons Science and Technology Committee. III Report 1995. Human genetics: The science and its consequences London. Vol I: 1-10

IATP, 1997. Intellectual property and biodiversity project. IPR Info Sheets MN, USA.

Ingrassia, A. 1997. Trade-related environmental measures in the field of safety in biotechnology In: *Transboundary movement of living modified organisms resulting from modern biotechnology: Issues and opportunities for policy-makers.* Mulongoy K.J. (ed.) Intl. Acad. Envir. Geneva. pp. 89-113.

Jain, H.K. 1994. Biodiversity Convention: More losers than winners. *Biotechnology and Dev. Monitor.* 21: 24.

James, C. 1998. Global status and distribution of commercial transgenic crops in 1997.*Biotech-nology and Dev. Monitor.* 35: 9-12 .

Jenkins, R. 1999. Bt. Crops are unsustainable *Biotechnology and Dev. Monitor.* 38: 24.

Johnson, P. 1993. The Duce syndrome: Buffalo bias' stunts exploitation of one of the most useful of domestic animals. *Ceres*, The FAO Review 141: 36-38

Jonas, D. and F. Kaferstein 1995. Manning dinner's defences *Ceres*, The FAO Review 153: 26-28.

Jovetic, S. 1994. Natural pyrethrins and biotechnological alternative. *Biotechnology and Dev. Monitor.* 21: 12-13..

Kate, K.T. 1995. Biopiracy or green petroleum?: Expectations and best practice in bioprospect-ing. ODA, UK. pp. 1-22.

Kelle, A. 1998. Biological weapons: Easy to produce and difficult to control *Biotechnology and Dev. Monitor.* 35: 18-21.

Kelves, J.K. 1993. Out of engenics: The historical politics of human genome, The code of codes. Harvard Univ. Press, pp. 1-20.

Kendall, H.W., R. Beachy., T. Eisner., F. Gould., R. Herdy., P. Raven., J.S. Schell and M.S. Swaminathan. 1997. Bioengineering of crops. Report of the world bank : panel on transgenic crops ESDS Monograph Series: 23. WB Washington DC.

Kleiner, K. 1995. Pesticide tree endsup in court. *New Scientist* 16 Sept 1995. p.7.

Kochen ,J. and G.V. Roozendaal. 1997. The neem tree debate. *Biotechnology and Dev. Monitor.* 30: 8-11.

Kollet, R .1995. Ambiguous genes. *Biotechnology and Dev. Monitor.* 23:24

Lacy, W.B. 1995. The global plant genetic resources: A competition cooperation paradox. *Crop Sci.* **35**: 335-345

Lang, T. and C. Hines 1995. The GATT debate: Let the readers judge. *Ceres*, The FAO Review 151: 19-23.

Leakey, R.E. 1994. The people yes, but... some caveats en route to the ideal protected system *Ceres*, The FAO Review 150: 29-31.

Lehmann, V. 1998. Patent on seed sterility threatens seed saving. *Biotechnology and Dev. Monitor.* 35: 6-8.

Lewis, R.G. 1993. Genetic freshness: The biotech tomato heads for market *Ceres*, The FAO Review 140: 10-12.

Loesch, H.V. 1996. Green Revolution protects the environment. *Biotechnology and Dev. Monitor.* 29: 24.

Lopez, M.B. 1993. After the Earth Summit: View point. *Ceres*, The FAO Review 139: 6-7.

Lopez, P.B. 1994. A new plant disease: Uniformity *Ceres*, The FAO Review 150: 41-47.

Madeley, J. 1993. Finding strength in diversity *Ceres*, The FAO Review 143: 38-39.

Madeley, J. 1995. UNEP joins ranks of CGIAR sponsors *Ceres*, The FAO Review 154: 8-9.

Manicad, G. 1996. Biodiversity conservation and development: The collaboration of formal and non-formal institutions. *Biotechnology and Dev. Monitor.* 26: 15-17.

Marical, G. and V.Lehmann, 1997. CGIAR : Evalutions and new directions. *Biotechnology and Dev. Monitor.* 33: 12-17

Martin, G.J., A.L. Hoare and D.A. Posey. 1995. *People and plants handbook. Sources for applying ethnobotany to conservation and community development.* WWF./UNESCO/RBG–Kew. pp.1-17

Martin, R.B. 1994. A voice in the wilderness *Ceres*, The FAO Review 150:24-28

McClellan, S. 1993. "The fishing decayeth....." *Ceres*, The FAO Review 142: 23-27.

Melchias, G. 1999. Bioethics: The ethics of bioscience. In: *The foundations of humanity* SJC. Tiruchirappalli, pp. 45-50.

Moffat, A.S. 1996. Biodiversity is a boon to ecosystems, not species. *Science* **271**: 1497.

Montecinos, C. 1995. We all (should) know: *Biotechnology and Dev. Monitor.* 22: 24.

Mugabe, J. and E.Ouko. 1994. Control over genetic resources *Biotechnology and Dev. Monitor.* 21: 6-7.

Mulongoy, K. 1997. Difficult perceptions on the international biosafety protocol. *Biotechnology and Dev. Monitor.* 31 : 16-19.

Mulvany, P. 1996. *Dynamic diversity: Farmers, herders and fisherfold safeguarding biodiversity for food security.* Intermediate Technology Development Group. UK.

Mulvihill, M. 1991. DNA+PCR+DVM = A chain reaction whose time has come *Ceres*, The FAO Review 132: 28-34.

Narang, R.S. 1993. The imbalance of Green Revolution: Reactions. *Ceres*, The FAO Review. 144: 41-42.

O' Brian, C. 1995. European parliament axes patent policy. *Science.* **267**: 1417-1418.

Ojwang, J.B. 1994. National domestication of the Convention on Bioligical Diversity. In: *Biodiplomacy: Genetic resources and international relations.* Sanchez V. and Juma C. (eds). Nairobi: ACTS Press pp. 304-308.

Osten, AVD 1996. Growing consensus on farming for food and for development *Ceres*, The FAO Review 157: 39-43.

Pandey, B. 1994. Hybrid seed controversy in India *Biotechnology and Dev. Monitor.* 19: 9-11.

Pandey, B. and S. Chaturvedi. 1994. Prospects for aquaculture in India. *Biotechnology and Dev. Monitor.* 21: 16-17.

Panos Media Briefing 1995. Genetic engineers target third world crops. The Panos Institute. London 7 : 1-23.

Perez, J.F. and J.J. Mendoza. 1998. Marine fisheries, genetic effects and biodiversity *NAGA,* ICLARM Oct-Dec. 1998 pp. 7-14.

Pilari, D. 1997. Policy issues related to the transfer and sustainable use of biotechnologies In: *Transboundary movement of living modified organisms resulting from modern biotechnology: Issues and opportunities for policy-makers.* Mulongoy K.J. (ed.) *Intl. Acad. Envir.* Geneva, pp. 3-11.

Pistorius, R. 1997. *In situ* or *Ex situ*? Conservation strategies in the 1980s and early 1990s. In: *Scientists, plants and politics: a history of the plant genetic resources movement.* IPGRI Roma. pp. 100-107.

Poole, N.J. 1997. International trade of transgenic crops In: *Transboundary movement of living modified organisms resulting from modern biotechnology: Issues and opportunities for policy - makers.* Mulongoy K.J. (ed.) *Intl. Acad. Envir.* Geneva. pp. 115-121.

Posey, D. and G. Dutfield. 1996. Beyond intellectual property. Toward traditional resource rights for indigenous peoples and local communities IDRC. Ottawa. Canada pp. 5-48 & 155-208.

Posey, D.A. and G. Dutfied. Are intellectual property rights useful? In: *Beyond intellectual property.* IDRC, Ottawa, Canada. pp 75-92.

Prat A.R.M./GRAIN, 1995. Fishing out aquatic diversity. *Seedling* **12**(2): 2-13

Prescott - Allen,C. and R. Prescott – Allen. 1990. How many plants feed the world? *Conservation Biology* 4(4): 365-374.

Radin, J.W. 1999. Technology protection system: Revolutionary or evolutionary. *Biotechnology and Dev. Monitor.* 37: 24.

RAFI, 1995. Conserving indigenous knowlege: Integrating two systems of innovation. UNDP pp. 1-54.

Ramprasad ,V. 1998. Genetic engineering and the myth of feeding the world. *Biotechnology and Dev. Monitor.* 35: 24.

Rappert, D. 1995. The US extension of plant variety protection: a critical evaluation *Science and Public Policy.* **22** (2): 95-105.

Raybould, A.F. and A.J. Gray. 1993. Genetically modified crops and hybridization with wild relatives: a UK perspective. *Journal of Applied Ecology,* **30**: 201-204.

Regal, P.J. 1997. The geography of Risk : special concerns for insular ecosystems and for centres of crop origins and genetic diversity. In: *Transboundary movement of living modified organisms resulting from modern biotechnology: Issues and opportunities for policy-makers.* Mulongoy K.J. (ed.) *Intl. Acad. Envir.* Geneva. pp. 159-169.

Reid, W.V. 1994. Biodiversity prospecting: strategy for sharing benefit. In: *Biodiplomacy: genetic resources and international relations.* Sanchez and Juma C (eds.) Nairobi: ACTS Press, pp. 241 268.

Reijntjes, C., B.Haverkort and A.Waters-Bayer. 1993. Inspecting the tool box : A look at the means for achieving substainable agriculture. *Ceres,* The FAO Review. 144: 24-27.

Rhind, D. 1997. What's what in Biotechnology? *Genetic Engineering and Biotechnology* . 2&3 : 1-9.

Rissler, J. and M.Mellon. 1993. Perils amidst the promise : Ecological risks of transgenic crops in a global market. Cambridge MA : Union of Concerned Scientists . pp. 1-92.

Rojas, M. 1999. The biotrade initiative: Programme for biodiversity based development *Biotechnology and Dev. Monitor.*38: 11-14.

Roozendal, G.V. 1996. Enhancing the nutritional qualities of crop: A Second Green Revolution ? *Biotechnology and Dev. Monitor.* 26: 12-15.

Ross, E.B. 1996. Malthusianism and agricultural development: false premises, false promises .*Biotechnology and Dev. Monitor.*26: 24.

Saouma, E. 1993. A view from the end of the twentieth century *Ceres,* The FAO Review. 143: 1-8.

Saouma, E. 1993. Farmers of the North and South: Winning together or losing out against each other? *Ceres,* The FAO Review. 144: 1-8

Seoul Conference 1995. Food, Culture, Trade and the Environment : WTO and sustainable Agriculture. Proceedings. pp. 11-16.

Shand, H. 1992. Genetic engineering of pyrethrins: Early warning for East African pyrethrum farmers. RAFI Communique.

Shands, H. 1991. Complementarity of *In Situ* and *Ex Situ* germplasm conservation from the standpoint of the future user. *Israel J. Bot.* **40**:521 - 528

Sharma, D. 1995. Food will be used as a weapon against India. *Ceres, The FAO Review.* 151: 39-41.

Shelton, D. 1995. Fair play, fair pay. Laws to preserve traditional knowledge and biological resources. WWF International Switzerland. pp 1-47.

Shepherd, AW. 1993. Glut or Glory? Matching on-farm production to market demand *Ceres, The FAO Review.* 140: 35-37.

Shepherd, D. 1994. All in the same Ark: Looking for truce in a tug of war *Ceres, The FAO Review.* 150: 17-23.

Shiva, V. 1995. Mistaken miracles *Ceres, The FAO Review* . 154: 28-35.

Shiva, V., A.H.Jafri., G.Bedi and R.Holla-Bhar. 1997. The enclosure of the commons. In: *The enclosure and recovery of the commons: Biodiversity, indigenous knowledge and IPR.* RFSTE. New Delhi, pp. 3-72.

Sperling, L. and M.Loevinsohn. 1995. Using diversity : Enhancing and maintaining genetic resources on-farm IDRC *Proc.* pp.1-124.

Tepfer, M. 1993. Viral genes and transgenic plants. *Bio / Technology.* **11**:1125-1132

Trip ,R .1997. Unproductive debates: The Green Revolution, biotechnology and agricultural diversity *.Biotechnology and Dev. Monitor.* 32:24.

TWN, 1996. Biosafety: Scientific findings and elements of a protocol. Report of the Independent Group of scientific and legal experts on biosafety. Penang, Malaysia. pp. 1-65.

van Loesch, H 1996. The Green Revolution people respond to Dr. Shiva *Ceres, The FAO Review* .157:50

van Noordwijk,M., T.P.Tomich., H.de Foresta and G.Michon. 1997. To segregate – or to Integrate? *The question of balance between production and biodiversity conservation in complex agroforestry systems. Ceres, The FAO Review.* 9 (1): 6-9.

van Wijk, J. 1994. Hybrids, bred for superior fields or for control? *Biotechnology and Dev. Monitor.* 19: 3-5 .

Villalobos, V. 1995. Brave new technologies *Ceres, The FAO Review.* 153: 18-20.

Visser ,B. 1994. The prospects for technical guidelines for safety in biotechnology. *Biotechnology and Dev. Monitor.* 20: 21-22.

Visser, B. 1998. Effects of biotechnology on agrobiodiversity *Biotechnology and Dev. Monitor.* 35: 2-7

Waltson, O. 1993. Letter from Thriplow farms. One man's reaction to Europe's new common agricultural policy. *Ceres, The FAO Review.* 142. 37-40.

Yusuf, A. 1994. Technology and genetic resources: Is mutually - beneficial access still possible. In: *Biodiversity prospecting- strategy for staring benefit. Biodiplomacy: Genetic resources and international relations.* Sanchez and Juma C (eds.) ACTS Press. pp. 233-240.

Zannoni, L. 1993. Trends in commercialisation of products of biotechnology In: *Transboundary movement of living modified organisms resulting from modern biotechnology: Issues and opportunities for policy - makers.* Mulongoy KJ (ed.) *Intl. Acad. Envir.* Geneva. pp. 79-87

Zolty, A. 1991. Desert rennaissance: Biotechnology may be a boon to the oasis- or its bane. *Ceres, The FAO Review.* 130: 37-45.

Zweifel, H. 1995. Modern biotechnologies in agriculture: Impact on women in the South *Biotechnology and Dev. Monitor.* 23: 10-13.

Index

Capacity building – 88, 137
Caracas Action Plan – 185
Caribbean – 19, 113, 159
CBD – 27, 59, 84, 86, 90, 92, 93, 105, 128, 144, 152, 188, 191, 200, 207
cDNA – 81
Celera – 77, 78
Cell culture – 100, 182
Central America – 10
Centres of diversity – 10
Centres of origin – 40
CGIAR – 22, 45, 53-55, 59, 72, 95, 190-195, 200, 219, 222
Characterization – 198
Charles DeLisi – 80
China – 10, 17, 19, 22, 65, 66, 102
Chromosome mutations – 4
Chymosin – 103
CIAT – 46
CIMMYT – 45
CITES – 216
Clearing house – 88
Cloning – 201, 202
COAG – 217
Coat protein – 109
Coelacanth – 69
Collection – 143
Commercial seed system – 44
Commercialization – 157, 158
Commodification – 154
Common heritage – 162
Community IPR – 166
Conservation – 13, 46, 85, 92, 181, 187, 188, 190, 197, 199, 202, 214, 217
Convention – 84, 89, 91, 94
Copyrights – 161
Coral reef – 5, 8, 24
Costa Rica – 6, 89
Cote d'Ivoire – 14
CPV – 115
Craig Venter – 77
Crop plants – 9
Cross resistance – 116
Crustaceans – 20, 21
Cryogenic preservation – 199, 209
Czechoslovakia – 13

de CODE Genetics – 79
Deforestation – 14, 26
Deliberate release – 120
Denmark – 129
Derwent's world patent index – 116
Differential survival – 203
Diffusion – 43
Discovery – 168

Diversity – 3, 43
DNA – 3, 4, 76, 79, 81, 82, 100, 107, 136, 145, 152, 153, 168, 169, 190, 200, 202
DNA transfer – 202
Domesticated fish – 72
Domestication – 16, 29, 61, 62, 73
Drift net fishing – 70
Drug – 80, 144, 145, 147
Dynamite fishing – 70

E. coli – 115, 129
E. gibbosus – 25
EAAP – 66, 217, 218
Earth Summit – 28
Ecosystem – 5, 12, 13, 26
Ecuador – 156
Elizabeth Dowdeswell – 84
Embryo – 200
Embryo bank – 201
Embryo collection – 200
Embryo transfer – 18
Endangered – 218, 221
Endangered animals – 25
Endemic flora – 26
Endophytes – 117
Environmental risk – 109
Epiphytes – 117
Equitable sharing – 85
Erosion – 46
Escapes – 126, 136
ESTs – 78, 81
Ethiopia – 8, 27
Ethnoscience – 34
Eugenics – 80
Europe – 16-19, 21, 64, 66, 78
European Commission – 72, 170
European Union – 64, 68, 69, 126, 129, 164
Evaluation – 137, 138, 198
Evolution – 203
Ex situ – 59, 93, 144, 182, 188, 190, 191, 193, 195, 197, 199, 202, 203, 209, 214, 218
Exotic – 22, 65
Extinction – 4, 17, 60
Extracting – 142

Factory farm – 65
Famine – 212
FAO – 3, 11, 13, 29, 53, 67, 102, 194, 197, 200, 217-222
FAO Commission on PGR – 56
Field gene bank – 190
Fish – 19, 21, 110
Fish conservation – 204
Fisheries – 69
Fishing – 69